EMPOWERED EDUCATORS

How High-Performing Systems Shape Teaching Quality Around the World

Linda Darling-Hammond

Dion Burns

Carol Campbell

A. Lin Goodwin

Karen Hammerness

Ee Ling Low

Ann McIntyre

Mistilina Sato

Kenneth Zeichner

With the assistance of Raisa Ahtiainen, Maude Engstrom, Jesslyn Hollar, Jiacheng Li, Ann Lieberman, Pamela Osmond-Johnson, Shane Pisani, Robert Rothman, Pasi Sahlberg, and Jacqueline Sohn

JB JOSSEY-BASS™

A Wiley Brand

Published by Jossey-Bass
A Wiley Brand

One Montgomery Street, Suite 1000, San Francisco, CA 94104-4594—www.josseybass.com

Jossey-Bass books and products are available through most bookstores. To contact Jossey-Bass directly call our Customer Care Department within the U.S. at 800-956-7739, outside the U.S. at 317-572-3986, or fax 317-572-4002.

Wiley publishes in a variety of print and electronic formats and by print-on-demand. Some material included with standard print versions of this book may not be included in e-books or in print-on-demand. If this book refers to media such as a CD or DVD that is not included in the version you purchased, you may download this material at http://booksupport.wiley.com. For more information about Wiley products, visit www.wiley.com.

Library of Congress Cataloging-in-Publication Data

9781119369608 (paperback)
9781119369615 (ePDF)
9781119369578 (ePub)

Cover design by Wiley
Cover image: © suriya9/Getty Images, Inc.

Printed in the United States of America
FIRST EDITION
PB Printing   10 9 8 7 6 5 4 3 2 1

CONTENTS

FOREWORD

We can probably agree that great schools, without exception, are staffed by great teachers. It follows that if one wants an entire nation, state, or province with great schools, then one must provide all those schools with great teachers. Few, I suspect, would disagree with that. But then the question arises, how can that be done?

Roll the clock back to the United States in the years leading up to the American Civil War. We know now that this was the period in which the outlines of the current American school system were taking shape under the pioneering leadership of Catherine Beecher and Horace Mann. Those communities that had any schools hired young men to tutor the children who were not working in the fields. Their wives were at home, and an increasing number of their daughters were working long hours in the mills for next to nothing. Those students who got any education got mostly drill and practice in the rudiments of reading, writing and, as they said, "'rithmetic."

Beecher and Mann had another idea. Send the men into the mills. Take the young women who had been working in the mills and put them in the schools. Although Beecher and Mann saw this move as building a profession for women, and advocated the creation of normal schools for professional preparation, the feminization of teaching typically took another turn as it played out across the country.

Scientific managers and town guardians often favored the move for financial reasons. They argued that schools could pay the women a pittance, because they were either single and living with their parents, and so did not need much pay, or they were married and it was up to the husband to provide for the family. They would not need much skill because they did not need to know much more than their students, and their students did not need any more than the basics. As the system grew, these young women were fired when they became pregnant, so it was hardly worth while investing in their development as teachers. Of course, it would take real skill and ability to manage this system, especially in the big cities, where there were lots of schools and lots of people and money to manage, but the managers would be men who would be paid a lot more than the teachers to tell the teachers what to do and how to do it. This was the model that was being used in America's burgeoning industrial enterprises with enormous success, and there was no reason why it should not work in the schools.

And it did. The United States used this model to set one new global benchmark after another in educational attainment. By the middle of the 20th century, it had the best educated workforce in the world. It had done it with a classic blue-collar model of work organization in its schools.

Educators from all over the world came to look at the American education system, learn its lessons, and take them home. Variations on the American model popped up everywhere.

But, as the 20th century drew to a close, the world was changing. Poor countries were learning how to use the model of schooling just described to deliver the same basic skills that schools in the more developed countries were delivering. But the graduates of those schools in these poor countries were willing to work for much less than their counterparts in the more developed countries. Jobs for people with only the basic skills in the more developed countries migrated to the countries where employers could get the same skills for much less. Hundreds of millions of people in the less developed countries were lifted out of poverty this way, but people in the more developed countries who had only the basic skills were in real trouble. Then the jobs of people who do mostly routine work began to be done by robots and other automated machinery. Between outsourcing and automation, the market for people with only the basic skills in the most developed countries was devastated.

That fact was a death knell for the blue collar model of school work organization. One country after another began to realize that cheap teachers responsible only for teaching the basic skills, working in schools in which they were expected to do what they were told to do by school administrators who were selected not for their ability as teachers but for their skills as managers, could no longer do the job that had to be done. A model in which teachers were expected to come from the lower ranks of high school graduates, to be educated in the lowest status higher education institutions, who were paid poorly, all of whom did the same job and had no career to look forward to, who were not rewarded at all for getting better at their work but simply for their time in service, while others, not them, were expected to figure out how to improve student performance—a model like that could never accomplish what now had to be done.

What now had to be done was to provide almost all students in the most developed nations with the knowledge, skills, attitudes, and values that only the elite students had been expected to develop before. All students would have to emerge from schools with the qualities that only the future leaders of society had been expected to have before if the nation was going to be able to maintain its standard of living. In an era like the middle of the 19th century in the United States, in which only a handful of people had any education beyond high school, it was obvious that only the high schools educating the future leaders of the whole society could afford to staff their schools with well-educated teachers. The blue-collar model of teaching was, in fact, the only model available to a country at that time that wanted to educate the masses.

But the blue-collar model of teacher work organization could not produce elite outcomes for the great mass of students. Only a professional model of teacher work organization could do that. So the search was on. What would such a model look like? Where would the future teachers come from? How would they be attracted to teaching? What sort of education would they need? How would they learn their craft? How would they be selected? Against what criteria? How would their work be organized? What sort of career could they be offered? What sort of incentives would they need to do the best work of which they were capable? How could their workplace be organized so that they would be constantly working to improve their skills, the curriculum, the schools, and student performance? What would schools look like if it was teachers, not managers or policy analysts or the research community, who was expected to lead the schools to higher performance? How would the answers to these questions change the kind of school leadership that would be needed? What, in other words, would a professional model of teaching look like when applied not just to an isolated elite school but to an entire country, province, or state?

That question—perhaps the single most important question facing educators today—is the question this book and the study on which it was based was designed to answer. Three years ago, my colleague, Betsy Brown Ruzzi, the director of NCEE's Center for International Education Benchmarking, and I asked Linda Darling-Hammond if she would be interested in leading a major international comparative study of teacher quality to look at how the leading countries were answering the kinds of questions just asked. Darling-Hammond, of course, is one of the world's leading education researchers and has had a lifelong interest in the teaching profession. She leaped at the chance. Such studies are usually done by a lead researcher with a gaggle of graduate students actually doing much of the field work. Darling-Hammond did not do that. She assembled a team of leading researchers from all over the world to join her in this very large research program. The result is a stunning piece of work, the result of a true collaboration among an all-star cast of researchers. It is everything we hoped it might be and more.

Don't look here for the one country, state, or province to be copied. What you will find is a picture in which the jurisdictions described tried first this and then that. Some had opportunities that others did not have. Some worked on this while others worked on that. As they were doing this, they looked over each other's shoulders for inspiration, ideas, and tools. Gradually, themes emerged. If you want a model, you will have to assemble it from those themes and the mosaic of policies and practices you will find in this volume and the others in the series of books from this project. And then you will have to adapt what you have learned to your own goals, values, and context.

There is plenty of inspiration here. Some of the key changes these countries made were nothing if not dramatic. Some countries look at their teacher education systems in despair, thinking there is no way that they can make the changes they ought to make in the education of teachers at the scale that is needed, given the politics. But look at how Finland decided to abolish all of its teacher education institutions at once and created in their stead a much smaller number of institutions, all of them at their research universities and all of them with a similar curriculum intimately tied to that nation's aims for its schools. Or look at Shanghai, which created out of whole cloth a career ladder system in which teachers get more compensation, more authority, more autonomy, and more status as they go up the ladder, in the process transforming what it means to be a teacher from the blue-collar model to the professional model. Or consider Singapore and Australia, where carefully considered standards for teachers and school leaders have been developed to drive their systems forward in the same way that the development of professional standards have characterized the professionalization of medicine, the law, engineering, accounting, and many other professions.

But be careful. Darling-Hammond and her colleagues point out that it is not any one of these innovations and others like them that account for high teacher quality. It is the whole system and the way it fits together that is most important. They point out that it is not just all the parts and pieces of the teacher quality system that account for the differences they observe in student performance; it is also the way that these teacher quality systems fit together with the larger design of the education systems of which they are a part. The issue of equity is a case in point. It is not just a matter of making sure that new teachers have had classes in which they are introduced to the essentials of teaching students from low-income and minority backgrounds or get some experience in doing that in their clinical work. Shanghai has designed its career ladder system so that it is virtually impossible to go up the ladder without having worked in a variety of schools serving low-income and minority students. In Singapore, one is very likely to find that the best teachers are the ones working in classrooms with the highest concentrations of low-income and minority students. Singaporean teachers are taught early diagnosis and intervention in order to make sure that vulnerable students do not fall behind. In Toronto, with one of the most diverse student populations in the world, equity considerations govern virtually every aspect of the continuing development of teachers. Australia is working with its teachers to make sure that the curriculum they develop provides rich opportunities for indigenous students to see themselves in the materials they use in the classroom.

What emerges from this composite picture is almost the antithesis of the world that Catherine Beecher and Horace Mann created more than a century ago. The leading jurisdictions are selecting their teachers from among the more capable of their high school graduates. They want to make sure that they are not only strong in academics, but that they can connect with young people and have a passion for teaching. They are upgrading the status of the higher education institutions that are responsible for preparing teachers, making sure that they have a deep, conceptually based understanding of the subjects they with teach and have really mastered the craft of teaching. The most advanced are creating real careers in teaching to match the kind of careers that are available in the high status professions. They are creating professional standards for teachers, paralleling the high standards set for professionals in the high status fields. They are reorganizing schools and changing the way they are managed so that teachers, far from simply doing what they are told to do in isolated classrooms, can instead work with one another in teams to design more and more effective experiences for their students. Teachers in these systems are increasingly seen as the engine for school improvement, not simply implementing the recommendations made by university researchers, but doing their own research, sharing it with their colleagues and advancing the field themselves, with the support of the research community. Teachers in these top performing countries are treated with respect not because these countries are mounting respect-for-teachers campaigns, but because they are treated like professionals, are expected to work to professional standards, and are producing professional results in a professional work environment.

This landmark study documents that transformation in detail.

MARC TUCKER, PRESIDENT
NATIONAL CENTER ON EDUCATION AND THE ECONOMY

ACKNOWLEDGMENTS

NO MAJOR PROJECT LIKE this one is completed without the participation and assistance of many people. We wish to acknowledge and thank the many individuals and organizations who generously donated their time and energy to help with the planning and implementation of the study and who shared with us their knowledge and experiences in the preparation of this book.

First, we'd like to thank Marc Tucker and Betsy Brown-Ruzzi at the National Center on Education and the Economy for conceptualizing and guiding this study and helping it come to fruition. We would also thank the advisors of the Center on International Education Benchmarking who provided thoughtful reviews and feedback about the drafts: Kai-ming Cheng, Michael Day, Sing Kong Lee, Tony Mackay, Barry McGaw, Ursula Renold, and Minxuan Zhang.

We acknowledge the contributions of the Ford Foundation to the components of this research addressing the uses of time in the different educational systems we studied. We also offer our thanks to Barnett Berry and the Center for Teaching Quality, whose teachers contributed their experiences and perspectives to this work.

We would like to give our sincere appreciation to the members of the project team—Sonya Keller and Jon Snyder—for their critically important help in organizing and managing the research process—and to Maude Engstrom for her excellent research assistance in summarizing key themes for the cross-case volume. We thank Kathleen Cushman, Ben Pender-Cudlip, and Justin Samaha for their wonderful work developing the many audiovisual items that accompany this volume, along with Brendan Williams-Kief and Jennifer Craw for their work on the project website.

In addition to the leaders of the case study teams, named as authors of this book, we want to gratefully acknowledge the other contributors to the teams: Raisa Ahtiainen, Jesslyn Hollar, Jiacheng Li, Ann Lieberman, Pamela Osmond-Johnson, Shane Pisani, Pasi Sahlberg, and Jacqueline Sohn. Robert Rothman assisted in drawing from their work for the cross-case analysis.

We'd also like to thank the many educational experts with whom we spoke. We acknowledge in particular the faculty and staff members of the Universities of Melbourne, Sydney, and Wollongong, and of La Trobe University; Shanghai and East China Normal Universities; University of Helsinki; Universities of Alberta, British Columbia, Calgary, and Ontario; and the National Institute of Education at Nanyang Technical University.

We are grateful to the many policy makers who gave their time to this project. This work would not have been possible without the cooperation of the ministries of education, teachers' federations, and other governmental and regulatory agencies in each jurisdiction. We give our thanks to the many senior staff members who provided important information on the context and goals of policy reforms, and we are grateful for their generosity with their time and thoughtful perspectives.

Special thanks go to the many schools, principals, teachers, staff members, and students who so generously opened their doors to us, provided us with information and materials, and allowed us to enter and observe their classes. In particular, we'd like to thank the staff members and students of Engadine High, Canley Vale Primary, Homebush West Primary, Footscray North Primary, Willmott Park Primary, and Rosanna Golf Links Primary schools in Australia; Myllypuro Primary, Poikkilaakso Primary, Langinkoski, Koulumestari, and Viikki Teacher Training schools in Finland; Shanghai Jiangsu Road No.5 Primary, Qibao Experimental Junior High, Pujiang No. 2 Elementary, and Qilun Elementary schools in Shanghai; and Kranji Secondary and Raffles Girls' schools in Singapore.

This work has benefited from all those who contributed their time, energy, and expertise toward this research. Any remaining errors or omissions are our own.

ABOUT THE SPONSORING ORGANIZATIONS

THIS WORK IS MADE possible through a grant by the Center on International Education Benchmarking of the National Center on Education and the Economy and is part of a series of reports on teacher quality systems around the world. For a complete listing of the material produced by this research program, please visit www.ncee.org/cieb.

CENTER ON INTERNATIONAL EDUCATION BENCHMARKING
LEARNING FROM THE WORLD'S HIGH PERFORMING EDUCATION SYSTEMS

The Center on International Education Benchmarking, a program of NCEE, funds and conducts research around the world on the most successful education systems to identify the strategies those countries have used to produce their superior performance. Through its books, reports, website, monthly newsletter, and a weekly update of education news around the world, CIEB provides up-to-date information and analysis on those countries whose students regularly top the PISA league tables. Visit www.ncee.org/cieb to learn more.

The National Center on Education and the Economy was created in 1988 to analyze the implications of changes in the international economy for American education, formulate an agenda for American education based on that analysis, and seek wherever possible to accomplish that agenda through policy change and development of the resources educators would need to carry it out. For more information visit www.ncee.org.

Stanford | Center for
Opportunity Policy in Education

Research for this book was coordinated by the Stanford Center for Opportunity Policy in Education (SCOPE) at Stanford University. SCOPE was founded in 2008 to foster research, policy, and practice to advance high-quality, equitable education systems in the United States and internationally.

ABOUT THE LEAD AUTHORS

 **Linda Darling-Hammond,** president of the Learning Policy Institute, is the Charles E. Ducommun Professor of Education Emeritus at Stanford University, where she founded the Stanford Center for Opportunity Policy in Education (SCOPE) and served as the faculty sponsor of the Stanford Teacher Education Program, which she helped to redesign.

Darling-Hammond is past president of the American Educational Research Association and recipient of its awards for Distinguished Contributions to Research, Lifetime Achievement, Research Review, and Research-to-Policy. She is also a member of the American Association of Arts and Sciences and of the National Academy of Education. From 1994–2001, she was executive director of the National Commission on Teaching and America's Future, whose 1996 report *What Matters Most: Teaching for America's Future* was named one of the most influential reports affecting US education in that decade. In 2006, Darling-Hammond was named one of the nation's ten most influential people affecting educational policy. In 2008, she served as the leader of President Barack Obama's education policy transition team.

Darling-Hammond began her career as a public school teacher and cofounded a preschool and a public high school. She has consulted widely with federal, state, and local officials and educators on strategies for improving education policies and practices. Among her more than 500 publications are a number of award-winning books, including *The Right to Learn, Teaching as the Learning Profession, Preparing Teachers for a Changing World* and *The Flat World and Education.* She received an EdD from Temple University (with highest distinction) and a BA from Yale University (magna cum laude).

 **Dion Burns** is a senior researcher with the Learning Policy Institute and research analyst at the Stanford Center for Opportunity Policy in Education. With a background in policy and quantitative analysis, his research has focused on international education policies, particularly those that promote high-quality and equitable learning opportunities.

Over the past 20 years, Dion has variously worked as a teacher in Japan, a higher education policy analyst in New Zealand, and an education diplomat with roles in Latin America and the Republic of Korea.

Carol Campbell is associate professor of Leadership and Educational Change and director of the Knowledge Network for Applied Education Research (KNAER) at the Ontario Institute for Studies in Education (OISE), University of Toronto. Her publications include *Teacher Learning and Leadership: Of, By and For Teachers*.

A. Lin Goodwin is the Evenden Professor of Education and vice dean at Teachers College, Columbia University, New York. She recently served as vice president of the American Educational Research Association (AERA)-Division K: Teaching and Teacher Education.

Karen Hammerness is the director of Educational Research and Evaluation at the American Museum of Natural History. She has previously contributed chapters about teacher education to a number of books, including *Teacher Education around the World: Changing Policies and Practices* and *Preparing Teachers for a Changing World*.

Ee Ling Low is professor of Applied Linguistics and Teacher Learning at the National Institute of Education, Nanyang Technological University, Singapore, where she is head of Strategic Planning and Academic Quality and elected member of the NTU Senate.

Ann McIntyre is an experienced principal, superintendent, and former director of Professional Learning and Leadership Development in New South Wales, Australia. In this role she led the development of professional frameworks, programs, and research. Ann's work is recognized for its impact on quality teaching, leadership, and school improvement.

Mistilina Sato is an associate professor of teacher development and science education at the University of Minnesota-Twin Cities. She is the inaugural holder of the Carmen Starkson Campbell Chair for Innovation in Teacher Development.

Kenneth Zeichner is the Boeing Professor of Teacher Education at the University of Washington, Seattle and a member of the National Academy of Education. His publications include *Teacher Education and the Struggle for Social Justice* (2009), and *Struggling for the Soul of Teacher Education* (2017).

ONLINE DOCUMENTS AND VIDEOS

Access online documents and videos at
http://ncee.org/empowered-educators

Link number	Description	URL
1-1	Video of professional learning practices at Kranji High School, Singapore	http://ncee.org/2016/12/video-professional-development-in-singapore/
2-1	Australian Institute of Teaching and School Leadership Chair Tony Mackay discusses key challenges Australia faced in making systemic educational change.	http://ncee.org/2016/12/interview-with-tony-mackay-part-1/
2-2	The Melbourne Declaration on the Educational Goals for Young Australians	http://ncee.org/2016/12/national-declaration-on-the-educational-goals-for-young-australians/
2-3	A report on Canada's approach to school funding	http://ncee.org/wp-content/uploads/2016/12/Alb-non-AV-9-Herman-2013-Canadas-Approach-to-School-Funding.pdf
2-4	Harvard University Visiting Professor Pasi Sahlberg discusses Finland's approach to curriculum and assessment.	http://ncee.org/2016/12/video-pasi-sahlberg-on-curriculum/
2-5	China National Plan for Medium- and Long-Term Education Reform and Development (2010-2020)	http://ncee.org/2016/12/china-education-plan-2010-2020/
3-1	Harvard University Visiting Professor Pasi Sahlberg discusses the process in Finland for recruiting and selecting teachers.	http://ncee.org/2016/12/video-pasi-sahlberg-on-teacher-recruitment/

Link number	Description	URL
3-2	Melbourne Graduate School of Education Deputy Director of Teaching and Learning Larissa McLean Davies describes how teacher candidates are recruited and selected to enter the Master of Teaching program.	http://ncee.org/2016/12/video-interview-with-larissa-mclean-davies-part-3/
3-3	Ontario College of Teachers Standards of Practice for the Teaching Profession	http://ncee.org/2016/12/ontario-standards-of-practice/
3-4	Alberta Education Teaching Quality Standards	http://ncee.org/2016/12/alberta-teaching-quality-standards/
3-5	The Australian Professional Standards for Teachers	http://ncee.org/2016/12/australian-professional-standard-for-teachers/
3-6	University of Helsinki Director of Elementary Teacher Education Anu Laine discusses the role of research in teacher education.	http://ncee.org/2016/12/audio-anu-laine-part-1/
3-7	Teacher Training Schools in Finland	http://ncee.org/2016/12/video-finnish-teacher-training-school/
3-8	Viikki Teacher Training School Teacher Sirkku Myllyntausta describes her role as a teacher and researcher	http://ncee.org/2016/12/audio-sirkku-myllyntausta/
3-9	NSW Department of Education and Communities' *Great Teaching, Inspired Learning* policy for building teaching quality	http://ncee.org/2016/12/great-teaching-inspired-learning/
3-10	Melbourne Graduate School of Education Dean Field Rickards describes the clinical teaching framework and academic supports in the Master of Teaching program.	http://ncee.org/2016/12/video-field-rickards/
3-11	Ontario policymakers, a teacher, and a university professor discuss policy changes, diversity, and action-oriented pedagogy in initial teacher education in the province	http://ncee.org/2017/01/audio-initial-teacher-education/

Link number	Description	URL
3-12	Singapore National Institute of Education's TE21—Teacher Education Model for the 21st Century	http://ncee.org/2016/12/teacher-education-model-for-the-21st-century/
3-13	Video of a day in the life of a Singaporean teacher	http://ncee.org/2016/12/video-day-in-the-life-of-a-singaporean-teacher/
3-14	Victorian Institute of Teaching Director of Special Projects Fran Cosgrove describes the cycle of teacher inquiry that supports teacher mentorship and registration.	http://ncee.org/2016/12/audio-fran-cosgrove-on-mentorship/
3-15	NSW Secretary of the Department of Education and Communities, Michele Bruniges, discusses NSW's policies and approach to building teacher quality.	http://ncee.org/2016/12/video-michele-bruniges-on-teacher-quality/
4-1	Austral Public School Assistant Principal Daniel McKay discusses how teacher professional learning is supported in his school.	http://ncee.org/2016/12/video-daniel-mckay/
4-2	Raffles Girls School Director of the Center for Pedagogical Research and Learning Mary George Cheriyan describes "professional learning space" and the "create, implement, review" cycle for educators.	http://ncee.org/2017/01/video-mary-george-cheriyan-on-professional-learning/
4-3	Kranji Secondary School Principal Tan Hwee Pin describes the time her teachers have for professional learning during the school day.	http://ncee.org/2016/12/video-tan-hwee-pin-part-1/
4-4	Alberta Teachers' Association Framework for Professional Development in Alberta	http://ncee.org/2016/12/a-framework-for-professional-development-in-alberta/

Link number	Description	URL
4-5	Victoria's Teacher Learning Network Executive Officer Michael Victory discusses TLN's approach to professional learning in leadership, classroom management, IT, teaching practices, and early childhood.	http://ncee.org/2016/12/video-michael-victory-part-1/
4-6	Qibao Middle School Teaching Contest Evaluation Form	http://ncee.org/2016/12/qilun-primary-teacher-annual-evaluation/
4-7	Helsinki assessment of teacher personal performance	http://ncee.org/2016/12/finland-teacher-evaluation-form/
4-8	NSW Teacher Performance and Development Framework	http://ncee.org/2016/12/nsw-performance-and-development-framework/
4-9	NSW Principals Estelle Southall and Annette Udall discuss the differentiation and personalization of teachers' professional learning in schools.	http://ncee.org/2016/12/video-estelle-southall-and-annette-udall-part-1/
4-10	Singapore Ministry of Education Teacher Growth Model fact sheet	http://ncee.org/2016/12/teacher-growth-model-tgm/
4-11	Kranji Secondary School Senior Teacher Rosmiliah Bte Kasmin describes how teacher evaluation supports professional growth in Singapore.	http://ncee.org/2016/12/video-rosmiliah-bte-kasmin/
4-12	Qilun Primary School student evaluation of teachers survey	http://ncee.org/2016/12/qilun-primary-students-evaluation-of-teachers-survey/
5-1	Description of the Singapore National Institute of Education teaching and learning e-portfolio	http://ncee.org/2016/12/teaching-and-learning-e-portfolio/
5-2	Australian Institute of Teaching and School Leadership Chair Tony Mackay describes the various planks of AITSL's platform for high-quality teaching and leadership, system-wide.	http://ncee.org/2016/12/video-tony-mackay-part-4/

Link number	Description	URL
5-3	Overview of the Ontario Teacher Learning and Leadership Program	http://ncee.org/2016/12/teacher-learning-and-leadership-program-overview/
5-4	Quick facts regarding Ontario's Leadership Strategy	http://ncee.org/2016/12/ontario-leadership-strategy-quick-facts/
5-5	The Australian Professional Standard for Principals	http://ncee.org/2016/12/australian-professional-standard-for-principals/
5-6	Bastow Institute of Educational Leadership Director Bruce Armstrong discusses government investment in developing high-quality teaching and school leadership across the system.	http://ncee.org/2016/12/video-bruce-armstrong-part-1/
5-7	University of Melbourne Director of Education Research John Hattie describes his efforts to help school leaders analyze the impact on students of teachers' effectiveness in meeting standards.	http://ncee.org/2016/12/audio-john-hattie/
6-1	University of Helsinki Director of Elementary Teacher Education Anu Laine describes the extra resources available for teachers of students from low socioeconomic backgrounds.	http://ncee.org/2016/12/audio-anu-laine-part-2/
6-2	Alberta Education guide to K–12 education funding in Alberta	http://ncee.org/2017/01/education-funding-in-alberta/
6-3	Ontario government guide to the grants for student needs in Ontario	http://ncee.org/2016/12/ontario-guide-to-funding-for-student-needs/
6-4	A review of funding for schools in Australia	http://ncee.org/2016/12/review-of-funding-for-schools-gonski/

Link number	Description	URL
6-5	University of Alberta Vice-Dean Randy Wimmer describes the community-based aboriginal teacher-education program he initiated, and the challenges of bringing large numbers of teacher candidates into diverse professional contexts.	http://ncee.org/2016/12/audio-randy-wimmer/
6-6	Ontario Ministry of Education Director of Student Success Rob Andrews describes the province's strategy for supporting students experiencing persistent achievement challenges.	http://ncee.org/2017/01/audio-rob-andrews-part-1/
7-1	Australian Institute of Teaching and School Leadership Chair Tony Mackay discusses improvement and innovation as a networked ecosystem that constructs new knowledge about teaching and learning.	http://ncee.org/2016/12/video-tony-mackay-part-3/
7-2	Training requirements for Shanghai teachers in the role of *banzhuren*.	http://ncee.org/2016/12/training-of-banzhuren/
p. 159	Video illustrations of professional practice under the Australian Professional Standards for Teachers	http://aitsl.edu.au/australian-professional-standards-for-teachers/illustrations-of-practice/find-by-career-stage
p. 184	Ontario Teachers' Federation profiles the Ontario Teacher Learning and Leadership Program	http://www.youtube.com/watch?v=3DCiHTSaZu8&feature=youtube

TEACHING POLICY AROUND THE WORLD

Three teachers huddle around a laptop (Link 1-1) in the school library at Kranji Secondary School in Singapore. Rosmiliah, a senior teacher, and her two colleagues are engaged in an intense discussion of geographic information systems (GIS) and how to incorporate them into their teaching of geography. The trio constitutes just one of many teacher groups working on year-long projects to create new and innovative learning resources.

Along with each of their colleagues, these teachers will share their research findings at an annual learning festival attended by academics, teacher educators, and other practitioners, with awards given for the best projects. Rosmiliah laughs as she explains that none of the teachers was initially familiar with GIS, but by working together, they had incorporated it into a field research project with students, who found the new lessons fun and engaging. She explains:

> Being a teacher, if you just keep on doing the same things every time without knowing what others are doing, or different ways to do it, you may be a bit boring—students may not find your lessons engaging. . . Teaching is alive . . . so the teacher is always learning as well.

In addition to these professional learning community groups, all teachers at Kranji take part in the school-wide "Learn and Grow" professional development workshops held fortnightly, in which the senior teachers introduce and model specific pedagogical strategies in "Skillful Teacher" workshops. In their 15 hours per week of non-teaching time, teachers plan together and may engage in lesson study or action research within their departments. Beginners receive regular mentoring from senior teachers like Rosmiliah. As teachers gain experience, they have opportunities to expand their skills and climb a career ladder that makes their expertise available to others. This includes teachers in a dozen other schools that learn together in a network, or cluster, and those who attend sessions facilitated by master teachers at the Singapore Teachers Academy.

This rich learning environment for teachers is not the work of a single innovative school or principal: Kranji is much like any other neighborhood school in Singapore. The opportunities for teachers to collaborate and engage in professional learning are embedded systemically in Singapore's education policy.

Although Singapore is well known internationally for its strong investment and thoughtful designs for education, it is not alone. A growing body of research has found that high-performing countries have in common a set of strategies for developing, supporting, and sustaining the ongoing learning and development of their teachers and school leaders (Barber & Mourshed, 2007; Lee, Lee, & Low, 2013; Tucker, 2011). These countries not only train individual educators well, but also they deliberately organize the sharing of expertise among teachers and administrators within and across schools so that the system as a whole becomes ever more effective. And they not only cultivate innovative practices but also they incorporate them into the system as a whole, rather than leaving them as exceptions at the margins.

This book describes how this seemingly magical work is done: how a number of high-performing education systems create a coherent set of policies designed to ensure quality teaching in all communities—and how the results of these policies are manifested in practice. Across three continents and five countries, we examined seven jurisdictions that have worked to develop comprehensive teaching policy systems: Singapore and Finland, the states of New South Wales and Victoria in Australia, the provinces of Alberta and Ontario in Canada, and the province of Shanghai in China.

Serving increasingly diverse student populations while seeking to meet more challenging learning standards geared to 21st-century expectations, each of these jurisdictions has focused intently on how to develop and support higher-quality teaching across all of its schools. This book describes how governments in these places have carefully developed, planned, and implemented what we call a *teaching and learning system* and the lessons that can be learned from these systems.

What Kinds of Policies Affect Teaching?

Creating such a system does not actually require magic. It requires purposeful policies in a number of areas that shape the teaching force and the work of teachers:

- o *Recruitment:* identifying and selecting individuals with the right blend of academic abilities and personal attributes to become effective teachers

- o *Teacher preparation:* providing candidates with deep content knowledge and understanding of pedagogy, together with the clinical learning that translates these into quality teaching

- o *Induction and mentoring:* ensuring that early-career teachers have the opportunity to observe, plan with, and learn from experienced teachers as they enter the profession

- o *Professional learning:* ensuring ongoing learning opportunities for teachers to continually develop and improve their practice and to share their expertise

- o *Teacher feedback and appraisal:* creating systems for providing feedback to teachers about their practice and for furthering teachers' ongoing development as professionals

- o *Career and leadership development:* providing pathways for teachers that support individual growth and the development of strong educational leaders

These policy areas are mutually supportive. Recruitment strategies that select capable individuals well suited to teaching may help initial teacher education programs produce high-quality teacher graduates, even as high-quality preparation serves as a magnet for talented candidates. Induction and mentoring practices that effectively aid teachers' transition to the classroom are known to support retention in the profession, helping teachers gain in experience and effectiveness (Darling-Hammond, 1998; Ingersoll & Strong, 2011). Opportunities for veteran teachers to offer mentoring can also enhance their career satisfaction and retention as well as their ongoing learning and growing expertise. Effective feedback can inform professional learning, highlighting areas for development that support quality teaching. As teaching becomes a public activity—with educators sharing and receiving feedback on their practice—the profession as a whole is strengthened.

Beyond these areas of teacher policy, it is important to understand how other educational policies inform and enable quality teaching and learning to take place.

○ *School curriculum, assessments, and accountability* systems shape what teachers are expected to teach and how students are expected to show their learning—which can greatly influence instruction.

○ *School funding strategies* shape the resources and supports teachers have available to do their work and the degree to which teachers themselves are equitably distributed.

○ *School organization and scheduling* influence the time teachers have available to collaborate and learn from each other.

These elements play out within a social and political context that shapes school conditions, supports for children and families, and the design and implementation of policies. We illustrate how these components interact in Figure 1–1.

Figure 1–1 Policies in a Teaching and Learning System

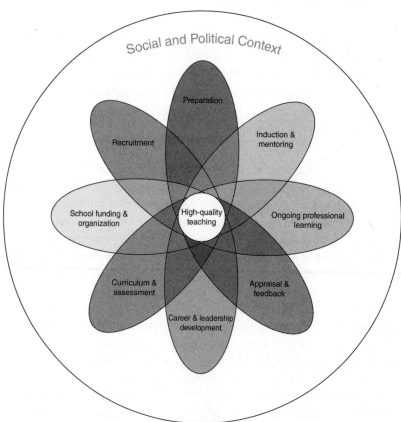

Responding to different educational challenges, countries and provinces differ in their relative emphasis on elements of the policy system and the manner in which policies are implemented. For example, as we show in subsequent chapters, Finland has placed particular emphasis on effective recruitment strategies and strong teacher preparation; in Singapore, collaborative professional learning and well-developed career pathways are key levers; in Shanghai, intensive mentoring of beginners and development of all teachers' practice is facilitated by school designs that provide significant time for collaboration and learning. Though the emphasis and balance of policies may vary, none of these functions is neglected in well-functioning policy environments.

Every country faces differing circumstances and contexts for education. Moreover, implementation strategies necessarily vary, because each context poses different challenges that must be addressed in order to avoid the "slip between the cup and the lip" that can undermine policy intentions when initiatives make their way to schools. However, common elements and themes emerge in these settings that, taken with the proper analytical grain of salt, can yield important lessons for improving education policy and teaching quality across other nations and settings.

We know that the factors shaping teaching and student outcomes are complex, and so we have sought to avoid facile explanations or silver bullet solutions. Instead, building on our examination of hundreds of documents and in-country interviews at every level of these systems, coupled with in-depth observations in schools, we provide rich descriptions of the policies and their implementation in these educational systems. (See Appendix A for a description of the study's methodology.) We further examine how these approaches contribute to well-developed teaching practices and in turn facilitate learning that prepares students for the growing complexity of 21st-century economies. Through this investigation, we aim to uncover lessons and principles that might inform the way policy makers and practitioners think about educational policy as it may apply to their own settings.

Why Study International Teaching Policy?

Research into educational performance around the globe increasingly points to the role of a strong teaching workforce in achieving a high-performing system. In a now well-known study of 25 education systems, researchers Barber and Mourshed (2007) found that these countries had several features in common. First, policies were designed to find people with the right skills and attributes to become teachers. Competitive salaries helped make the profession attractive to potential candidates, and high standards were set for entry into and graduation from initial teacher education programs. Together these helped raise the status of teaching, creating a virtuous cycle for ongoing recruitment.

Second, these systems developed teacher education programs that promoted the integration of theory with the building of practical skills, and they established policies for ongoing learning that helped teachers identify areas for growth, learn from each other, and improve their instructional practices. Coaching and professional learning opportunities helped support ongoing teacher development and instructional leadership.

Third, these systems created strategies to ensure that all students, not just some, had access to high-quality instruction. As the report notes:

> Getting the right people to become teachers and developing them into effective instructors gives school systems the capacity they need to deliver the improved instruction that leads to improved outcomes. High-performing school systems go further than this and put in place processes which are designed to ensure that every child is able to benefit from this increased capacity. (Barber & Mourshed, 2007, p. 34)

These processes can include not only the equitable distribution of well-qualified educators and overall school funding but also the additional instructional, health, and welfare supports that enable students to benefit from quality teaching. Studies from the Organization for Economic Cooperation and Development (OECD) find that allocating resources to better address students' needs helps disrupt the usually strong relationship between students' socioeconomic background and their achievement (OECD, 2013a, 2013b).

Although there is widespread agreement that attention to educator recruitment, preparation, and development matters, less is understood about how countries and states create and manage such systems in very different contexts and how they integrate their teaching policies with their approaches to curriculum, assessment, accountability, and school design—creating a comprehensive teaching and learning system. We take on these questions in this study.

Policy systems that support high-quality teaching practices are of intense importance in an era characterized by rapid knowledge expansion and change. Researchers at the University of California at Berkeley have shown that more new knowledge was created between 1999 and 2003 than in the entire history of the world preceding—and knowledge growth continues exponentially (Lyman & Varian, 2003). Technology knowledge is doubling every 11 months, and technology advances are continually automating routine functions that once created low-skilled jobs. Not only can computers check you in at the airport and check you out at the grocery store, they can also, together with robotics, clean houses, conduct surgery, and steer self-driving cars.

University of Oxford researchers estimated that 47% of more than 700 present-day occupations in the US economy are susceptible to being computerized (Frey & Osborne, 2013). And many of the fastest-growing (and highest-paying) jobs in today's economy did not exist 10 years ago: mobile application developer, digital strategist, market research data miner, social media consultant, and sustainability expert (Casserly, 2012).

Students entering school today will leave to work in jobs that do not yet exist, using knowledge that has not yet been discovered and technologies that have not yet been invented, facing complex problems our generation has been unable to solve. As a consequence, the top skills demanded by employers are not merely following directions and counting change but the abilities to make sense out of complex information and events, think creatively to solve novel problems, work well with others, engage effectively in cross-cultural contexts, and manage many forms of media as well as quantitative data in sophisticated ways. Students today need much more than simply to recall a canon of received knowledge. They need to be able to find, analyze, synthesize, evaluate, and apply knowledge to new ideas, answers, and solutions; communicate in multiple forms, use new technologies, and collaborate with others; and become able to learn on their own throughout life.

Meanwhile, growing international migration is creating increasingly diverse societies. Young people, especially, are also likely to engage in multiple online communities. Each of these brings people with different perspectives and cultures into closer proximity and contact. Such exchanges yield new ideas, innovations, and possibilities, as well as transforming traditional notions of community, citizenship, and democracy.

The kind of teaching required to support contemporary learning goals in this context is very different from what was required when the goal was merely to "cover the curriculum" and "get through the book," enabling some students to succeed if they could and others to fail. In order to enable very diverse students to learn the higher-order skills once reserved for a tiny few, teachers need a range of new skills. They must understand content more deeply and flexibly; they must understand the science of learning—how children learn and develop in cultural contexts, generally and individually, within and across distinctive subject areas; they must understand how to support language acquisition and use for native and nonnative students; they must develop teaching strategies that foster analysis and reasoning; and they must continually incorporate appropriate technologies into their teaching practice.

"Chalk and talk" methods used to impart facts will need to give way to methods for engaging students in applied learning, facilitated by teachers. Teachers will be increasingly called on to collect and analyze a range of assessment data to ensure all students are learning and provide differentiated teaching to students of varying abilities in the same classroom. All of these expectations have implications for how teachers are trained, the supports that they receive early in their careers, and their ongoing professional learning to help them develop and maintain effective teaching practices.

Beyond teachers' work in classrooms—and through the other places and modalities that will no doubt evolve—educators must learn how to redesign schools and education systems to support these goals. Governments must reconceptualize how they think about education, the role of schools, and what and how students are taught. It is therefore critical to pay attention not just to single policies but also to the ways in which policies interact and how they function as a policy *system* that together provides an enabling environment in which quality teaching and learning can occur and evolve to meet new demands. We take up all of these issues in this book.

With all of these factors in mind, we focus on *teaching* because it is where the rubber hits the road, so to speak—where the direct engagement between students and the content and processes of their learning occurs and can be most effectively leveraged. Teachers facilitate this process, and the strategic moves they make—in selecting and orchestrating materials, activities, examples, and supports—are the primary mediators of learning.

Why Study These Jurisdictions?

The jurisdictions we chose to study have made considerable investments in developing teaching and learning systems that include a coherent approach to supporting teaching quality. All of them have also demonstrated considerable success on international indicators of educational quality that emphasize the kinds of higher-order skills needed in contemporary societies, such as OECD's Program for International Student Assessment (PISA). Further, most of these education systems include significant linguistic, cultural, and racial and ethnic diversity, and all of them have exhibited strong achievement and growing equity for students who are lower income, immigrants, and members of long-standing minority groups.

For example, the populations of Australia and Canada include large numbers of immigrants (28% and 21%, respectively) (ABS, 2015; Statistics Canada, 2013), far more than in the United States (approximately 13%). They are also working to reduce achievement gaps for their significant aboriginal or First Nations populations and those living in rural or remote communities. Singapore is a multiethnic nation within which the three largest groups—Chinese, Tamil, and Malay—define three national languages that are explicitly preserved while English is taught in school. All students are supported to become bilingual English speakers. Other immigrants with a wide array of additional languages are also supported to preserve their mother tongue whenever possible while learning English and one of the other national languages.

Shanghai's Chinese population features many language dialects and groups of widely varying income and educational experiences, as is common throughout China. Roughly 20% of Shanghai's student population in grades 1 through 9 is composed of children of migrant families, reflecting a national trend of mass rural migration to the industrial centers of the nation (OECD, 2011, p. 96). And Finland, commonly thought of as a homogeneous country, has a growing number of immigrants, speaking more than 60 languages, with the largest number of children from Bosnia, Britain, China, Estonia, Germany, India, Iran, Iraq, Russia, Serbia, Somalia, Sweden, Turkey, Thailand, United States, and Vietnam (Statistics Finland, 2014b). In some urban schools, the number of immigrants and children with a home language other than Finnish is close to 50% (Sahlberg, 2007, p. 149).

All of these jurisdictions have high rates of educational attainment, with high school graduation rates generally exceeding 85% and college-going rates climbing rapidly. Recognizing that many factors other than schools influence educational achievement and attainment, including nations' investments in children's welfare, we note that student achievement in all of these jurisdictions exceeds the OECD average in reading, mathematics, and science as measured by the PISA (see Table 1–1). The PISA tests go beyond recall and recognition of information, emphasizing the ability of students to apply knowledge to new circumstances—the kind of competencies of increasing relevance to 21st-century learners.

In addition, these jurisdictions produce proportionately greater numbers of high achievers, shown here in Figure 1–2 by the proportions of students scoring at levels 4, 5, and 6 on PISA, reflecting a greater ability to solve complex problems.

Table 1–1 PISA 2012 Mean Scores and Rank

Jurisdiction	Mathematics		Reading		Science	
	Rank	Mean Score	Rank	Mean Score	Rank	Mean Score
Shanghai	1	613	1	570	1	580
Singapore	2	573	3	542	3	551
Finland	12	519	6	524	5	545
Canada	13	518	9	523	10	525
Alberta		517		525		539
Ontario		514		528		527
Australia	19	504	14	512	16	521
Victoria		501		517		518
New South Wales		509		513		526
OECD		494		496		501
United States	36	481	24	498	28	497

Source: OECD (2014c). Used with permission.

Equally important is the extent to which each jurisdiction provides equality of educational opportunity. A growing focus on equity is linked to an increasing recognition that for countries to compete in the context of greater economic and social globalization, all students—not just some—must have the necessary skills to be successful in the modern workplace and society (Tucker, 2011).

Figure 1–2 PISA 2012 Proficiency Levels

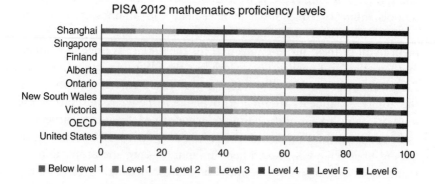

Source: OECD (2014c). Used with permission.

Figure 1–3 Relationship of Student Performance and Equity

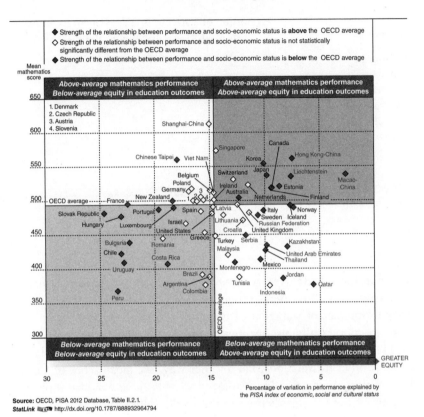

Source: OECD, PISA 2012 Database, Table II.2.1.
StatLink http://dx.doi.org/10.1787/888932964794

Note: Percentage of variation of performance explained by the PISA index of economic, social, and cultural status.
Source: OECD (2013a). Table II.2.1. Used with permission.

One broad measure of equity is the relationship between socioeconomic status and achievement. A lower correlation signals greater equity, because socioeconomic status is less strongly related to student performance. As shown in Figure 1–3, our study jurisdictions are found primarily in the upper-right-hand quadrant, indicating both above average achievement and a greater-than-average equity quotient (measured by the impact of socioeconomic status on mathematics score).

In Finland, Canada, Singapore, and Australia, the proportion of variance in achievement explained by socioeconomic status of students was

Table 1–2 PISA 2012 Variation in Score Attributable to Socioeconomic Status

Jurisdiction	Proportion of Variance in Achievement Explained by Student Socioeconomic Status (%)
Finland	9.4
Canada	9.4
Alberta	8.9
Ontario	9.6
Australia	12.3
New South Wales	12.8
Victoria	9.0
Singapore	14.4
OECD	14.8
Shanghai	15.1

Source: OECD (2013a). Used with permission.

less than the OECD average (14.8%), whereas Shanghai's measure of equity was just above that average (15.1%)[1] (see Table 1–2). However, the performance of Shanghai's students was so high that the proportion of socioeconomically disadvantaged students scoring at the upper levels on PISA was still significantly higher than that of the entire population of most other jurisdictions. Put another way, the mean score of Shanghai's socioeconomically disadvantaged schools alone would still place it among the top five jurisdictions in the world (OECD, 2013a, p. 257).

We recognize that this relationship can be affected not only by the educational opportunities children experience but also by the extent to which there are wide economic disparities across households in a given jurisdiction: The greater the disparities in children's living conditions, the greater the effect of these disparities are expected to be, so educational access is a function of how schools provide educational opportunities and how children are supported by the society at large to take advantage of those opportunities.

What We Found

Although each country and province has a different history, culture, and context for education, we found many commonalities in how they approach policy making in support of quality teaching. A key goal in all of the jurisdictions was to develop a strong teaching profession, including a commitment to "invest in knowledgeable practitioners who can make sound decisions about how to shape education for the specific clients they serve" (Darling-Hammond, 2009, p. 46).

A professional approach suggests that policy is directed toward the development of a teacher workforce that is highly educated and empowered to make decisions about teaching for the best interests of their students, based on knowledge accumulated from their training and from what they learn about the wisdom of practice from their in-service experiences and sharing of expertise with colleagues. It also suggests that teachers are accountable not only to students and parents but also to each other as professionals to maintain professional standards. Our findings reflect several themes common across these jurisdictions:

1. *A high social regard for teaching:* In virtually all of these jurisdictions, positive views of teaching reflected in public surveys and government statements are also reflected in compensation that is competitive with other professions requiring comparable education. In all of the jurisdictions, starting salaries for teachers are above international averages, and all have significant increases within the first 10 years of teaching. In some jurisdictions, teacher unions negotiate for salaries; in others, the government sets high salaries and raises them consistently without a negotiating process. In some cases, administrators and teachers belong to the same association (Singapore, Australia, and Alberta). In all jurisdictions, unions serve as a voice for the profession, partner with universities or government agencies in advocating for and implementing professional standards, and help shape professional learning opportunities.

2. *Selectivity into the profession:* This high status enables teaching, as a rule, to be selective. Some jurisdictions exert a high bar at initial entry with rigorous selection of candidates into teacher training, others emphasize selective graduation and hiring policies, and some use a blend of the two. The criteria for selecting teachers into the profession include a strong capacity for working with children and appropriate professional dispositions, often including a demonstration of research and pedagogical skills, along with academic ability.

3. *Financial support for preparation and professional learning:* In all of the jurisdictions, preparation is free or substantially subsidized for teacher candidates so that most or all of the costs are covered. In some, candidates also earn a salary or stipend while undergoing preparation. In addition, government support is available for ongoing professional development. As a result, rather than acquiring only as much training as they can afford, teachers typically have ready access to high-quality

learning opportunities and schools can expect them to enter with substantial expertise that they continue to expand.

4. *Professional standards that outline teaching:* Professional standards outlining teaching competencies undergird preparation, professional licensure or registration, professional development, and appraisal in each jurisdiction. These common expectations are focused not only on technical knowledge and skills with respect to content and pedagogy but also on dispositions for learning and collaborating to serve students well. The vision of teaching and learning embedded in these standards is one that values the whole child and his or her development across physical, social, emotional, physical, and moral domains—anticipating that the teacher's role is to support this development. The establishment of such standards as a means to organize professional expectations and learning has been advancing rapidly around the globe and had occurred in various ways in each of our jurisdictions. In addition, among the nations we studied, those without a current system for teacher registration, accreditation, or licensure were actively exploring a means to assess and certify teachers as ready for practice.

5. *Preparation and induction grounded in well-defined curriculum content and well-supported clinical training:* All of the jurisdictions offer thoughtful curriculum guidance (national in small countries and state or provincial in larger ones) that has shaped the learning of teachers as students themselves and that shapes their learning and practice once they enter the profession. In every jurisdiction, these curricula have been recently revised to better reflect 21st-century skills and competencies for students. The curricula for initial teacher education typically focus on content pedagogy tied to the national or state curriculum, as well as an understanding of learning and child development. Teachers receive strong content preparation for the areas they will teach and increasingly strong preparation for teaching diverse learners—including students with special needs and new immigrants.

We also found an increasingly intense focus on extended *clinical training* for teacher candidates. Finland has long trained teachers in model schools connected to the university in master's programs. Today, virtually all of the other jurisdictions are developing or expanding school-university partnerships to provide clinical training that bridges theory and practice, and several are expanding the reach of graduate-level preparation. In Finland, Canada, and Australia, the most extensive clinical supervision typically takes place during initial teacher education, even as support is extended into the first year of teaching through mentoring or induction programs. In Singapore and Shanghai, beyond the student teaching teachers undertake during their preservice preparation, they receive even more intensive mentoring when they begin their careers from trained senior teachers, using the advantage of a reduced workload to engage in collaborative planning and coaching with veterans as well as seminars to deepen their practice.

6. *Teaching as a research-informed and research-engaged profession:* Teacher education and professional development in these jurisdictions are typically based on—and further encourage—research about student and teacher learning. In many cases, strategies such as Finland's model schools; Singapore's and Shanghai's use of lesson study, action research, and other teacher inquiry approaches; or Canada's leadership grants to teachers have sparked new lines of research about teacher development. In addition, the training that new teachers receive is increasingly designed to help them both use research and become researchers about classroom practice—with their work often published for other teachers' and researchers' use. As a consequence, teaching practice itself is becoming more research-engaged and deliberately reflective, with teachers conducting inquiries and action research with colleagues to meet specific teaching challenges. The collection and use of evidence to inform teaching practice is further supported by professional teaching standards and the design of professional development.

7. *Teaching as a collaborative, not isolated, occupation:* Teaching in the countries we studied is viewed as a team sport, not an individual act of courage. Teachers are expected to plan and problem-solve collaboratively, and they are generally afforded time to do so. Teaching practice is "de-privatized" with opportunities for teachers to observe others' classes, be observed, and mentor others. In this way, teacher knowledge and expertise are valued. In most cases, teaching as collaborative professional engagement is explicitly articulated in teaching standards and policy documents that set expectations for the work of teachers, and expectations for contributing to the learning of colleagues are often part of the teacher appraisal process. Beyond teacher sharing within schools, most jurisdictions also sought to foster teacher collaboration across schools to extend quality practices system-wide. This often takes the form of school networks (or pairings) for professional learning. Teachers and principals share expertise within these networks. Some jurisdictions also sponsor subject matter networks or other topical groups that are engaged in professional learning together.

8. *Teacher development as a continuum:* Each of the jurisdictions treats teacher professional learning as a continuum toward ever more effective work in support of student learning and, over time, toward the learning of colleagues as well. Collaboration with colleagues as well as commitment to ongoing learning are key aspects of the evaluation processes used in these jurisdictions, and they are means for identifying teachers as leaders. Teacher evaluation processes are connected to teacher growth and development rather than punitive accountability. And because entry and early induction are so well supported, there is no expectation that eliminating incompetence is a major goal of evaluation. Teaching is regarded as a learning profession, with opportunities for even senior teachers to continually learn new skills and increase their knowledge.

9. *Opportunities for leadership:* There are efforts in every jurisdiction to develop teacher leadership. In a growing number of countries (Singapore, China, and more recently Australia and Canada), teaching and leadership standards articulate knowledge and skill expectations at different career stages, laying out an ongoing pathway for learning with supported paths to leadership across the span of the career. In Singapore and Shanghai, there are highly developed career ladders, with opportunities to become a senior, master, or mentor teacher or a principal or administrator. In Singapore, yet another career track prepares and enlists teachers as specialists in curriculum, applied psychology in education, and educational research, evaluation, and measurement. Australia is developing a similar career ladder system, and teachers in Finland and Canada have opportunities to engage in research, mentoring, curriculum leadership, and school improvement activities as part of their role. In Ontario, a pathway to teacher and administrative leadership has been developed and extensive support for teacher research has been provided. In Finland, teacher leaders have prominent roles in teacher education and research. Each jurisdiction has formal or informal opportunities for teachers to develop pedagogical innovations and participate in school decision making.

10. *Systems organized to support quality teaching and equity:* All of the jurisdictions we studied developed systemic supports for quality teaching that provide an infrastructure to support the work of the individuals in the profession. The availability of national or state curriculum, in each case designed by members of the profession, provides a centerpiece for teachers' work and collaborative planning. This curriculum guidance is generally lean, offering a road map for teachers to meet the needs of their students, not a straitjacket. Stable systems of mentoring and professional

learning with reliable funding are part of this infrastructure, along with scheduled in-school and professional development time, which enable higher-quality teaching across the board with greater equity in learning as a result. Jurisdictions share a focus on fiscal and social justice with equitable funding and a conscious focus on traditionally underserved communities in their funding schemes, teaching standards, and professional development emphases.

Developing Both *Teacher* Quality and *Teaching* Quality

These jurisdictions recognize that, in building a system, it is important not only to develop skills on the part of individual practitioners but also to create the conditions under which practitioners can use their skills appropriately. Thus, they attend to *teacher* quality and *teaching* quality. *Teacher quality* might be thought of as the bundle of personal traits, skills, and understandings an individual brings to teaching, including dispositions to behave in certain ways, including attributes such as the following:

○ Strong content knowledge related to what is to be taught

○ Knowledge of how to teach others in that area (content pedagogy) and skill in implementing productive teaching practices

○ Understanding of learners and their development, including how to support students who have learning differences or difficulties and how to support the learning of language and content for those who are not already proficient in the language of instruction

○ General abilities to organize and explain ideas, observe and think diagnostically, and use adaptive expertise to make judgments about what is likely to work in a given context in response to students' needs (For a summary of studies, see Darling-Hammond, 2000; Darling-Hammond & Bransford, 2005; Wilson, Floden, & Ferrini-Mundy, 2001.)

Most educators, parents, and policy makers would also include important dispositions in this list, such as the willingness to

○ Support learning for all students

○ Teach in a fair and unbiased manner

○ Adapt instruction to help students succeed

○ Strive to continue to learn and improve

○ Collaborate with other professionals and parents in the service of individual students and the school as a whole

Teaching quality, as distinct from teacher quality, refers to strong instruction that enables a wide range of students to learn. Such instruction meets the demands of the discipline, the goals of instruction, and the needs of students in a particular context. Teaching quality is in part a function of teacher quality—teachers' knowledge, skills, and dispositions—but it is also strongly influenced by the context of instruction, including factors external to what the teacher brings. Key to considerations of context are the curriculum and assessment systems that support teachers' work, the opportunities to learn from and work with colleagues, the fit between teachers' qualifications and what they are asked to teach, and teaching conditions. An excellent teacher may not be able to offer high-quality instruction in a context where he or she is asked to teach a flawed curriculum or lacks appropriate materials. Similarly, a well-prepared teacher may perform poorly when asked to teach outside the field of his or her preparation or under poor teaching conditions—for example, without adequate teaching materials, in substandard space, with too little time, or with classes that are far too large. Conversely, a less-skilled teacher may be buoyed up by excellent materials, strong peer support for lesson planning, and additional specialists who work with students who may, for example, need extra help to learn to read.

Even when teachers have equivalent skills, there is little doubt that the quality of instruction experienced by students is greater in a school with high-quality and plentiful books, materials, and computers; a coherent, well-designed curriculum that teachers have built together; a team of teachers working in tandem on similar norms and practices, paying attention to students' needs; and adequate facilities and resources than it is when they must learn in overcrowded, unsafe conditions with insufficient materials, poorly chosen curriculum, teachers struggling in isolation from one another, and no instructional supports.

These jurisdictions have understood that strong teacher quality may heighten the probability of effective teaching, but it does not guarantee it. Initiatives to develop teaching quality and effectiveness must consider not only how to identify, reward, and use individual teachers' skills and abilities but also how to develop teaching contexts that enable good practice. The teaching and learning systems they have developed acknowledge that, if teaching is to be effective, the policies that construct the learning environment and the teaching context must be addressed along with the qualities of individual teachers.

Organization of This Book

We articulate and elaborate each of these themes in the remainder of this book. We begin in Chapter 2 with an analysis of the ways in which education is organized and supported in each of the five countries in our study. We describe the education context within which these policies sit, including the funding arrangements and governance structures in each country. We discuss how each jurisdiction takes an integrated approach to curriculum, instruction, and assessment policy that creates a teaching and learning system. The chapter also outlines the broader context in which policy making occurs, including the major educational challenges and debates raised in each jurisdiction.

Chapter 3 looks at entry into the career, examining specific strategies for educator recruitment, preparation, and early induction into the field. Our discussion addresses how each jurisdiction attracts high-quality individuals into teaching and employs strategies to distribute them equitably and address potential areas of teacher shortages. It then looks at initial teacher education programs and how these are increasingly influenced by a foundation of professional teaching standards. The chapter also describes the ways in which teachers are inducted into the profession, receiving mentorship to extend and guide their early career learning.

The focus of Chapter 4 is the way each jurisdiction approaches teacher professional learning and developing teacher knowledge. The kind of professional learning undertaken is often linked to state or national teaching standards and tied to student learning and school improvement. We discuss the range of professional learning strategies available, including time for professional collaboration, coaching, and mentoring, and the role of government in providing for or supporting teacher learning. We also outline the various approaches to teacher feedback and appraisal and the ways in which these are linked to teachers' professional development.

In Chapter 5, we look at how each jurisdiction structures careers in teaching and develops teacher and administrative leadership. We look at the range of supports available for leadership development and how these leaders become part of the human capital for the teaching and learning system.

Chapter 6 examines how these jurisdictions structure broader education improvement initiatives and organize their systems to promote equity in access to high-quality teaching.

Chapter 7 zooms back out to look at the development of education policy internationally. It discusses where the countries have been evolving and learning from global exemplars, where they see challenges, and how they are viewing and acting on the next horizons for improvement in their own settings. We conclude by summarizing lessons that might be drawn from this research about what matters and what works in developing strong teaching, as well as principles that emerge from policy systems that enable high-quality teaching.

Creating an effective system of policies to support teaching quality can have transformative potential. In just 50 years, for example, countries such as Finland and Singapore have vaulted to among the top-performing educational systems, despite the fact that each had a very underdeveloped and inequitable education system those decades ago, with among the lowest rates of educational attainment in their regions. Although they have very different populations, histories, and social and economic challenges, what they have in common is a policy vision grounded in an ethic of equity and a belief in the power of a professional and effective teaching force. This has helped produce teaching environments similar to that of Kranji Secondary School: a commitment to collaboration and continual improvement. As Singapore's former prime minister Goh Chok Tong noted in a speech announcing his "Thinking Schools, Learning Nation" initiative:

> [This initiative] will redefine the role of teachers . . . Every school must be a model learning organization. Teachers and principals will constantly look out for new ideas and practices, and continuously refresh their own knowledge. Teaching will itself be a learning profession, like any other knowledge-based profession of the future. (Goh, 1997)

NOTE

1. A well-publicized criticism of Shanghai's outcomes with regard to equity is that the proportion of migrant students in PISA (at age 15) is not representative of the number of migrant students at all age ranges and may also exclude migrant students in schools outside the public system. Migrant students are more likely to come from less affluent backgrounds and have access to fewer educational resources. We discuss these issues in later chapters.

2

CONTEXTS FOR TEACHING
AND LEARNING SYSTEMS

EACH OF THE PLACES WE STUDIED has created supports for effective teaching in a particular national context with its own history, social and economic contexts, and political considerations. All have undertaken these initiatives not as a string of disconnected activities but as an effort to create a teaching and learning *system.*

A *system framework* recognizes that societies can support effective teaching in part by constructing attractive teaching careers, selecting talented individuals, ensuring they are well prepared, and developing career pathways that foster ongoing learning experiences for teachers. At the same time, to enable all students to experience such teaching, societies must also figure out how to govern and finance schools so that educators have the authority to use their knowledge to enact successful practices as well as the resources they need to staff and organize successful schools. Curriculum guidance and materials, along with assessments, shape the kind of learning and teaching expected and possible. The discretion principals and teachers have to shape instruction and allocate resources to meet diverse student needs can influence their ultimate effectiveness. Research, opportunities for innovation, and means for sharing knowledge create possibilities for ongoing improvement and progress.

Each of these policies and the overall approach to policy making is informed by the particular context and challenges associated with a jurisdiction's demography, geography, and economy, as well as the distribution of opportunities for students of different backgrounds. In this chapter we provide a snapshot of each of the jurisdictions we studied and the nature of its policy framework and context.

Although each jurisdiction is distinctive in its own ways, it is useful to note that all of them have, since the 1990s, embraced a conception of learning that reflects what are generally called the *21st-century skills*—and moved very purposefully to incorporate higher-order think-ing, complex problem-solving, and competent performance into the cur-riculum and assessment system. Each has also reshaped standards for teachers to reflect the pedagogies needed to teach these new standards to the increasingly diverse populations each jurisdiction serves. And each is moving assertively to enhance equity and opportunity for students who need additional support to meet these goals and expectations.

Australia

Australia is a diverse, multicultural land of contrasts. It is geographi-cally vast—about two-thirds the size of the United States—with a pop-ulation of 23.5 million citizens (just under the population of Texas), most of whom live in the eastern and southeastern coastal cities. How-ever, outside the metropolitan areas, many remote schools are a several-hour drive from the nearest city. This creates challenges for education, including attracting educators to remote areas and providing training and professional learning opportunities. The cultural context is continu-ously changing, because international migration has been the main driver of population growth since the turn of the 21st century (ABS, 2015): Indeed, about 28% of the population was born overseas.

New South Wales (NSW) and Victoria are Australia's two most popu-lous states, together accounting for over half the total population. At 7.5 million people, New South Wales has a population similar in size to Washington state; Victoria's 5.8 million is close to that of Wisconsin. Each is quite urbanized, with about 90% of the population living in cities. In Victoria, nearly three-quarters of the population lives in the greater Melbourne area, and more than half of all residents have a par-ent born abroad. In Victoria and New South Wales, more than a quarter of students in government schools speak a language other than English in the home: Mandarin, Cantonese, Vietnamese, Greek, and Italian are among the common home languages for students in these states. Indige-nous Australians comprise about 2.4% of the population nationally and about 6% of students in New South Wales. Greater equity for diverse students forms a significant focus of educational policy efforts at the national and state levels.

Governance and Funding

Public education has historically been a state function: Education systems are administered by the governments of Australia's six states and two largest territories; however, much of the funding is federal. States receive their funds from national taxes and receive additional targeted funds through partnership agreements with the Australian (national) government. In addition, teacher training in Australia takes place largely in the 40 nationally funded research universities. This gives the Australian government a noticeable role in an otherwise state-based system. About one-third of students attend schools in the Catholic or independent sectors. Although nominally private, schools in each of these sectors also receive the majority of their funds from the Australian government. The schools must offer a curriculum that meets the objectives of the Australian national curriculum, and they participate in NAPLAN, the national testing program.

Since 2008, Australia has moved toward the creation of nationally consistent policies in education, motivated by growing political and public concerns about educational quality and equity (Link 2-1). Although more equitable than many nations, significant achievement gaps exist across states and regions, by school system, and by socioeconomic and indigenous status. For example, the difference in PISA mathematics performance between students in metropolitan and remote areas in 2012 was estimated to be equivalent to nearly 2 years of schooling (Thomson, De Bortoli, & Buckley, 2014).

The policy vision for achieving a high-quality and equitable education system is articulated in the *Melbourne Declaration on Education Goals for Young Australians* (MCEETYA, 2008) (Link 2-2), which has two overarching goals:

○ Goal 1: Australian schooling promotes equity and excellence.

○ Goal 2: All young Australians become successful learners, confident and creative individuals, and active and informed citizens.

The movement to a nationally consistent approach to education policy has included these aspects:

○ *Curriculum and assessment:* The Australian Curriculum, Assessment and Reporting Authority (ACARA) was established in 2008 and has developed a national curriculum framework and a national assessment and public reporting strategy.

○ *Teaching quality:* The Australian Institute of Teaching and School Leadership (AITSL) was established in 2009 and has developed national standards for educators and a framework for all aspects of the teaching and leadership career, from preparation through induction, professional learning, and career advancement. States are implementing these standards and frameworks in locally appropriate ways.

○ *Funding:* National partnership agreements were created between the Australian (federal) and state governments on funding for educational improvement and a nationally consistent, more equitable approach to per-student funding in schools. The increased investments have thus far been partially implemented.

Curriculum and Assessment

Since 2013, states been progressively implementing the Australian curriculum framework, which specifies eight learning areas reflecting subject matter disciplines and seven general capabilities encompassing the "knowledge, skills, behaviors and dispositions that, together with curriculum content in each learning area and the cross-curriculum priorities, will assist students to live and work successfully in the twenty-first century" (ACARA, 2015). The capabilities include these skills:

○ Literacy

○ Numeracy

○ Information and communication technology capability

○ Critical and creative thinking

○ Personal and social capability

○ Ethical understanding

○ Intercultural understanding

In addition, three cross-curricular priorities reflect national aspirations for how Australians live together and in their region. These priorities are Aboriginal and Torres Strait Islander histories and cultures, Asia and Australia's engagement with Asia, and sustainability. The national curriculum functions much like student learning standards and curriculum frameworks have functioned in the United States, creating a road map for student learning goals and topics, which is implemented with locally designed and selected materials.

Each state is charged with aligning state curricula with the Australian curriculum, implementing the resulting version of these learning expectations and credentialing against it in senior secondary schools, where many states have qualifications systems. These allow students to demonstrate their competencies in a wide range of academic and vocational content areas through open-ended examinations that include performance tasks or portfolios. In the lower grades (3, 5, 7, and 9), ACARA conducts national assessments in literacy and numeracy (NAPLAN), the results of which are available on the MySchool website, where parents and the community can see summary demographic, financial, and achievement data for each school. The data show cohort gains over 2 years and comparisons with schools that have similar demographic profiles but are not used to rank or label schools or allocate rewards and sanctions.

After some significant policy arm wrestling at the national level and in some states, states such as NSW have reinforced that the primary role of the test data is to guide school improvement and that the data are intended to be used as an evidence base to identify successful practices in schools and to allocate system resources to meet areas of need. This view was explained by a former official in the NSW government:

> When systemic assessment programs are strongly resourced and clearly aligned to teaching and learning they are more likely to be well received by teachers and schools. In NSW, the provision of diagnostic information linked to curriculum resources and professional learning has enabled the assessment programs to be perceived as another source of credible data to guide the development of learning programs.

Teachers and Teaching

Despite strong support by parents and local communities for individual teachers and schools, the teaching profession as a whole in Australia has historically not been regarded as a high-status occupation (Crowley, 1998). However, this appears to be rapidly changing, with improvements in the standing of teachers an explicit aim of policies at the national and state levels. Increases in salaries have raised teachers' entering wages to levels comparable with lawyers and other professionals. Victoria's current education minister James Merlino (2015) notes, "We are committed to raising the status of the teaching profession, and attracting and retaining the best, high-quality professionals to Victorian government schools."

One part of this has been the translation of the new professional teaching standards into a career ladder framework that states are adopting and adapting to recognize and better use the skills of excellent teachers. In this context, New South Wales recently moved to extend the top salary range above AU$100,000 (roughly equivalent to the US dollar at that time) for those attaining the highly accomplished teacher level. These teachers have opportunities to share their expertise without having to leave the classroom for administration. New South Wales also has added time for collaboration and planning to teachers' schedules. There and throughout Australia, quality teaching is increasingly understood in terms of the national professional teaching standards, which incorporate not only professional knowledge and practice but also professional learning and engagement with colleagues.

Investments in more extensive and clinically based preparation for teachers, stronger induction for beginners, and more widely available professional learning opportunities have also been undertaken during the last decade. Professional learning takes place within and across schools. Grade-level, disciplinary, and other learning teams are common in schools for lesson planning and review of student work, as well as school improvement planning. School networks are a feature of Australian schooling and serve as mechanisms for resource sharing, teacher and school leader professional collaboration and capacity building, and the spreading of effective practices across schools. Together with national policies increasingly underpinning teaching quality, they play an important equity role, helping support learning and greater opportunity across schools. In addition to the new, more equitable funding scheme, equity initiatives also include incentives to draw qualified educators to hard-to-staff communities and provide centrally supported coaches, instructional specialists, and special programs to high-needs schools.

Canada

Similar to Australia, Canada has a federalist system that places responsibility for education at the provincial level. Spread across 10 provinces and three territories, Canada is a country of nearly 36 million people, a little smaller than California in population, though larger than the United States in territory. Although by land area it is the second largest country in the world, 80% of the population lives close to its southern border with the United States. Canada's population is multicultural and multilingual, with about 21% having emigrated from other nations and 11% speaking a home language other than English or French, the two official languages that are also the major languages of schooling (Statistics Canada, 2013).

Within Canada, we focused on Alberta and Ontario, two provinces with multilingual and diverse populations. Among Alberta's 4.2 million citizens, roughly 18% are immigrants—a proportion greater than that of the United States. About 10% of students speak a primary language other than English. In addition, about 9% are identified as First Nations, Métis, and Inuit (FNMI) children. At 13.5 million people—a little larger than Illinois—Ontario is Canada's most populous and internationalized province. It is home to more than 40% of all the nation's immigrants and is ethnically and linguistically diverse, with more than 100 languages spoken (Statistics Canada, 2013). This diversity is also seen in the school system, where some 27% of students were born outside Canada, more than the proportion of immigrants in neighboring New York State (Krogstad & Keegan, 2014).

This population is highly educated, with more than half (53%) having earned a tertiary degree, the highest of any OECD country (OECD, 2014b). Canada typically ranks in the top 10 nations in the world on reading, mathematics, and science: Alberta and Ontario are among the highest-performing of Canadian provinces. Educational achievement is also relatively equitably distributed, with socioeconomic status accounting for just 9% of the variation in outcomes of achievement on PISA 2012 mathematics—well below the OECD average of 14.8% and nearly as equitable as Finland. As Parkin (2015) notes, "Canada is one of only a very few countries that combines overall high achievement, a larger than average immigrant population, and no significant achievement gap between immigrants and non-immigrants" (p. 20).

This equity is supported by a range of social services available to Canadians. All citizens receive free health care and a range of other social services, including a universal childcare benefit to offset the cost of preschool education. As a consequence, even when children come from families with low incomes, most experience less deprivation than they might in many other countries. The government provides support for low-income families in the form of childcare subsidies, rent support and affordable housing, and public health care insurance.

Governance and Funding

Unlike most other OECD countries, Canada has no federal education ministry. Ministries of education in each of the provinces are responsible for setting the policy and legislative frameworks and operating their own school systems. Professionally staffed districts administer schools under the guidance of locally elected boards. In Ontario, for example, each school board is run by a board of trustees composed of elected community members, First Nations appointees, and a student representative. Each school has a school council elected annually and composed of parents, students, staff members, and community member volunteers. All teachers are members of the Ontario Teachers' Federation, an umbrella group for the four sector unions.

There is a federal presence in the form of the Council of Ministers of Education Canada, which meets twice annually and sets a long-term vision for education while playing a coordinating role across provinces and territories. The council facilitates the national Pan-Canadian Assessment Program, which serves to benchmark and inform the public on student achievement in the provinces. It also functions as a mechanism for information sharing, which contributes to some similarities in policies across provinces (Mehta & Schwartz, 2011). Its Learn Canada 2020 policy statement (Council of Ministers of Education, Canada, 2008), which covers early childhood through adult learning, flags areas for national attention. These include, for example, Aboriginal education, minority and second-language programs, and working on national-level performance indicators and learning assessment programs.

Canada's history has produced separate systems of French- and English-speaking schools, which are publicly supported, and private schools of various kinds. In Alberta, about two-thirds of the nearly 2,200 schools are public. The remaining third consist of separate schools (typically Protestant or Catholic), Francophone, charter, private, and band schools for FNMI students. Except for the band schools on the First Nations reserves, which are federally funded, all of these separate schools receive provincial government funding. Funded private schools use the provincial achievement tests and diploma examinations.

In Ontario, 95% of school-aged children attend one of the four publicly funded education systems: English public, English Catholic, French public, or French Catholic. These are all considered public schools. French-immersion schools serve about 5% of Ontario's more than 2 million public school students. School districts in Ontario vary in size from over 250,000 in Toronto to just a few hundred students in rural areas. The small number of private schools that are not government funded can operate independently of the ministry. Those wanting to offer credits toward the Ontario secondary school diploma are inspected and must also use the provincial literacy test in secondary school. Use of the provincial tests in grades 3, 6, 9, and 10 is voluntary for other private schools.

Both provinces have a wide range of initiatives designed to address diversity and close achievement gaps, aimed at ensuring qualified teachers in all communities, culturally responsive curriculum, instructional resources for multilingual maintenance and acquisition of the language of instruction, and well-resourced instructional and social support systems for students. In Ontario, for example, an initiative that provided underperforming schools with additional resources, technical assistance, and professional development supports led to the number of these schools falling from 20% to about 6% even though the threshold for intervention was raised and achievement gaps between first-language English speakers and English language learners were reduced. The current policy vision extends the goals of high achievement, greater equity, and increased public confidence to include promoting students' well-being (Government of Ontario, 2014).

Provinces have different funding schemes for schools (Link 2-3), but all of them seek to equalize educational resources at the local school level and provide additional supports for students with greater needs. This includes factors such as socioeconomic background, First Nations status, geographic location of the school, and disability status. Strong support for education characterizes both provinces. In Alberta, for example, until 2015 the province was led for 90 years by successive conservative governments, each supportive of public education and teachers. This long period of political stability has fostered strong relationships between government and education organizations in the province, resulting in a high level of cooperation, which has fostered a sustained commitment to educational progress. Strong relationships are further enhanced by all teachers and principals belonging to the same educators' union.

As with Alberta, a striking feature of governance in Ontario is the high level of trust and cooperation that exists across and within educational agencies. Since 2003, a core element of the school improvement strategy has been to work with teachers to build confidence in the public schools system, including "job-embedded capacity-building" and the sharing of best practices that are already occurring within schools (Levin, 2014). Consistent with Ontario's theory of action emphasizing the development of shared leadership and capacity building at all levels of the education system, a key feature of the ministry's approach is a blending of policy and educational knowledge that has become embedded in a staff model that combines government officials and experienced educators working together in the ministry and in partnership with the education sector. As one analysis noted, "The key ideas are less about 'hard' concepts like accountability and incentives and more about 'softer' ideas like culture, leadership, and shared purpose" (Mehta & Schwartz, 2011, p. 158).

Curriculum and Assessment

There is no national curriculum in Canada; each province has developed curriculum guidance and programs of study that help organize teaching and teacher development. Alberta's ministry is presently revising the curriculum to encompass 21st-century skills as part of an education vision to "prepare students to be successful in a future world that will be defined by global interaction, competition, engagement and networks." In Ontario, the Ministry of Education has approached these challenges by establishing a continuous cycle of curricular review, with the aim of keeping the curriculum always current and developmentally appropriate. The process is research-based, involving analysis by educational experts, consultation with the field, and providing training to school board teams during implementation (Ontario Ministry of Education, 2013).

Alberta and Ontario assess students periodically (in grades 3 and 6, plus high school) with provincial assessments. These and in-school formative tools are intended to enable assessment for learning. Alberta Education has signaled that outcomes from new student learning assessments, replacing the provincial achievement tests applied in grades 3, 6, 9, and 12, will not be used for evaluating teachers or ranking schools. Instead, the assessments will be conducted early in the school year so that the data can be used to inform student learning during the school year. The new assessments, redesigned in consultation with a broad range of education stakeholders, reduce the emphasis on multiple-choice questions and aim to more effectively assess competencies such as the ability to apply knowledge to different scenarios.

Ontario's province-wide tests, given in grades 3 and 6 (reading, writing, and mathematics); 9 (mathematics); and 10 (literacy) provide targeted feedback to school boards, schools, and students to support improvement. The Ontario Ministry of Education also provides resources to schools and teachers on approaches that promote "assessment for learning" and "assessment as learning," involving strategies such as self- and peer assessment to promote learning and revision and means for providing feedback to students for improvement. Teachers are encouraged to use methods ranging from "formal and informal observations, discussions, learning conversations, questioning, conferences, homework, tasks done in groups, demonstrations, projects, portfolios, developmental continua, performances, peer and self-assessments, self-reflections, essays, and tests" (Ontario Ministry of Education, 2010, p. 28).

Both provinces offer professional development support for teachers to develop and enact the curriculum. Alberta's ministry provides resources for teachers to adapt lessons to meet curricular standards. Ontario created a province-wide literacy and numeracy initiative, combining professional development with materials and coaching. This initiative is widely seen as having helped raise the proportion of students achieving at expected levels in reading, writing, and mathematics from 54% to 72% over the period of a decade (Levin, 2014).

Teachers and Teaching

Teaching is a profession that is well respected by the Canadian public. A 2013 survey conducted by the Alberta Teachers Association found that 9 in 10 teachers agreed that they are very committed to teaching as a profession and that in public they are proud to say that they are teachers. The overall respect for the teaching profession is reflected in teacher salaries, which begin above those of other occupations that require tertiary-level education, although they flatten out sooner. There is a substantial surplus of teachers in Ontario and a healthy supply in Alberta, except for remote schools, for which the provinces have created recruitment incentives.

Teachers in Canada are well prepared for teaching, increasingly at the master's degree level. There is increasing importance placed on strengthening the clinical aspects of teacher training with many programs moving to extend the length of school placements. Ontario has recently doubled the required length of the clinical experience portion of teacher training program and increased the minimum length of teacher education programs, encouraging providers such as the Ontario Institute of Studies in Education to move their teacher education programs to the master's level, further integrating education research and practice into preparation.

Induction programs are particularly well developed, with all new teachers in Ontario working with trained mentors as part of the 2-year New Teacher Induction Program. Mentors and mentees receive shared release time for collaborative planning, classroom observation, or assessment of student work designed to enhance teachers' practice, efficacy, and support their commitment to continuous professional learning.

Professional development is a largely teacher-driven activity in each of the Canadian jurisdictions. Both provinces have sponsored large-scale innovation and action research projects conducted by teachers to develop, study, and disseminate successful practices. These have had a profound effect on schools as the provinces have also sponsored networks, conferences, publications, and other means for knowledge sharing. The teachers' associations are also involved in the development of many professional development programs and are often actively involved in partnerships with government to facilitate their implementation.

Professional learning policy seeks to foster an environment of collaborative professionalism in which teachers collectively engage in personal reflection and dialogue about improving their teaching practice. The result in each jurisdiction is a culture of schooling that recognizes teacher knowledge and provides opportunities for teachers to identify and develop their professional capabilities as part of a broader strategy of school improvement.

Finland

With a population of 5.49 million people, Finland is about as populous as Minnesota, but its presence in international discussions of education has been much larger. Once the least well-educated country in Scandinavia, it is now one of the most highly educated in the world: More than 99% of students now successfully complete compulsory basic education, and about 90% complete upper secondary school. Two-thirds of these graduates enroll in universities or professionally oriented polytechnic schools. Finland ranks near the top among all the OECD nations on the PISA assessments in mathematics, science, and reading. The country also boasts a highly equitable distribution of achievement, even for its growing share of immigrant students.

Finland has been called "a model of a modern, publicly financed education system with widespread equity, good quality, large participation—all of this at reasonable cost" (Sahlberg, 2010, p. 324), partly because of the way the schools are designed and teachers are supported. It is also because of the strong social supports for children and families that enable all children to come to school ready to learn, without the challenges that many experience in less well-supported contexts.

More than 98% of funds for education at all levels comes from public sources (OECD, 2015). The Finnish Ministry of Education and Culture sets the national policy vision, while its more than 3,700 schools are administered by just over 300 municipalities across the country. Municipalities are regarded as self-governing entities that fund schools via municipal taxes. Because these vary, the central government equalizes funding through subsidies to municipal governments, which constitute about one-third of all education funding. The federal role is organized to ensure educational opportunity and guide the general direction of schooling through the national curriculum. However, almost all of the decisions about how to achieve the goals are taken up by local municipalities and schools, which have considerable room to innovate.

The reforms that accomplished Finland's gains began in the 1970s, first by eliminating the practice of separating students into very different tracks based on their test scores and by replacing the highly prescriptive curriculum that the system was based on. A new common curriculum was developed, teacher education was improved and extended, and social supports for children and families were enacted, including health and dental care, special education services, and transportation to schools.

Policy makers decided that if they invested in very skillful teachers, they could allow local schools more autonomy to make decisions about what and how to teach. By the mid-1990s, the country had ended the highly regulated system of curriculum management (reflected in older curriculum guides that had exceeded 700 pages of prescriptions). The current national core curriculum is a much leaner document—featuring fewer than 10 pages of guidance for all of mathematics, for example—which guides teachers in collectively developing local curriculum and assessments. Recent curriculum reforms have emphasized teaching students how to think creatively and manage their own learning.

Equity as a Core Principle

Equity and education for all constitute the core elements of the strategic vision for education in Finland. Since 2000, Finland has achieved among the top scores on PISA and other international assessments, yet with some of the lowest achievement gaps between students from more and less disadvantaged backgrounds. Although there was a sizable achievement gap among students in the 1970s, by 2006, Finland's between-school variance on the PISA science scale was only 5%, whereas the average between-school variance in other OECD nations was about 33% (OECD, 2007). The overall variation in achievement among Finnish students is also smaller than that of nearly all the other OECD countries.

This is true despite the fact that immigration from nations with lower levels of education has increased sharply in recent years, and there is more linguistic and cultural diversity for schools to contend with. Schools seek to support students' native languages and culture whenever they can. This means that, along with Swedish and Russian, there are many students among the fastest growing groups of immigrants speaking Arabic, Bosnian, Somali, Thai, Turkish, and Vietnamese, among others. Some schools in Helsinki have as many immigrants as they have native Finnish students. Yet, achievement has been climbing in Finland and growing more equitable.

The principle of equity is also evident in schooling for students with disabilities. All students in Finland have a right to enroll in their local school, with the system adapting to meet the needs of the students. With extensive teacher training in how to teach diverse students, Finland has extended the availability of special education services to a broad range of students; many children receive targeted support for learning, particularly early in their educational career, setting them up for later success.

Curriculum and Assessment

The central Finnish National Board of Education (FNBE) develops curricular frameworks, evaluates the quality of education, and provides support and guidance in key areas of education. National curriculum frameworks designed by FNBE are lean documents that describe flexible standards; schools have a significant responsibility in developing and implementing the curriculum (Link 2-4), including in the selection of textbooks. The national curriculum aims to provide not only the skills needed by professionals but also the competencies to equip students for a rapidly changing economy and society (Sahlberg, 2015b). Unlike many countries, Finland has avoided narrowing the curriculum in other subjects in order to strengthen literacy and numeracy, instead "giving equal value to all aspects of an individual's growth of personality, moral, creativity, knowledge, and skills" (Sahlberg, 2010, p. 333). There is a strong emphasis on inquiry, metacognitive skills, and developing students' capacities to guide and assess their own learning.

The national framework curriculum provides teachers with recommended assessment criteria for "good" grades in each subject and in the overall final assessment of student progress each year. Schools and teachers then use those guidelines to craft a more detailed curriculum and set of learning outcomes at each school as well as approaches to assessing benchmarks in the curriculum. According to the FNBE (June 2008), the main purpose of assessing students is to guide and encourage students' own reflection and self-assessment. Consequently, ongoing feedback from the teacher is very important. Teachers give students formative and summative reports through verbal and narrative feedback.

A salient feature of educational practice in Finland is that there is no universal standardized testing used to evaluate students or schools. Samples of schools and students, as in the NAEP assessment in the United States, are assessed based on government national assessment plans to inform curriculum and school investments. Aside from the voluntary matriculation exam taken by 12th graders in general upper secondary schools—an open-ended set of tasks organized by the Matriculation Examination Board and developed and scored by education experts including teachers—assessments are school-based.

These school-based assessments are curriculum-embedded activities intended to engage students in research and inquiry. Currently all schoolchildren are also encouraged to conduct self-assessment of their learning (Schwartz & Mehta, 2011). Thus assessment *for* learning—which guides student reflection and revision—is used as often as assessment *of* learning. This requires teachers to be skilled in the creation of assessment activities that provide actionable feedback to teachers and students and is a central focus of teacher training programs. Finland's use of these school-based, open-ended tasks embedded in the curriculum is often touted as an important reason for the nation's success on the international exams (Finnish National Board of Education, 2007; Lavonen, 2008).

Teachers and Teaching

Teaching is a highly regarded profession in Finland and one of the top occupational choices of young people. Entering salaries are comparable to those of other professions. However, the greater draw appears to be the high esteem with which the profession is held, the desirable working conditions, and the trust that allows teachers to be creative and innovative in their work.

Entry into initial teacher education is highly selective. Only about 1 in 10 primary school teacher education candidates is selected annually. Along with an application, essays, and in-person interviews, candidates must pass an entry examination that tests their ability to read and interpret recent education research, a process that is reinforced during the 5-year initial teacher education programs in the country's research universities, which are entirely free of charge and offer a living stipend. Students graduate with a master's degree in education or the subject that they primarily teach in school (Sahlberg, 2015b).

Teacher education programs include extensive academic course work on pedagogy and other educational sciences—with a strong emphasis on using research based on state-of-the-art practice—and extended periods of clinical experience in a school associated with the university. These teacher training schools are intended to develop and model innovative practices, as well as to foster research on learning and teaching. Teachers are trained in research methods so that they can "contribute to an increase of the problem-solving capacity of the education system" (Buchberger & Buchberger, 2004, p. 10).

Teachers learn how to create challenging curriculum and how to develop and use performance assessments that engage students in research and inquiry on a regular basis. Teacher training emphasizes learning how to teach students who learn in different ways, including those with special needs. The egalitarian Finns reasoned that if teachers learn to help students who struggle, they will be able to teach all students more effectively and, indeed, leave no child behind.

Within teacher training schools, student teachers participate in problem-solving groups, a common feature in Finnish schools. The problem-solving groups engage in a cycle of planning, action, and reflective evaluation that is reinforced throughout the teacher education and is, in fact, a model for what teachers will plan for their own students, who are expected to do similar kinds of research and inquiry in their own studies.

This process continues in the schools where teachers engage in ongoing inquiry and knowledge sharing to improve instruction. In Finland, similar to other high-achieving nations, schools provide time for regular collaboration among teachers on issues of instruction. Teachers typically meet at least one afternoon each week to jointly plan and develop curriculum, and schools in the same municipality are encouraged to work together to share materials. Indeed, the entire system is intended to improve through continual reflection, evaluation, and problem-solving at the level of the classroom, school, municipality, and nation.

Shanghai

Like Finland, Shanghai has become a focus of international education attention because of its surprising appearance at the very top of the PISA rankings in education in mathematics, science, and reading when it became one of the participating Chinese jurisdictions in 2009. It is one of the world's most populous cities—at over 24 million people, about the population of Texas—and is mainland China's most international-ized city, stemming in part from its colonial history as a major regional business and export hub. The school system in Shanghai supports about 1.5 million students in its 1,624 primary, junior and senior secondary, and specialized education schools. A further 300 nonpublic schools also operate within the city.

Residents of Shanghai have the highest mean income and longest life expectancy of those living in any other province in China. Participation in tertiary education is high, and the number of higher education institutions has rapidly multiplied. As elsewhere in China, education in Shanghai is seen as the primary vehicle for social mobility. And although Shanghai's wealth and the foresight of its leaders have put it at the forefront of Chinese provinces with respect to developing a top-flight education system, it is entirely part of the Chinese system as a whole, simultaneously informing and implementing reforms and practices that are part of the national approach to education.

In recent years, China has been dramatically increasing its nationwide investments in education, focusing especially on strategies to improve the compensation, preparation, and ongoing professional learning for teachers. Much of its energy has focused on improving schools and staffing in remote, rural communities so that they can begin to approach the standards of the more advanced urban areas. However, the nation has also been promoting innovation aimed at a 21st-century curriculum and has looked to provinces such as Shanghai to lead the way in demonstrating what this new Chinese education can be.

Governance and Funding

Education in Shanghai, as in the rest of China, is formally overseen by the national Ministry of Education, which sets the policy vision and legal framework for education and regulates national exams, which are an important part of the Chinese tradition in education as across all civil service fields. Provinces in China may develop policies based on ministry guidelines and are responsible for the distribution of funds.

China's policy vision is set out in the National Plan for Medium- and Long-Term Education Reform and Development (2010–2020) (Link 2-5) (Communist Party of China Central Committee and the State Council, 2010), made with broad public consultation and establishing education as the main driver of national development. It aims to dramatically accelerate investment in education and human resources nationwide:

> In line with the requirements to reach out to modernization, the world and the future, and to meet the demands for building a moderately prosperous society in all respects and an innovative country, it is imperative to regard cultivation of people as a fundamental mission, draw strength from reform and innovation, improve education equity, carry out quality oriented education in an all-round way, push forward scientific education development from a new historical starting point, and speed up the transition from the world's largest education system to one of the world's best, and from a country with large scale of human resource to a country rich in human resources. (p. 6)

A core strategy for building the country's economic engine is to invest in the quality of its workforce. The scale of the effort is enormous. As the 2020 plan emphasizes, "We must cultivate and bring forth quality workers by hundreds of millions, competent professionals by tens of millions, and a large number of top-notch innovative personnel" (p. 8). A second key goal is to address inequities within the overall national system of education, among regions and communities as well as within schools. Education Minister Yuan Guiren was quoted at an official government meeting in March 2013 as saying, "My dream is to ensure that we can teach students in accordance with their aptitudes, provide education for all people without discrimination, and cultivate every person in this nation to become a talent" (Roberts, 2013).

A third goal is to move the curriculum toward 21st-century skills—an objective that Shanghai is helping to enact and lead. Shanghai occupies a unique status within education policy in China. It is used as a launching point for rolling out new education policies and is also a test bed for innovations that inspire national policy. It is one of four province-level municipalities, and as such, can create a more unified system of education policy. The Shanghai Municipal Education Commission is the body charged with setting education policy within the province and responding to national laws.

Educational funding in China is decentralized, with local governments primarily responsible for funding, supplemented by national funds (about 17% of the total) to help equalize disparities. The Municipal Education Commission in Shanghai seeks to equalize funding between rural and urban schools within its boundaries. Shanghai has also sought to equalize opportunities for the migrant students who have arrived with their families to take advantage of the economic opportunities of the city. The number of migrants has tripled since 2000 to comprise nearly 40% of the resident population. Such workers are critical to the local economy, because Shanghai has a low birth rate and aging population. At the same time, the influx of migrants has created challenges for its schools. It is estimated that the children of migrant workers account for about 20% of the student population in the city. Depending on their registration status (a complex process that operates throughout China),[1] migrant students are either educated by the Shanghai district or by private schools serving those not registered locally.

Shanghai has established that migrant children are "our children" and has made efforts to ensure a quality education experience for children of migrant families (OECD, 2011, p. 96). The Municipal Education Commission is making an effort to reduce the number of schools designated as private schools for migrant children and enroll them in regular public schools. Specific public schools are now designated within districts for migrant children. In addition, the Municipal Education Commission has announced that it will help supplement the funding private schools receive from the national government when they are registered as a school serving a province where its migrant population is from.

As of 2010, all school-age children in Shanghai attend 9 years of compulsory education including all of the children living with parents who are migrant workers (Shanghai Municipal Statistics Bureau, 2011). Shanghai was the first province in China to achieve 100% elementary and junior secondary school enrollment and, today, has achieved almost universal secondary school attendance, even among its migrant student population (OECD, 2011). Access to higher education has also opened up dramatically for students in Shanghai. In 2004, 75% of secondary graduates continued to higher education with 45% attending universities and 30% attending other types of postsecondary education (Cheng & Yip, 2006).

Curriculum and Assessment

Shanghai frequently pilots curricular reforms for later dissemination nationwide. In the 1990s, Shanghai was the first province to implement a national curriculum that broadened beyond traditional subject areas and included change toward more active kinds of pedagogy aimed at critical thinking and problem-solving (Tucker, 2014). National reform efforts in China have continued in this direction, focusing on encouraging more innovative and creative thinking and encouraging students to follow their interests and potential. A key part of the national 2020 plan is its call for major changes in curriculum:

> Our concept of education and our teaching contents and methodology are relatively outdated, schoolwork burdens on primary and middle school students are too heavy, the promotion of quality education arrested, our students are weak in their adaptability to society, and innovative, practical and versatile professionals is in acute shortage. (p. 6)

The 2020 plan proposes to address these concerns by calling for more student-oriented approaches to teaching: updating the school curriculum in order to allow students to address authentic, real-world problems; promoting less focus on examination preparation; and engaging students in more creative and self-regulated activities. This call for a shift in curricular focus has been characterized as China's efforts to shift away from examination-driven schooling to supporting students in developing creativity and innovative thinking—a shift that requires deep cultural change in how success is viewed and understood by students and their families.

Traditionally, achievement on examinations has been highly valued. As one commentator noted, "Success in examinations is seen as the only respectable success" (Cheng, 2011, p. 24). Hard work in studying is a prevalent cultural value, and student engagement with in-class lessons is high. Students also spend significant time studying outside of school hours, and many students have private tutors. China's national 2020 plan calls for reducing heavy schoolwork burdens that cause stress and sleep deprivation. At the municipal level, Shanghai has sought to limit homework and encourage increased physical exercise for students (Cheng, 2011).

In Shanghai, there has been a sustained effort to shift pedagogy toward more student participation in class rather than traditional lecture-style teaching under the banner of "returning class time to students." In a learning culture with a long history of focusing on recollection of content in preparation for exams, this more constructivist style of teaching "overturns the old orthodoxy of exam preparation and teachers' absolute authority over the information they convey. These changes add up to a sea change in classroom pedagogy" (Cheng, 2011, p. 35). The changes are highly visible in the teaching competitions that Shanghai uses to exemplify and spread best practices throughout the system, as well as in the curriculum of teacher education programs.

Although there are only two external exams—the *zhongkao* (senior high school entrance examination) and the *gaokao* (national higher education entrance examination)—they affect the work of teachers and the experience of students in important ways. There is pressure on teachers to direct their teaching to success on the examination. In some cases, teachers may receive financial bonuses for their students' strong performance, some teacher preparation programs include training in preparing students for the examination, and there is temptation to direct teaching in secondary school toward exam preparation. This places the exams in tension with the curricular reforms aimed at developing more critical and creative thinking skills.

Shanghai led examination reform in China, being the first province in the nation permitted to develop its own examination and tailoring it to local curricula. This has since been extended to other parts of the country. Ongoing examination reforms are aimed at reducing the enormous stress of the *gaokao* and bringing the examination in closer alignment with the curriculum. This has included eliminating multiple-choice questions and increasing the number of applied problems regarding critical analysis and defense of ideas.

Teachers and Teaching

In China, teachers are viewed by students as elders and models responsible for moral and emotional guidance, as well as an authority in their disciplinary content:

> Under the current curriculum reform in Shanghai, "giving a student a cup of water" [teaching] means more than just imparting a set of knowledge and ability to the student. The teacher is also expected to promote the desirable emotions, attitudes and values in their [sic] students using appropriate processes and methods. (Tan, 2013, p. 34)

Teaching in China is regarded as a well-respected profession, though salaries are low and shortages exist in many rural areas. Recent national legislation requires that teachers be paid no less than the average of other public servants in each province. Teachers in Shanghai are the highest paid in the nation, as much as twice as high as in other regions. A career ladder for teachers enables them to progress based on highly developed assessment processes through a four-tiered ranking system, which is also tied to responsibilities and compensation.

Nationwide, many teachers have a 2-year associate's degree from a normal college and provinces are working to meet the new requirements pressing for bachelor's degrees for all secondary teachers. In Shanghai, education levels of teachers are higher: Virtually all secondary teachers and most primary school teachers hold a bachelor's degree, and about 6% of the secondary school teachers hold a master's degree. Recent reports suggest that "possessing a Bachelor's degree with . . . teacher professional training has become the new threshold for all the new entrants to the teaching profession in Shanghai" (Zhang, Xu, & Sun, 2014, p. 146).

The two universities supplying most of Shanghai's teachers (East China Normal University and Shanghai Normal University) offer 4-year programs that start candidates off immediately with studies in educational sociology, philosophy, and psychology and include content pedagogical training, child development, and teaching methods. In addition to their broad study of all the subjects they will teach, elementary candidates specialize in a content area from among the social sciences, math and natural sciences, or performing and fine arts, as do secondary teachers.

A growing emphasis on clinical training has expanded the amount of practicum and student teaching candidates receive in the third and fourth years of their program.

This is just the beginning of entry to the career, however. Candidates must pass a set of rigorous examinations to graduate and then undertake additional examinations, interviews, and exhibitions of their skills to be hired in Shanghai. Once hired, they experience intensive mentoring from a veteran teacher. Reflected in the phrase "the old bring along the young," senior teachers are regarded as having much to offer the ongoing professional education of teachers. Beyond the basics of classroom management, experienced teachers in Shanghai work with novices on sophisticated pedagogical skills, such as asking good questions of their students in order to know on a continual basis whether students are understanding the material, a kind of ongoing formative assessment of student learning (Tucker, 2014).

Teachers in Shanghai typically participate in each of three school-based collaboration groups, which together serve to support teacher learning and address student learning and well-being. Teaching and research groups, known as *jiaoyanzu,* conduct research, discuss new pedagogies, and provide observation, mentoring, and feedback for colleagues. Smaller lesson-preparation groups jointly plan and refine lessons and solve teaching problems. Grade-level teaching groups address issues common to students, including student welfare (Zhang, Xu, & Sun, 2014).

These activities are facilitated by considerable noninstructional time, with most teachers directly teaching students about 15 hours a week at the primary level and just 12 hours a week at the secondary level. The remaining time may also be spent on grading papers, meeting with students, or conducting school-based research, which is something all teachers do. As Tucker (2014) noted in an earlier study, "Teachers are taught research methods during their professional preparation and are expected to use those research methods as they work in groups to systematically improve their teaching practices" (p. 28). Teachers' research is published and shared with others and is an expectation for moving up the career ladder.

The quality of instructional practice is highly valued and routinely celebrated. Lessons are frequently viewed by parents and colleagues from their own or another school, providing many opportunities for discussion and feedback on their teaching. Teachers may also be selected to represent their school to participate in teaching competitions in which lessons are delivered to students and judged by panels of experts. The walls of schools frequently feature the pictures and awards received by highly performing teachers, aimed at encouraging teaching research and for teachers to continually improve their teaching.

Singapore

Sitting at the southern end of the Malaysian peninsula, Singapore is a country of some 5.5 million people. It has a population comparable to the state of Minnesota, but in an area a little smaller than the size of New York City, making it one of densest nations in the world. Singapore is a regional and global hub for commerce and trade and is an internationalized nation in which foreign residents make up about 29% of the population. Its multicultural and multilingual society is composed primarily of Chinese (76%), Malay (15%), and Indian (7.5%) peoples (Singapore Department of Statistics, 2015), whose mother tongue languages—Mandarin, Malay, and Tamil—are taught in all schools. Although English is the language of instruction, it is the home language for a minority of students, all of whom are expected to be fully bilingual and many of whom speak more than two languages.

Singapore aims to develop internationally minded, culturally competent citizens with a high degree of literacy and technical expertise. With almost no natural resources, it regards its citizens as its most valuable resource, placing education as a central concern in policy and government investment. There is a belief in the importance of education for every individual, for the economy, and for nation building.

Singapore has experienced one of the most significant transformations of any country internationally, moving in the half century since its independence in 1965 from a nation where education was the province of a tiny, affluent minority to a thriving state with among the highest levels of student achievement in the world. Today, about 75% of young people complete a postsecondary technical or college degree; the remainder receive a well-resourced up-to-date postsecondary vocational education through the Institute of Technical Education that prepares them for work, which is increasingly likely to be in a high-tech or service field in one of the many multinational corporations settling in Singapore.

Building a Modern Economy and Diverse Society

Singapore has invested in the creation of a strong public education system, bringing together a diverse range of schools that existed pre-independence (Stewart, 2011). About 75% of schools in Singapore are government operated. The next largest category is government-aided schools, often religiously affiliated, many of which date to the era before independence. These are also regarded as public schools, and they can receive up to 95% of their funding from public sources. There are seven independent, specialized secondary schools that can select students; they receive a small amount of government aid, and their student tuition is subsidized based on need, so that any admitted can afford to attend. All of these schools must adhere to the same curricula and assessments as government-operated schools.

In part because of its small size, education administration in Singapore is centralized, with the Ministry of Education directly administering schools, simultaneously taking on what would elsewhere be the functions of a nation, a state, and a city or school district. This allows for a tight alignment of policy among schools, the ministry, and the National Institute of Education, the country's only teacher training facility. This close tripartite relationship is known as *PPP*—linking policies, practice, and preparation.

The country's 365 schools are organized into 30 clusters, each composed of about 10 to 13 schools, which are administered to help ensure fidelity of policy implementation and leveraging of quality. They are an important mechanism for the sharing of good practices across schools and a platform for professional learning. Teachers and principals are expected to contribute to the effective functioning of their school and school cluster. With a well-developed career ladder to recruit and train highly talented and knowledgeable teacher leaders and system leaders, the ministry and the clusters are staffed by educators who have progressed from the classroom and who deeply understand how all the aspects of the system operate. These career pathways ensure that expertise is developed and shared within the education system.

Fostering Innovation and Equity

Since 1997, Singapore's vision for education has been to reform the system to prepare the country for increasingly rapid changes in the global economy. As noted by then–prime minister Goh Chok Tong, "it will be an intensely global future" in which "knowledge and innovation will be absolutely critical" (Goh, 1997). The "Thinking Schools, Learning Nation" initiative launched in 1997 sought to transform curriculum, assessment, and teaching to develop a creative and critical thinking culture within schools by explicitly teaching and assessing these skills for students. It sought to create a reflective culture among teachers as well, who are supported to conduct action research, lesson study, and other teacher-inquiry methods on their teaching so as to continually revise their teaching strategies in response to what they learn.

This initiative was married to a commitment to integrating technology into all aspects of education, fostering greater feedback from schools to the Ministry of Education to continually inform policy making and enabling schools to identify and develop the capabilities of each student (Goh, 1997). A key feature of the governance of education in Singapore is a commitment to learning for all students. The philosophical approach regards all students as being diverse learners with different potentials, with the role of government as one of equalizing educational opportunities to enable students to reach that potential (Teh, 2014).

The push to create thinking schools and students equipped for a 21st-century economy has resulted in changes to teaching and learning that are aimed at going beyond academic skills to building character and life skills that can help students lead successful lives. This approach has encapsulated curriculum and assessment. The number of examinations and standardized assessments was reduced, with national examinations occurring at the end of grade 6 (primary school leaving examination), grade 10 (O levels), and grade 12 (A levels). The examinations were always open-ended, including structured essays and problem solutions. They now include projects and investigations that students undertake during the school year that are designed by the Singapore Examinations Board with the help of teachers and are scored by teachers with a moderation process that supports consistency. Science courses, for example, include the requirement for a scientific investigation that students must design, conduct, analyze, and write up, which is part of their examination score.

The "Teach Less, Learn More" policy introduced in 2004 aimed to further reduce the quantity of content in the curriculum and open up time for inquiry. The curriculum framework was revised to emphasize 21st-century skills and competencies including critical and creative thinking, global awareness, civic literacy, and cross-cultural skills (Ministry of Education, Singapore, 2015). There is an increased emphasis on problem-based learning and project work in class in Singapore. School-based assessments can incorporate multiple indicators to assess student progress against the competencies. Students are also encouraged to participate in self-assessment and to play a greater role in their learning process.

Teachers and Teaching

Teachers in Singapore enjoy high respect from society. This is not only due to the cultural context but also to policies that have underscored the importance of education in society and promoted the status of teaching as a career.

Teaching is well compensated. Not only are new teachers paid a salary similar to beginning accountants and engineers but also initial teacher education is fully paid for, and teacher candidates are salaried while still in training. Most teachers have at least a bachelor's degree and about a third possess a master's degree qualification. All preservice teacher education takes place at the National Institute of Education; an increasing share of teachers pursue the graduate-level route into teaching. Not surprisingly, teacher education is highly selective, with only the top one-third being shortlisted and another two-thirds of these not making it through the selection interview. Teacher education is underpinned by values, skills, and knowledge considered integral to teaching and emphasizes a learner-centered approach to teaching with strong content specialization as well as pedagogical training.

All teachers receive a formal induction program on graduation, involving ongoing professional learning courses, a symposium, and school-based mentoring from more experienced teachers or teacher leaders in the school they enter. Mentoring extends beyond beginners: 40% of all lower secondary teachers are engaged in some mentoring or coaching activity (OECD, 2014d). In addition to mentoring, teachers often participate in small-group lesson study, action research, and other teacher-inquiry projects. These small teacher groups or professional learning teams may examine their teaching practice and student learning, foster innovative teaching practices, or develop curricular resources for their departments and other teachers. Time for such sustained collaboration is set aside. A school staff developer at each school ensures that professional development for the teachers is customized to teacher needs and supports school goals. This role also involves planning and implementing whole-school structured professional learning programs with teacher leaders.

Beyond the schools, teacher leaders also support other teachers in the fraternity of professional learning. They take on roles as pedagogical leaders, instructional mentors, and professional learning leaders. As pedagogical leaders, they are experts in the teaching and learning of their subject disciplines; as instructional mentors, they develop less-experienced teachers in becoming more effective teachers; and as professional learning leaders, they plan and facilitate professional learning activities for other teachers in the fraternity. For example, learning communities of teachers are set up and led by teacher leaders to facilitate teacher collaboration within and across schools in projects involving pedagogical innovation and subject mastery. AST (Academy of Singapore Teachers) and other academies and language centers, as well as the National Institute of Education, create systems of expertise that strengthen every part of the teacher development process.

As in Shanghai, Singaporean teachers teach students directly for relatively fewer hours each week than those in other countries (about 17 as compared to the OECD average of 19), although their work week is a long one. This highlights the expectations of teaching as involving not just classroom instruction but also time spent planning engaging lessons as well as reviewing and refining them, grading and providing feedback to students, and engaging in collaborative professional learning and research. The cocurricular activities for students are school based and they are managed by the teachers. Monetary and nonmonetary rewards are used to incentivize high performance, balanced with an evaluation system that also emphasizes feedback and support for teachers, mentorship, and ongoing professional growth.

Summary

The jurisdictions in this study are diverse in many respects. They range from small city states such as Singapore to geographically large territories such as Australia and Canada and from populations of just 4 million in Alberta up to 24 million in Shanghai. Nonetheless, there are important similarities in the approach to educational policy making across these jurisdictions:

o *Central purpose and local innovation:* There is a balance between centralization and decentralization of educational functions. Governments set a long-term policy vision around which policy making can cohere—connecting funding, curriculum, instruction, assessment, and teacher development in ways that aim to produce a well-functioning system that is always improving. Meanwhile, local innovation is enabled by capacity building and freedom from excessive top-down mandates.

o *Resources pointed toward equity:* There are mechanisms for the more equitable distribution of resources. These can take the form of equalizing allocations from the national or state government, increased funding for schools with more disadvantaged students, targeted resources for student learning, and investments in educators who can meet diverse student needs.

o *Curriculum and assessment for 21st-centuries competencies:* Each jurisdiction has revised its curriculum to increasingly emphasize 21st-century competencies, including communication and second language skills, creativity, and critical thinking and problem-solving abilities. In each jurisdiction, there is also a movement toward more formative modes of assessment and assessment for learning.

o *Teaching as a valued profession:* A wide variety of supports for teaching—from competitive salaries and subsidized preparation to job-embedded professional learning opportunities and recognition for accomplished practice—make teaching a desirable and productive career in the eyes of teachers as well as the public.

Each jurisdiction establishes the conditions in which teacher knowledge is valued, and there are opportunities for teachers to collaborate, share knowledge, and engage in collaborative professional learning directed toward improving student learning. In addition, schools and teachers are provided with a measure of discretion in making decisions that affect classroom learning. That is, despite the great differences in educational contexts, each jurisdiction has developed—and is continuing to strengthen—policies that can enhance teachers' professional capital, taking advantage of teachers' individual knowledge and strengths and also of the collective capacity of the teacher workforce (Hargreaves & Fullan, 2012).

In Chapter 3, we take a closer look at the first slice of the policy pie: how each jurisdiction recruits high-potential individuals into teaching; prepares them with the knowledge, skills, and practice to be ready for the classroom; and how new teachers are inducted into the profession to bridge the worlds of teacher education and the workplace.

NOTE

1. The *hukou* is a national system of household registration for families based on their permanent residence or land ownership. Within this system, families register in their home provinces, and although they may migrate to other parts of the country, their permanent residence is identified as the province where they are registered. A family's *hukou* status determines their access to social systems, such as health care, education, welfare, and housing opportunities in a given province.

3

RECRUITING AND PREPARING PROFESSION-READY TEACHERS

A KEY ELEMENT IN THE STRATEGY that high-performing countries employ to ensure all students have access to well-qualified teachers is making sure teachers are carefully selected and prepared right from the start. The jurisdictions we studied do so in three ways: encouraging highly capable individuals to consider teaching and screening the applicants carefully to ensure that the most committed and able pursue a teaching career, preparing prospective teachers well so that they are ready to teach on their first day, and supporting the development of their teaching practice early in the career. Although these jurisdictions expect teachers to continue learning—and, as later chapters show, provide ample opportunities for them to do so—the initial recruitment, preparation, and induction of teachers is a critical step toward a highly qualified profession.

The specific practices for recruitment, preparation, and induction vary in their details from country to country. Some place a stronger emphasis on one aspect than on others. For example, some jurisdictions—such as Finland and, increasingly, Australia and Canada—make sure teachers' initial preparation offers intensive clinical training, whereas others—such as Singapore and Shanghai—provide more extensive and heavily mentored clinical training during the first year on the job. In these latter cases, the career ladder systems that place expert mentors in every school support this model (see Chapter 5). But all countries provide strong content and pedagogical preparation and expect teachers to be ready to teach well before allowing them to practice independently. All of the systems have continued to strengthen preservice preparation and induction. Furthermore, they manage the preparation and distribution of educators with a strong commitment to equity so that all students can be taught by capable, caring teachers.

This chapter examines the practices of recruitment, preparation, and induction in the five countries we studied. It describes features that are unique to each and underscores themes that are common to all. Among these common themes are competitive compensation and subsidies for preparation that make teaching attractive and preparation affordable, professional standards that guide programs and teacher learning opportunities, strong preparation in content and pedagogy connected to the common curriculum and diverse students to be taught, and well-mentored clinical experiences.

Recruiting the Best

In the countries we studied, teaching is, by and large, a profession held in high esteem. Recruitment of teachers is not a problem; so many individuals flock to teaching, the challenge is selecting the most promising applicants from those who seek slots in preparation programs. Teacher compensation in high-performing systems tends to be comparable to that of other well-regarded professions, as we detail in the following sections.

At the same time, government-subsidized tuition for teacher education students makes it easy to lure individuals to teaching who might otherwise look for professions that might be more lucrative. In the jurisdictions we studied, tuition for teacher candidates is completely free or largely subsidized by the government, making it possible for people to pursue teaching careers without incurring significant debt. In addition, some provide stipends or salaries to teacher candidates while they are in training.

Financial Compensation

In the jurisdictions we studied, salaries fell at or near the average received by other college graduates across occupations (generally between 90% and 105% of the average for college-educated workers). By contrast, US teachers earned, on average, about 70% of what other college graduates earned (OECD, 2014a). A competitive pay scale reinforces the prestige in which teaching is held in these systems; at the same time, the financial rewards serve as an incentive for highly capable individuals to enter teaching.

When we conducted our study we found, for example, that—with the exception of some remote sites—there was a large surplus of teacher candidates in Canada, where trained beginning teachers sometimes take substitute teaching jobs for years before they can land a full-time position. In Alberta, teachers were among the highest paid of all professions in the province. Utilities and oil and gas extraction were the only two job categories with higher wages (Alberta Learning Information Services, 2013). Starting teachers earned CA$58,000 in 2012, and teachers with 10 years' experience could earn CA$92,000, further augmented by generous benefits (Alberta Education, 2014). (The Canadian dollar was roughly equivalent to the US dollar at that time, placing these beginning salaries about 60% higher than the average starting teacher salary in the United States in that year.)[1]

Ontario teachers are also very well paid and can increase their salaries by earning master's degrees or completing additional qualifications. As a result, the salary curve for teachers rises more sharply than it does for other professions. In 2011, the Ontario salary of CA$66,893 after 5 years of teaching was above the 75th percentile of average salaries for comparable individuals with a university degree who were working one full-time job; after 10 years of teaching, teachers were close to the 90th percentile of salaries within the university-educated group (Johnson, 2013).

In Australia, teachers are also generally well paid. A government-supported survey of occupations in 2012 found that new graduates who entered teaching ranked seventh among 27 professional occupations in their level of compensation, just behind several medical fields and engineering but ahead of law; computer science; biological, veterinary, and other sciences; pharmacy; and accounting (Graduate Careers Australia, 2013). Although teacher salaries have tended to fall behind those of other professions later in the career, states have been revising their salary structures to significantly increase the pay of veteran teachers who meet standards of accomplishment in the new career ladder. For example, New South Wales recently revised its salary structure in ways that will significantly increase the pay of well-qualified teachers who demonstrate higher levels of the professional teaching standards. Building on a starting salary for teachers that is high relative to that of other professions—close to AU$60,000 in 2012—the new system, that went into effect in 2016, enables teachers who attain the highly accomplished level or higher to earn a salary of more than AU$100,000.

Singapore's starting salary for teachers is roughly equivalent to the starting salary of other university-educated workers, comparable to that of civil service engineers and accountants, and teachers start receiving a full monthly salary when they begin preservice education. Candidates who are mid-career professionals earn starting salaries that recognize their previous working experience. Salary growth over the career remains competitive; annual increments are based on performance, potential, and advancement on the three-pronged career tracks.

Since 2009, China has required districts to keep the average salary of all the teachers above the average salary of all public servants in the same district (in accordance with the Teacher Law of 1993). Shanghai offers among the highest salaries in the country. Although teacher salaries in other parts of China have been much lower, the Chinese government has recently made large investments in boosting salaries and creating other incentives, such as housing subsidies, across the other provinces, especially in poor rural areas. In addition, a career ladder (see Chapter 5) guides teacher promotion that is linked to compensation.

Finnish teacher salaries are very close to national average wages and on par with those with similar levels of education (graduate degree) employed in the public sector. However, there is a significant range in teacher earnings based on the level of school (primary, middle, or upper secondary school) and the length of service. Nonetheless, because the status and working conditions of the occupation are attractive, there are many more applicants for preparation than there are slots available. Finland has recently added an element in the teacher pay system that enables school principals to provide teachers with small bonuses or increases in salary if the teachers are doing a particularly good job.

In all of these cases, candidates are also financially supported in their study of education, which influences recruitment and retention. As Sclafani and Lim (2008) point out about Singapore:

> How does Singapore get high-performing students to apply? It is not just future salary, although salaries are competitive with those of engineers in the civil service. It is a combination of factors. The most immediate is that the Ministry pays all tuition, fees and a monthly stipend to undergraduate teaching candidates. For those who enter teacher preparation at the graduate level, the stipend is equivalent to what they would have made as college graduates in a civil sector job. Since this must be repaid if the candidate fails the program or leaves the profession before the stipulated period . . . it is also a powerful motivator for serious commitment to the program. (p. 3)

Successful applicants to teacher preparation are not only salaried during their preparation but also are assured of employment on successful program completion.

Finnish teacher education is also tuition-free, and candidates earn a stipend while they are in training. In Ontario, the government covers about 60% of the cost of candidates' preparation. In Australia, most teacher education students attend college in Commonwealth-supported slots. In 2012, the Commonwealth subsidy for teacher education covered more than two-thirds of the cost in a public university, beyond which additional scholarships are available for teachers in high-need fields.

Attractiveness of the Profession

The attractiveness of teaching is more than financial. Recruitment is also influenced by teaching's reputation as a high-status field. In Finland, teaching is the top-choice profession for college students (Liiten, 2004). Teaching is highly ranked in Singapore as well, and there is a very low attrition rate, less than 3% annually. A survey conducted by the Ministry of Education found that teachers' top three reasons for staying in the profession include a positive professional culture, good remuneration that is competitively benchmarked, and ample opportunities for professional development and career growth.

Teachers in Alberta have long felt well supported and respected through many decades of largely conservative governments. A 2013 survey conducted by the Alberta Teachers Association found that about 9 in 10 teachers agree that they are very committed to teaching as a profession and that in public they are proud to say that they are teachers (ATA, 2014, p. 56). In this same survey, about two-thirds of teachers reported that they experience no or low stress due to any sense of lack of control over their professional practice (personal communication, J. C. Couture, September 2014).

In Ontario, initiatives after 2003 have substantially improved the status and attractiveness of teaching because an era of teacher bashing and disinvestment in public education was replaced by a supportive approach from the provincial government. As a consequence, retirements and other forms of attrition have declined to about 4% annually (about half the rate in the United States), whereas entry into teacher education increased, resulting in a surplus of teachers and a highly competitive market. A survey by the Ontario College of Teachers (2011) found that new teachers are highly committed to their careers; of those in their first 5 years, approximately 9 in 10 indicated that they will definitely or probably be in the teaching profession 5 years hence. A public opinion survey conducted at OISE every 3 years meanwhile showed that Ontarians have a high regard for the teaching profession and support the public education system (Hart, 2012). As Rhonda Kimberley-Young of the Ontario Teachers Federation put it:

> Kids coming out of high school now, heading into university, if they think, "I think I want to go into teaching," it's because they have had that good experience themselves. And they think, "That would be a

nice place to work." Of course, it's the "I want to make an impact on young people's lives." I think that's what draws you to the profession at a base level, but just that comfort level with "this is a respected profession. I have a good feeling about public education."

Her colleague Lindy Amato added:

People are proud to say, "I am a teacher." People feel that pride.

Michael Salvatori, at the Ontario College of Teachers, agreed:

Teachers are still among the most trusted of professions and I think that helps. You want to be part of a profession where you know the public has a good opinion of the professionals.

A virtuous circle has been created in which the public supports the education system and students' own positive experiences in schools encourage them to become teachers who want to further support and contribute to a strong public education system with positive benefits for future students. As Lori Foote of the Ontario Federation of Secondary School Teachers noted:

For the most part, although we have issues that we all work on and we try to improve in our school system, most people have a pretty good experience, and they [aspiring teacher candidates] see the value of education. They understand that education is a great balancing factor: if you want to have a life that is fulfilling for yourself and that you can move forward and you can achieve things, then you need education. I think people get caught up in that passion and they want to share that passion and they want to ensure that others have the same opportunities that they did through education. In Canada, we are so very lucky that it is a universal education system. And that's part of the tenets we believe in: universality, comprehensiveness, proficiency, and accountability. I think people understand that [teachers] build the future on education and they want to be a part of that.

Teachers in China are revered as elders, role models, and those whom parents entrust to shape the future for their children. In the Tao traditions of ritual, the phrase "heaven-earth-sovereign-parent-teacher" is repeated and becomes ingrained in how people see themselves holistically governed and supported. Thus, teachers are viewed as special people in the lives of students, not only in their formal education but also in how they exemplify the life of scholarship, hard work, and success in life through success in one's studies. In addition to this significant historical and social prestige, teaching is viewed as a stable, good-paying, and relatively high-status occupation. In surveys of occupational prestige, teaching is ranked above occupations such as corporate managers and mid-level military officers and on par with doctors (Dolton & Marcenaro-Gutierrez, 2013; Li et al., 2004, as cited in Ingersoll, 2007). Teaching is viewed as a stable career that generates a stable salary, and jobs like this are in high demand in China's educated workforce.

Selection Practices

In the jurisdictions we studied, selection into teaching is typically based not only on academic merit but also on evidence of commitment to and capacity to work well with children and, often, to collaborate well with other adults. Interpersonal and communication skills are evaluated, along with conceptual, analytic, and problem-solving abilities. We saw sophisticated selection practices across the jurisdictions we studied, some of which we highlight here.

Selecting Teachers in Finland

The prestige of the teaching profession is particularly pronounced in Finland. Among young Finns, surveys of high school graduates show that teaching is consistently the most admired profession (Martin & Pennanen, 2015; see also Ministry of Education and Culture, 2012). Finnish officials publicly recognize the value of teachers, and the country's policies show that they trust teachers' professional judgment in schools. Finns regard teaching as a noble, prestigious profession—akin to medicine, law, or economics—and one driven by moral purpose rather than material interests.

As a result, annually about 20,000 students apply for about 4,000 slots in teacher education institutions. In 2016, for example, more than 8,000 people applied for 800 available slots for primary teaching positions; at the University of Helsinki, there were about 2,000 applicants for 120 positions. The number of applicants in primary school teacher education programs has grown by 18% since 2010 (Finnish National Board of Education, 2014).

The process of selecting students from these vast pools is a rigorous one (Link 3-1). First, primary education applicants must take a national exam known as the VAKAVA, developed by faculty members from the eight research universities that offer teacher education programs. First instituted in 2006, the VAKAVA is a 3-hour written exam consisting of questions based on five to eight research articles that students must analyze and interpret. This begins to create a research-based profession from the very beginning of the selection process.

In 2013, for example, the VAKAVA included seven articles—among them a study that examined children's discourse in mathematics classrooms and research that investigated children's use of social media and how they portrayed themselves to others. Candidates have approximately 6 weeks to read and study the materials before the exam, which is given at the same time in all eight universities in May.

Candidates taking the VAKAVA indicate which university they would like to attend, and the university then selects for additional consideration, from among those who have passed the exam, about three times the number of candidates it expects to admit. These candidates engage in interviews and additional assessments designed to evaluate their interest in teaching on a holistic basis.

There is no common interview or selection protocol among universities. At the University of Helsinki, candidates are interviewed individually and in groups by professors and lecturers of the Department of Teacher Education. In the group interview, three to four candidates are given a text to read or an illustration about teachers and their work and prepare to discuss together how they might introduce and discuss it in a group situation. The group of prospective candidates is observed by teacher educators, who are watching for motivation, willingness to work together, and other characteristics. Teacher educators also then interview the candidates individually and rank order their choices.

Those who are not selected can apply again the following year. A recent survey of candidates taking the VAVAKA found that 56% were taking it for the first time, 28% were taking it for the second time, and 18% were taking it for the third time. Alternatively, candidates can apply for kindergarten teaching where the competition is somewhat less fierce.

Selecting Teachers in Singapore

Singapore's process is also rigorous. Grounded in the systemic approach that typifies Singaporean education, teacher recruitment is a single, statewide selection process, jointly managed by the Ministry of Education and the National Institute of Education. It places emphasis on candidates' academic achievement, communications skills, and motivation for joining the profession, and it relies on school partners to be key decision makers in the selection process. Students who want to become teachers must

**Figure 3–1 The Process of Teacher Recruitment
in Singapore**

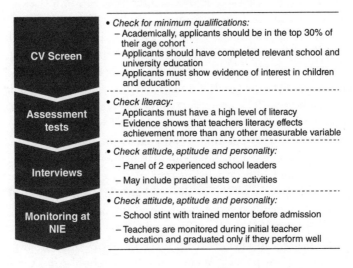

Source: Barber and Mourshed (2007). Updated based
on more current information.

go through a four-step process before entering a preparation program. Only one of three shortlisted applicants makes it through the selection interview, which is just the third of the four steps. A study by McKinsey and Company (2007) summarized the recruitment process in Figure 3–1.

First, the Ministry of Education selects candidates based on their academic record. Candidates who meet that requirement are then required to take and pass the relevant entrance proficiency tests. Of particular importance is English proficiency, which is a key requirement of teacher preparation programs at the Ministry of Education. (English is one of four official languages in Singapore and is the language of instruction in schools.)

Those who make the short list based on academic qualifications and English proficiency are then invited for interviews. The interview is conducted by a panel led by currently serving or recently retired principals or vice principals. Interviewers look for good communication skills, deep passion for teaching, and potential to be a good role model to their future students. According to Sclafani and Lim (2008),

> the Ministry is looking for and finding those young people who have a passion for helping others. Community service is part of every student's education in Singapore, and assignments of working with

younger students or peers who need tutors help teachers identify students who should be encouraged to be teachers. (p. 3)

If found suitable for teaching by the interviewers, candidates are then required to attend the Introduction to Teaching Program (ITP) before they are sent to spend time as a contract teacher in the schools. The ITP is run by the Academy of Singapore Teachers, an organization created by the Ministry of Education to provide teacher-led professional learning for teachers. This program is an introductory course that provides all contract teachers with an awareness of the expectations and ethos of the profession and the fundamentals of teaching. These include adopting a growth mind-set, lesson planning and enactment, assessment for learning, use of technology, and classroom management.

The school stint, during which candidates are paid, can range from a few months to a year. Under the guidance and supervision of their school mentor (usually a more experienced teacher or a teacher leader) and their reporting officer (usually the head of department or subject head), the contract teachers take on teaching duties other than grading examinations or test papers. At the end of their school stint, candidates are assessed on their suitability to become a teacher. Only if they receive a good recommendation from the school and pass that assessment can they enter teacher preparation. And even during their preparation, they are continually monitored and can be removed for poor performance, although this rarely happens.

Selecting Teachers in Canada

In Canada, teacher education is also selective. Fewer than half of aspiring candidates are accepted into programs in Alberta and Ontario. At the largest institution, the Ontario Institute for Studies in Education at the University of Toronto, only one in four candidates is selected. To enter teacher education in Ontario, candidates must demonstrate competencies set by the Ontario College of Teachers' Standards of Practice. Each university implements these in its own way; criteria for acceptance typically include academic standards and evidence of competencies is evaluated in entry interviews, teaching statements, discussions about experiences with children, and evidence of teaching.

In order to increase diversity in the teacher population, teacher candidates who can bring knowledge of First Nations issues and connections with First Nations communities and students into their teaching practices are a priority. This is also the case in Alberta, where candidates in the nine teacher-preparing institutions typically must succeed in pre-admissions courses in teacher education, sit for interviews with faculty, do volunteer work, and, sometimes, complete a portfolio. There are also checkpoints along the way at which candidates may be counseled out of the program if they are not meeting expectations.

Selecting Teachers in Shanghai

Although there are shortages of teachers in some parts of China, teaching in Shanghai is oversubscribed. The two preparation institutions in Shanghai—East China Normal University and the Shanghai Normal University—can afford to be selective at entry and throughout their 4-year teacher education programs. Those who successfully complete the course work and clinical experiences must apply for a teacher qualification certificate issued by the national government in order to be eligible to teach. There are seven types of teaching certificates: kindergarten, primary school, junior secondary, senior secondary, secondary vocational, secondary vocational internship advisor, or higher education. These certificates also have a subject matter specialization based on the candidate's field of study.

To be certified, teachers must pass a new three-part national certification exam that, as of 2014, replaced the previous local exams. First the candidate must pass written examinations in pedagogy, psychology, and teaching methods. Candidates who are successful then participate in an interview process with master teachers and local school district officials who themselves are typically former teachers. During this interview, candidates demonstrate their teaching ability in specific subject matter instruction, show their teaching process skills, and may be asked about their classroom management and classroom questioning techniques. Finally, all teachers must also pass the Mandarin language test (with speaking and listening components).

To be hired in Shanghai, candidates must also pass yet another district-level exam constructed by content area specialists on the district research staff who are highly respected former teachers. Each subject area has a director who writes questions for and grades the exam and participates in the interview process for the potential hire. The exam contains content knowledge questions in the area of specialization, questions about other subject areas, and questions about pedagogy.

After passing the district-level exam, the candidate participates in an interview with a panel of content area experts from the district office. The interview questions can range from specific content knowledge questions, to questions about how to teach particular concepts, to students and pedagogical questions, such as "what do you think is most important in preparing a lesson?" In many interviews, the candidate is asked to teach a short lesson to the interview panel on a topic that the panel has selected. The bar for achieving a teaching position in Shanghai is a high one, requiring deep knowledge of content, an understanding of pedagogy, and a reflective orientation toward teaching work.

Selecting Teachers in Australia

In Australia, the competition for teacher education positions has been somewhat less intense, varying across institutions. However, Australia's new standards for accreditation of initial teacher education programs now require institutions to select from the top 30% of applicants in literacy and numeracy, and graduates must meet registration standards in order to enter the profession after graduation.

Although many universities have long included other personal qualities and attributes as part of selection, there is a move to make these practices more sophisticated and more widespread. Strong support for the use of "more sophisticated selection processes" was one of the findings of the recent federal report by the Teacher Education Ministerial Advisory Group, and new selection guidelines were added to the accreditation processes for initial teacher education programs in 2016; these will apply to all new candidates from 2017 (TEMAG, 2015; AITSL, 2015a). The strengthening of selection processes was supported by union representatives we spoke with, who suggested that initial teacher education policy should seek to achieve strong academic abilities in candidates as well as aptitude for teaching, such as strong communication skills (personal communication with Australian Education Union representatives A. Mulheron, S. Hopgood, and A. Gavrielatos, January 27, 2014).

In addition to these federal initiatives, there are also innovative selection initiatives under way at some universities. For example, at the University of Melbourne, candidates are evaluated based not solely on academic transcripts and working experiences but also on their disposition and suitability for teaching, based on a set of tasks that evaluate candidates' abilities and perspectives ranging from literacy, numeracy skills, and spatial reasoning to communication style, persistence, cultural sensitivity, and ethics. Some of these traits are measured in a recently introduced teacher selector tool, which rates candidates on several dimensions, including conscientiousness, agreeability, openness, and persistence (see Figure 3–2). The outcomes are used in conjunction with

Figure 3–2 Teacher Selector Tool

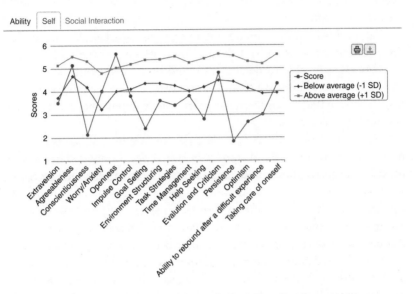

Source: Screenshot reproduced from https://teacherselector.com.au/.

other application materials in admissions decisions, and faculty members are studying how differences in scores are related to outcomes in teacher education and beyond.

As explained by MGSE deputy director of teaching and learning, Larissa McLean Davies (Link 3-2), the balance of these strengths is important in the selection process:

> We spent many hours actually looking at the profiles of the candidates coming in and looking at where their strengths were . . . It's not an overall score at the end. It's a much more nuanced way of looking at different bands (on the Teacher Selector dimensions) in combination with GPA.

Preparing Professionals

Standards for Practice: A Framework for Teacher Learning

Once teachers have taken the first step into the profession, the question is whether their training can truly prepare them for the challenging work ahead. For some, teaching ability is an ineffable trait; teachers either have it or they don't. To those who hold that view, the best way to ensure high-quality teaching is to allow people who want to teach to become teachers, measure their performance, and weed out those who are not successful.

High-performing systems do not operate on this belief. They act on the conviction that there is a distinct body of knowledge and skills all teachers must be able to demonstrate and that teachers can learn these competencies and improve their performance. Just as many systems profess to believe that all children can learn, these systems believe all teachers can learn as well.

Moreover, these systems articulate the knowledge and skills teachers must demonstrate in a set of standards of practice. Grounded in research on effective instruction, these standards, similar to those for students, spell out what teachers should know and be able to do in clear ways that can guide teachers' preparation, practice, assessment, and professional growth. They make clear the expectations for teachers as well as for those who support them, so that teachers become increasingly effective.

In the United States, the articulation of teaching standards began in the 1980s with the creation of the National Board for Professional Teaching Standards, which outlined standards for accomplished teaching and developed assessments to measure whether teachers could demonstrate those standards. In addition, states participating in the Interstate New Teacher Assessment and Support Consortium established related teaching standards for beginning teacher licensure. The idea has spread across the globe and is now a feature of virtually all high-performing countries.

With the exception of Finland, where universities got together to set standards and curriculum expectations for teacher education some time ago, each of the jurisdictions we studied has adopted standards in recent years that describe the knowledge and skills that teachers are expected to learn and display. In Singapore, the statement of Graduand Teacher Competencies has been developed by the National Institute of Education, which is the primary teacher education institution in the nation. In Canada, the provinces set standards for the teaching profession: In Ontario, it is the College of Teachers, and in Alberta, it is the Ministry of Education. In Australia, the profession-led Institutes of Teaching in Victoria and New South Wales play a similar role. As national standards have been adopted through AITSL, they are implemented through these state-level professional bodies. Shanghai's standards are set by the Chinese Ministry of Education.

The standards have many commonalities and feature some interesting cultural differences as well. For example, all of them include categories of standards focused on teacher commitment to students and their learning; professional knowledge and skills—including skills of reflection used to evaluate practice; and commitment to collaborate with other professionals and continue learning to improve their practice. In addition, some (e.g., Alberta, Singapore, and Shanghai) emphasize teachers' responsibilities to develop all the aspects of children's development—moral and ethical as well as cognitive, social, emotional, and physical. Singapore's standards also include skills of self-management, people management, and innovation and entrepreneurship—signals of the country's desire to create expectations for a dynamic, highly motivated, and leadership-oriented teaching force.

Canada

In addition to technical knowledge and skills, these standards treat teachers' moral and ethical commitments to students and their learning—and, by extension, to teachers' own ongoing reflection and learning—so that they can always improve their ability to meet student needs. For example, in Ontario, the Standards of Practice for the Teaching Profession (Link 3-3), developed by the Ontario College of Teachers, include the following:

- ○ *Commitment to students and student learning.* Members are dedicated in their care and commitment to students. They treat students equitably and with respect and are sensitive to factors that influence individual student learning. Members facilitate the development of students as contributing citizens of Canadian society.

- ○ *Professional knowledge.* Members strive to be current in their professional knowledge and recognize its relationship to practice. They understand and reflect on student development, learning theory, pedagogy, curriculum, ethics, educational research and related policies, and legislation to inform professional judgment in practice.

- ○ *Professional practice.* Members apply professional knowledge and experience to promote student learning. They use appropriate pedagogy, assessment and evaluation, resources, and technology in planning for and responding to the needs of individual students and learning communities. Members refine their professional practice through ongoing inquiry, dialogue, and reflection.

In addition, the Ontario standards, similar to those in several other countries we studied, explicitly address teacher responsibilities to contribute to the well-being of the school as a whole and to be members of professional learning communities:

○ *Leadership in learning communities.* Members promote and participate in the creation of collaborative, safe, and supportive learning communities. They recognize their shared responsibilities and their leadership roles in order to facilitate student success. Members maintain and uphold the principles of the ethical standards in these learning communities.

 Alberta's Teaching Quality Standards (Link 3-4), established in 1997, are similar: They describe desired knowledge, skills, and attributes for teachers throughout their career, and they guide teacher certification, professional development, supervision, and evaluation. They emphasize viewing children holistically, understanding contextual factors that influence learning, and incorporating that understanding in adaptive decision making. One purpose of the standards is to evaluate teacher education programs. Every 5 years, the Professional Standards Branch of the ministry completes an efficacy report, similar to an audit, of each university's program, ensuring that the institution meets the teaching quality standards. This process includes surveys of current students, alumni, and employers of program graduates.

The standards are also used to guide professional growth. In 1998, a teacher growth, supervision, and evaluation policy was developed to support the teaching quality standards. Each school year, every teacher completes an annual professional growth plan that (1) reflects goals and objectives based on an assessment of learning needs by the individual teacher; (2) shows a relationship to the teaching quality standards; and (3) takes into consideration the education plans of the school, the school authority, and the government. This annual plan must be submitted for review or approval to either the principal or a group of teachers delegated by the principal. In these ways, the standards are threaded throughout the teaching career.

Australia

As in Canada, teaching standards were historically a state function in Australia. In 2009, following work on national standards and curriculum for students, the federal government created a body known as the

Australian Institute for Teaching and School Leadership, which began an effort to develop national standards for teachers and school leaders.

To develop the standards, AITSL drew on the substantial body of research on instruction and leadership and consulted with a broad range of stakeholders, including regulatory officials, unions, and focus groups of teachers and school leaders. The standards were adopted by the agency's board, which represented all segments of the schools and profession. Thus the standards from the start had broad buy in and were seen as legitimate by all parties.

The standards describe action across three teaching domains (Link 3-5)—professional knowledge, professional practice, and professional engagement—covering seven standards:

o Professional Knowledge

　　1. Know students and how they learn.

　　2. Know the content and how to teach it.

o Professional Practice

　　3. Plan for and implement effective teaching and learning.

　　4. Create and maintain supportive learning environments.

　　5. Assess, provide feedback, and report on student learning.

o Professional Engagement

　　6. Engage in professional learning.

　　7. Engage professionally with colleagues, parents and caregivers, and the community.

These standards outline what teachers are expected to know and be able to do at each of four different career levels: graduate, proficient, highly accomplished, and lead. Among their purposes are to make explicit the elements that constitute high-quality teaching to support a common discourse about the expectations for teachers within the profession and among other education stakeholders (AITSL, 2011). In addition, the standards are intended to foster a developmental approach to teaching, supporting an ongoing process of reflection and learning. States have adopted the standards and are figuring out how to use them best in their processes of accreditation and registration, as well as professional learning, appraisal, and recognition.

Shanghai

China's Ministry of Education released two sets of professional teaching standards in 2011, one for primary teachers and one for secondary teachers. These standards were developed to align with laws governing education and to give stronger guidance to teacher preparation programs about the professional expectations for teachers. These standards are organized into four broad categories and then further specified into 61 basic requirements or teaching standards.

The first broad area focuses on establishing a student-centered approach to teaching. These standards speak to respecting the rights and individual personalities of the students, understanding physical and developmental needs of the students, and caring for and protecting the students. The second broad area focuses on the teacher's ethics. The standards include expectations of the teacher to serve as a role model and to have a love of the work they do with career aspirations and strong professionalism.

The third broad area focuses on the theoretical and practical aspects of teaching. These knowledge and skills standards include general pedagogical knowledge, such as classroom management, understanding student thinking, understanding cultural characteristics and behaviors of students, and understanding overall life development and values formation. They also include disciplinary knowledge and pedagogical content knowledge, such as methods and strategies for teaching specific content subjects.

The final broad area focuses on the teachers' lifelong learning and contribution to the ongoing development of the whole educational enterprise. These standards specify that teachers should work with their colleagues to share experiences and resources. Teachers should also take initiative to "collect and analyze relevant information, and constantly reflect and improve education and teaching" (Ministry of Education of the People's Republic of China, 2011; Wu, 2014).

To do this, teachers should identify practice-based needs and problems and address them through exploration and research. This research is frequently published and widely disseminated beyond an individual teacher's classroom or school.

Singapore

In Singapore, standards for teacher education were established to support the 21st-century competencies established for students and the nation's new vision of teaching and learning that is "student-centric and values-driven" (Heng, 2012). The National Institute of Education has established a framework for teacher preparation that articulates the values, skills, and knowledge needed of a 21st-century teaching professional who can develop learners who are problem-solvers, critical thinkers, and contributors to the community. Interestingly, this framework focuses especially on three sets of values—learner centeredness, a teacher identity that aims for high standards and strives always to improve, and service to the profession and the community—as well as skills and knowledge. These are articulated in the "V³SK" framework, which communicates that technical knowledge exists to be used in the service of the learner.

Alongside this framework are the graduate teacher competencies (GTCs), which outline the professional standards, benchmarks, and goals for graduates of the initial teacher education programs at the National Institute of Education (see Table 3–1). These competencies are modeled after the Ministry of Education's teacher appraisal and development system—the enhanced performance management system—and specify three dimensions of preservice teacher professional performance: professional practice, leadership and management, and personal effectiveness.

Table 3–1 GTC Framework from NIE

Performance Dimension	Core Competencies
Professional Practice	1. Nurturing the whole child 2. Providing quality learning of child 3. Providing quality learning of child in CCA 4. Cultivating knowledge: 　i. with subject mastery 　ii. with reflective thinking 　iii. with analytic thinking 　iv. with initiative 　v. with creative teaching 　vi. with a future focus
Leadership and Management	5. Winning hearts and minds 　i. Understanding the environment 　ii. Developing others 6. Working with others 　i. Partnering parents 　ii. Working in teams
Personal Effectiveness	7. Knowing self and others 　i. Tuning into self 　ii. Exercising personal integrity and legal responsibilities 　iii. Understanding and respecting others 　iv. Resilience and adaptability

Source: Singapore NIE (2009).

Acknowledging the human qualities and commitments needed to teach with concern for the child and colleagues, the competencies begin, as does the performance management system, with "nurturing the whole child," and they specify areas of knowledge and skills to accomplish that. They continue with "winning hearts and minds," including helping to develop others, and they conclude with "knowing self and others," including integrity, respect, resiliency, and adaptability.

For in-service teachers, the Teacher Growth Model (TGM) guides the professional growth and learning for teachers. The TGM is organized to address five learning outcomes: the ethical educator, the competent professional, the collaborative learner, the transformational leader, and the community builder. Competencies associated with each outcome are enumerated within the model. Teachers use the TGM to examine their professional learning needs. There are programs and activities that are themed according to each outcome and competency. Teachers can select the area that they would like to be developed and participate in the tagged professional learning courses and activities.

Preparation That Enables Professional Practice

High-performing countries provide teacher candidates with strong preparation to provide them with a solid foundation for teaching. There are relatively few universities providing training in most of the jurisdictions we studied—eight in Finland, nine in Alberta, two in Shanghai, one in Singapore, for example—and these invest substantial effort in preparing teachers to meet high standards. Because attrition rates for teachers are quite low in many of these jurisdictions, universities are not trying to prepare a large number of teachers who will enter and leave the profession quickly. They are investing in individuals who generally will stay in the profession for a substantial career. This reduces the total number of teachers needed and enables these societies to invest more thoughtfully in that group.

In concert with governments, teacher-preparing universities are continually engaged in improving their own practices. A major aspect of this self-improvement in recent years has been to extend the duration and rethink the design of clinical experiences to make them more tightly connected to course work and program goals and more expertly supervised. Stronger clinical training occurs within preservice preparation and, increasingly, once teachers are in their first year of practice, as part of a strong mentoring program. We describe both of these as part of the learning-to-teach process.

Finland

We begin with Finland as the acknowledged world leader in initial teacher education (Sahlberg, 2015b). Finland began its education reform effort many decades ago by moving teacher education to universities in 1971 and placing it in master's degree programs by 1978–1979. At this time, many other countries in the world did not even require a bachelor's degree for all teachers, and even today, Finland is one of only a few countries that require a master's degree for all teachers—although many leading nations are now moving much more rapidly in this direction.

It is not the length of study that is most noteworthy, however. It is the nature of the highly intellectual and deeply clinical preparation all Finnish teachers receive that is extraordinary.

To begin with, the 5-year program, which comprises undergraduate and graduate study, is highly rigorous. As we described, entrants must complete an examination that engages them in reading and interpreting primary research on teaching. For a primary school teacher qualification, students must complete course work in the disciplines they will teach (which includes not only Finnish, mathematics, history, and science but also drama, music, and physical education); pedagogical course work; course work on communication and language development; and course work in research and analysis (Link 3-6) (which also includes the writing of theses for the bachelor's and master's degrees).

Rather than taking course work divorced from pedagogy, primary candidates' broad and deep subject matter studies are integrated with how that content is taught. For instance, during the first year of the primary teacher education program, students take rigorous course work in the teaching of different subject areas that they will eventually teach, from mother tongue to science to mathematics. Simultaneously, students must take pedagogical courses, including a methods (or didactics) course; two courses on child development (tailored for teaching, loosely translated as "Interacting With and Awareness of Pupils" and "Introduction to Educational Psychology"); and engage in a series of gradually lengthening placements in a teacher training school.

During those initial visits, student-teachers are learning how to observe children through assignments that require them to chart social relationships, interview children, and apply what they are learning in their child development courses. They are also asked to observe teachers' teaching and classroom interactions. Students are simultaneously taking course work in the teaching of all the subjects that they will eventually teach (60 credits)—they also typically choose to also take a certain number of "pure" content courses (such as mathematics or Finnish) as part of their "minor subject" and "optional studies" (75 credits). This preparation—with a focus on the *teaching* of subject matter rather than pure content courses—has been in place since the late 1970s (Uusiautti & Määttä, 2013). The fact that the content is studied through a lens of teaching develops "pedagogical content knowledge" (Shulman, 1986).

The preparation also emphasizes learning how to teach students who learn in different ways and teaching diverse learners, including those with special needs. It includes substantial emphasis on "multiculturality" and the "prevention of learning difficulties and exclusion" in courses such as "Facing Specificity and Multiplicity: Education for Diversities" and "Cultural Diversity in Schools," along with a course on "Education and Social Justice" as well as on the understanding of learning, assessment, and curriculum development.

Finnish teacher education also includes substantial clinical requirements intended to provide lengthy opportunities to learn in real clinical practice. At least two of three clinical placement periods are at teacher training schools associated with the university's teacher education program. Much like teaching hospitals in medicine, these schools are designed to be staffed by expert teachers who can demonstrate research-based practices and who also continually engage in research and inquiry, connecting theory and practice. All eight universities throughout Finland that offer teacher education degrees have teacher training schools associated with them—there are 11 teacher training schools in total. They also work with other partner or field schools, which are organized to support teacher learning but are run by the municipalities directly.

The teacher training school is an important and unique feature of Finnish teacher education. As university units, teacher training schools are funded through the Ministry of Education and Culture, which has a separate budget line for all teacher training schools that it allocates to the universities as part of annual agreement between the universities and the ministry. The funding for these teacher training schools is equivalent to that of regular public schools, with the exception of extra money for supervising student teachers.

Teacher training schools are public schools that serve neighborhood children and are subject to national curriculum and teaching requirements just like any other municipal school. However, they are administered by the faculty members of teacher education, who are engaged in hiring the principal and staff members and designing the curriculum, pedagogy, and, often, the architecture so that they support both pupils and student teachers in their learning.

For example, the current site for Viikki—a teacher training school associated with the University of Helsinki (Link 3-7)—was built in 2003 with special features that would support learning about teaching. The school has a "comprehensive school" serving children in grades 1–9 and general upper secondary school. An associated kindergarten abuts the main building so that children can also attend as 5- and 6-year-olds. However, the main purpose of the school is also to support the learning of prospective teachers: Principal Kimmo Koskinen estimates that at any one time, the school typically has between 30 to 36 student teachers placed in various classrooms throughout the grades.

Among the special features of the school is a suite of rooms for student teachers, including a room with tables for meetings among student teachers, lockers and bookcases for materials and resources, a coatroom, and lunch space. An entire room equipped with the latest technology and designed for meetings between student teachers and practice teachers underscores the importance that is placed on analyzing teaching.

In one of our visits, we observed student teachers meeting with their practice teachers in the room to debrief a lesson plan and to talk about next steps. This attention to the cycle of planning, action, and reflection and evaluation is modeled throughout teacher education, demonstrating what full-time teachers do in planning for their own students. Graduates are expected to eventually engage in similar kinds of research and inquiry in their own work as teachers. These meeting sessions underscore the notion that learning in practice does not happen on its own without opportunities for teachers to analyze their experiences, relate experiences to research, and engage in metacognitive reflection. In some ways, it models what the entire system is intended to undergo: a process of continual reflection, evaluation, and problem-solving at the level of the classroom, school, municipality, and nation.

Student teachers work in pairs, co-planning lessons that they alternately teach and that they debrief together with their master teachers. When the student teachers embark on their own research, they work with faculty members who sponsor research groups of three to seven students investigating issues close to the interests and expertise of the faculty member, for example, the teaching and learning of mathematics, science, or other topics.

The teachers in these schools are especially selected; the expectation is that they are highly accomplished and experienced teachers who are actively engaged in research. At Viikki, most have completed or are working on doctoral degrees and are involved with multiple research projects. For example, Sirkku Myllyntausta, who has taught at Viikki for

26 years, is involved in an international project on math pedagogy in 12 different countries and a study with the research group of the University of Eastern Finland on design-oriented pedagogy (Link 3-8). She has also been writing textbooks on religion for 3rd, 4th, and 5th graders, along with a group of four other teachers, and just published a book of creative writing with a colleague. She explained that working at a teacher training school had in fact been a kind of dream for her since she herself was a student teacher.

Sirkku described the benefits of being a teacher training–school teacher as a combination of the value of sharing professional expertise, staying updated with new educational research, being challenged intellectually, and constantly learning:

> I think the main thing is that after having this long experience as a teacher and having this very deep interest in teaching and interacting with pupils, I feel it is very meaningful to share all of that, and also my occupational skills. In addition, I enjoy discussions with students. I also feel that as a training school teacher it is crucially important to be aware of the latest research in education and the up-to-date teaching methods to be able to apply them in a class with students and to reflect upon your methods. And you know it kind of keeps me going. It is so fascinating to have this daily cooperation with the students because of the way they challenge me and my occupational skills.

Sirkku's colleague, Anni Loukomies, explained her role as a kind of bridge between theory and practice to help student teachers learn about the relevance of theory to real classroom practice—which is the major point of the entire teacher preparation experience. She noted that often the student teachers come thinking that "real practice" is somehow divorced from theory.

> Many student teachers see the theoretical studies and the practice here at school as completely distant and different from each other. And they are like, "Okay, now we are going to get rid of the theory and now we're starting to really practice."

But, she explained, her work is to help candidates see the relationships.

> As supervisors, we try to find out . . . a relevant way of saying to them that . . . now this is the place where you should be combining what you have been studying beforehand. [So] through which concepts should you be reflecting what you are doing here? And what are the phenomena that you meet here? If I had to describe my position in two words, I would say that I'm a bridge between theory and

practice. And I have to somehow distribute that idea to the student teachers and be an example of how to reflect the issues from practical life with theoretical terms.

As these examples suggest, a key feature of teacher education in Finland is the emphasis on research, inquiry, and analysis of teaching and learning—which includes the study of research methods and a master's degree thesis. These competencies are considered central to the development of professional teachers. This means that all courses integrate educational research, and for primary teachers, educational science is their major and the focus of their 5 years (Kansanen, 2007; Krokfors, 2007; Toom et al., 2010). They must take courses in research methods and inquiry, including a course in qualitative methods and one in quantitative methods, and must also write bachelor's and master's theses (for a total of 70 of 300 total credits). Many students go on to earn doctorates, and most continue to teach in Finland's highly educated profession of teachers. Many of these features of Finnish teacher education have been spreading to other countries.

Australia

The Finnish idea of creating much stronger connections between universities and partner schools—and between theory and practice—has taken root in several ways in Australia. In Victoria, a growing proportion of teachers prepare in graduate-degree programs (required for secondary teachers and increasingly common for primary teachers), and these are moving toward 2-year, rather than 1- year, models allowing for much more extensive clinical training as well as course work. Most master's level teacher education programs also require or encourage a substantial research component, often a practice-based research project intended to develop inquiry skills needed to generate, analyze, and act on evidence as a basis of professional practice.

Policy Levers for Teacher Education Improvement

Across Australia, several policy levers have been used to improve the quality of initial teacher education since the mid-1990s. Movement toward a nationally consistent teacher registration process began in 2011. In New South Wales and Victoria, state laws have required teacher registration since the mid-2000s. To be registered, teachers must provide evidence of meeting the required competencies for teaching as measured against state standards and, since 2013, national teacher professional standards. Programs must also be accredited to prepare teachers against the same standards, and accreditation requirements have also been put in place to leverage change.

There are a number of federally led initiatives under way to strengthen the quality of initial teacher education. The recent move to national standards has created pressure to move programs to the graduate level as well as to phase out the once-common diploma of teaching—a 1-year, graduate program—in favor of 2-year master's degrees, a move that has received support from several quarters, including the Australian Education Union (AEU, 2014). This enables more time for serious clinical training, and strengthened accreditation requirements will require consistent agreements between universities and schools regarding the level of supervision and support for teacher candidates in practicum settings.

The move to extend time for teacher education is also translating into more intensive opportunities for content specialization. Secondary teachers generally prepare in a major and a minor content field of specialization. Historically, primary school teachers have been trained as generalists, typically receiving a broad preparation to teach all but specialist subjects, such as languages other than English, music, and physical education. The recent Teacher Education Ministerial Advisory Group report recommended that teacher education programs offer a specialization, such as mathematics, a science, or an additional language (TEMAG, 2015). The intent of the specialization is that teachers will be able to share this knowledge with colleagues to build school capacity in these subject areas.

A number of universities already offer a level of subject specialization. For example, the master of teaching (primary) at the Melbourne Graduate School of Education allows candidates to elect a specialization in mathematics or science teaching, the content of which comprises a quarter of the total program (personal communication, S. Dinham, January 15, 2014). Teacher candidates at Monash choose one of three discipline studies streams—leadership in English and literacy, leadership in mathematics, or languages other than English—designed to strengthen their own capabilities in the selected area. The requirement that all schools offer a language other than English is reflective of the diversity of the student population in Victoria, and this has increased the need for teachers with second-language skills. Thus students in this stream study their language of choice within the relevant department in the university. Those in literacy or mathematics specialize in the fundamentals of that discipline with a focus on the communication of concepts.

Other national and state initiatives have increased entry standards for new teacher candidates. Each of these steps can be viewed as part of a historical passage of increasing teacher professionalization that has taken place progressively over almost a century but has accelerated in the new millennium.

In line with these moves, New South Wales has undertaken a set of ambitious reforms. Starting in 2007, all teacher education programs there have undergone a rigorous assessment process designed to improve the quality of graduate teachers and ensure they have met the state's professional teaching standards. More recently, a new policy, known as Great Teaching, Inspired Learning, was enacted to offer a cohesive strategy to transform the way that teachers in New South Wales are selected, prepared, developed, evaluated, and compensated. In 2012, NSW initial teacher education requirements were further revised to incorporate the nationally agreed-on accreditation requirements for programs.

The Great Teaching, Inspired Learning reforms (Link 3-9) make several changes in initial teacher preparation. The policy defines teacher quality in terms of 21st-century "knowledge, understanding, skills and values," including deeper learning, creativity, interpersonal communication, problem-solving abilities, confidence, social connectedness, and lifelong learning (DEC, 2013). Teacher attributes are articulated as a balance of content knowledge, the ability to assess student needs, and capability to employ multiple teaching strategies.

Programs are expected to provide a rigorous intellectual preparation with strong subject discipline knowledge, as well as knowledge and skills in the key elements of teaching practice, including student learning and teaching strategies, classroom and behavior management, literacy, technology, Aboriginal education, special education, and education for students with diverse linguistic and cultural backgrounds. There is a strong focus on developing teacher expertise to interpret student assessment data, evaluate student learning, and modify teaching practice.

In addition, under the new policy, student teachers will be supervised by teachers who have attained the "highly accomplished" or "lead teacher" levels based on national standards for teaching. The supervising teachers, moreover, will be required to undergo specific professional development to prepare them for supervising teacher candidates. In addition, the new policy sets out expectations for outcomes of the placements and calls for the development of evaluation tools to assess candidates' experiences in a consistent way across all institutions of higher education in the state.

Research-Based, Inquiry-Oriented, Clinical Preparation: The MTeach Model

One national leader in the process of teacher education redesign has been the University of Sydney, which made significant changes to the quality of teacher preservice education well before governmental reforms were mandated. In 1996, the University of Sydney established Australia's first master of teaching (MTeach) program. The 2-year full-time program of study was developed in recognition of the importance of a high-level, inquiry-oriented professional study to enable teachers to meet the needs of the rapidly changing society and the profession.

The program is underpinned by a strong commitment to enable teachers to focus on their own ongoing learning as well as that of their students. This focus entails a strong commitment to social justice. The program entry is highly competitive. It continues to serve about 250 students annually and provides ongoing case-based inquiry through school experience, including an internship enabling teacher inquiry for a final action research study. The preservice teacher's learning is supported by a mentor who assists him or her to develop new and explicit professional understandings. The preservice teachers graduating from this program are highly valued by school and system leaders.

Another, more recent pioneering program that has stimulated reforms in many other universities is the University of Melbourne's Master of Teaching model, initiated in 2008 as the university moved from largely undergraduate- to entirely graduate-level programs and that now enroll over 1,200 candidates in early childhood, primary, and secondary teacher education. Launched in partnership with the Victorian Department of Education and Training (DET);[2] the Australian Department of Education, Employment, and Workplace Relations (DEEWR); and the Catholic Education Office in Victoria, the 2-year Master of Teaching, designed as a research-based clinical program, was influenced in part by the Teachers for a New Era program in the United States, which sees teaching as a clinical practice profession like many health professions (McLean Davies et al., 2012).

The program integrates master's-level academic study with practical work in collaborating partnership schools. It is designed to develop graduates who have the professional capabilities to meet the needs of individual learners through the use of data to plan, implement, and evaluate teaching interventions. Building on a strong foundation of curriculum, assessment, learning, and teaching, candidates learn to do the following:

○ Gather evidence about what learners know now and what they are ready to learn next o Create appropriate learning strategies to take the learner to the next level of knowledge

o Use evidence-based teaching interventions

o Evaluate the impact of their decisions on student learning

The process also encourages teachers to research and decide among possible interventions to advance learning, some of which may be not be familiar. This diagnostic approach expects teachers to evaluate what students need, evaluate practice options supported by research, make well-grounded decisions, and evaluate the results of their actions with the purpose of refining further (see Table 3–2).

The design of the MTeach approach is thus grounded in education research. Teacher candidates and graduate teachers interviewed for the project indicated that the incorporation of the diagnostic cycle and collection of data and evidence on student learning was already a part of their teaching practice.

They learn these practices in courses that are grounded in research and analysis and from tightly connected clinical practice in closely partnered schools. Rather than short blocks of school experience separated by long periods away from the school, candidates are in schools 2 days a week throughout each semester. The weekly school experience is supplemented with an additional 3 weeks of full-time teaching practice during each semester. These tight connections are made possible through school-university partnerships that function like teaching hospitals for medical students.

Candidates work with university-based "clinical specialists" and school-based "teaching fellows," who work with supervising teachers and teacher candidates to support their teaching practice. Together clinical specialists and teaching fellows review and give feedback on lesson

---

Table 3–2   Interventionist Practitioner Cycle of Inquiry

Aspire	What is the student ready to learn in _____ and what is the evidence for this?
Analyze	What are the possible evidence-based interventions and what is the associated scaffolding process for each?
Apply	What is the preferred process and why is it preferred?
Anticipate	What is the expected impact and how will you check?
Appraise	What happened and what resultant decision was made?

Source: Rickards (2012).

plans, observe lessons, and provide coaching. The two positions also work with mentor teachers in schools to support them in applying the clinical teaching methods in their mentorship roles and in turn helping to shape the culture of the school. All courses are connected to the practicum experience. Importantly, the clinical specialist and teaching fellow are in close communication with each other to support the teacher candidate's transition from academic studies to teaching and to see that candidates are effectively drawing on their practice experiences and that these are tightly integrated with their studies.

The clinical teaching framework of diagnosis, intervention, and assessment (Link 3-10) forms the basis for the evaluation of teacher candidates in the program. Each candidate's semester is capped with a clinical praxis exam. The MTeach program combines elements of each of the three core subjects—learners, teachers, and pedagogy; social and professional contexts; and language and teaching—together with candidates' elective subjects and the professional practice seminar, and it assesses teacher candidates on this basis. This is in contrast to traditional university settings in which each course of a program is usually assessed in a separate exam. The clinical praxis exam requires teacher candidates to identify student needs, identify and enact interventions, and evaluate the effects of their efforts.

o Was the learning need well identified and an appropriate intervention selected?

o What kinds of evidence of learning were collected, and how were these used to assess gains in student learning?

o What was the effect of the teacher and intervention on student learning?

o Was the intervention successful, and if not, why not? (Interview with Field Rickards, dean of Melbourne Graduate School of Education, May 2014)

Their findings from this research are then presented before a university-assembled panel consisting of faculty members and practitioners. Thus candidates' learning and readiness are assessed in an integrated way, based not solely on what they have studied but on how they are able to apply this knowledge in their teaching practice.

As one sign of the improved outcomes made possible by this model, the Australian Council for Educational Research found, in an external evaluation of the MTeach in 2010, that 90% of graduates felt well-prepared for their first teaching role (Scott, Kleinhenz, Weldon, Reid, & Dinhan, 2010). There is also early evidence that the MTeach graduates have higher rates of employment, stronger career commitment, and lower attrition. Principals report that graduates have had a significant impact on schools' educational programs. Many partnership schools are now working with the university to involve more of their teachers in the model so as to support whole-school change through an evidence-based approach. The University of Melbourne is now aligning its school leadership programs to follow a similar model, philosophy, and impact.

School Centers for Teaching Excellence

Other initiatives to strengthen clinical practice in Australia include the School Centres for Teaching Excellence (SCTE). This program was a federal initiative that was locally designed and implemented by the states. The Victorian program was launched by the state Department of Education and Training in 2010 to foster innovative clinical practice in initial teacher education. The initiative seeks to build school capacity to provide professional placement experiences for teacher candidates and more closely link theory and practice. The SCTE was developed in consultation with a range of education stakeholders, including Victorian universities, the Victorian Institute of Teaching, and principal and teacher associations, to transform clinical placements for preservice teachers so that they are more closely integrated with teacher education courses and with the life of the school. These more immersive residency models involve university faculty members working with teams of teachers and student teachers in schools—undertaking curriculum planning, school improvement strategies, and research, much like professional development school models launched in the United States and the teacher training schools developed in Finland.

Seven clusters were formed, each comprising one or more universities, several schools, and a DET regional office. In all, 6 universities, 65 schools, and about 1,000 preservice teacher candidates have taken part in the program (DEECD, 2014b). The clusters are funded by the National Partnership for Improving Teacher Quality and the Victoria DET. The pilot initiative was so successful that in 2014 the department expanded it and made it a permanent program. It is now called "Teaching Academies of Professional Practice."

The Australian Council for Educational Research found that the initiative has strengthened preparation through these steps:

○ *Partnerships and collaboration:* Relationships and communication between school and university educators have been strengthened by the increased contact that occurs in site-based models and by the presence of university staff members in schools. This has resulted in significant changes to practicum arrangements and university course content, as well as enhanced and strengthened school curriculum.

○ *Practicum models:* The SCTE model has enabled the development of on-site, practice-oriented models of teacher education, with greater emphasis on preservice participation in the life of the school. A typical pattern for the practicum is an extended period (often a semester), in which preservice teachers spend at least 2 days per week in a school, followed later by a more traditional block placement of 3 or 4 weeks. Preservice teachers are often invited to faculty and learning team meetings and are given the opportunity to consider policy and school focus areas. Placement of teams of preservice teachers in a school provides greater opportunity for mutual support.

○ *Mentoring:* Professional collaboration among teachers in schools has improved as result of new mentoring cultures that have developed out of SCTE mentoring initiatives. The team emphasis has enabled more collaborative models beyond the traditional teacher-supervisor role, in which one supervising teacher is paid for the supervision of one preservice teacher. The role of "expert mentor" has also been introduced on some sites.

○ *Course quality and design:* The school-university relationship enables courses to be designed with close connections to practice and tailored to local circumstances, such as rural needs, ethnic diversity, and socioeconomic disadvantage. Team teaching and integrated curriculum in schools are reflected in course arrangements, with preservice teachers also working in teams and on team projects; this has had positive effects on school curriculum. In some of these partnerships, teams of teachers worked on course development and delivery with teams of preservice teachers. Some preservice teacher assessment focused on this work, for example, practicum presentations and presentations of curriculum projects.

○ *Assessment quality:* Within SCTE programs, assessment of practicum performance has largely become a team exercise, with teams of mentors conferring in various ways to assess the performance of teams of preservice teachers. The assessment of practicum in SCTE programs is typically based on better information and greater consultation than in the past.

Canada

As in Australia, teacher education in Canada is also increasingly occurring at the graduate level. Similar to its pioneering peer institutions in Finland and Australia, the University of Toronto/Ontario Institute for Study of Education (UT/OISE) created a 2-year master's-level program for preparing teachers more than a decade before the province changed its policies, with significant clinical practice at partner schools integrated with academic and pedagogical studies. In this program, teacher candidates undertake their own research as well as using research generated by others. There is a strong program focus on equity, diversity, and social justice.[3]

UT/OISE teacher education candidates are expected to demonstrate capacities set out in the learner document:

o Knowledge of the learner (for example): "Understand that teaching includes responsibility for student learning."

o Teacher identity (for example): "Develop a personal philosophy of education that embodies principles of equity, diversity, inclusion, social justice, and environmental justice."

o Transformative purposes of education (for example): "Understand the roles teachers, learners, families, communities, schools, and systems play in this transformative process [of education]."

o Subject matter and pedagogical content knowledge (for example): "Make informed pedagogical decisions with the goal of success for all students based on knowledge of the learner, context, curriculum, and assessment."

o Learning and teaching in social contexts (for example): "Understand how systematic/institutional practices dis/advantage social groups/learners and ways that they can work with others to counter inequalities."

UT/OISE aspires for teacher candidates to become excellent teachers who are also critical, thoughtful, action-oriented learners. As faculty member Ann Lopez noted:

We engage in pedagogies, assignments, assessments, and evaluation all coming together to facilitate synthesizing. At the end of the day, [teacher candidates] should be able to bring together all of the components of the program, developing for themselves an understanding of what it means to be an effective teacher [and] being able to articulate that, reflect on what else they need to learn, what they need to

un-learn. If we've done that, we feel very good that our teacher candidates are able to make a difference. I think that one of the strengths
of our program is truly helping our teacher candidates to understand
that they are lifelong learners, not in a rhetorical way, but in a meaningful way and [to understand] how do they do that.

Other programs share many of the same goals, but few of them previously had the 2 years of time after the bachelor's degree within which
to accomplish them. Before 2015, when Ontario's requirements were
upgraded, this kind of model was not the provincial norm: Ontario
teachers generally completed 3 or 4 years of undergraduate study and
a year of teacher preservice education at a faculty of education before
becoming certified by the Ontario College of Teachers. Some programs
integrated education courses with undergraduate studies over a 4- to
6-year period. A few had launched 2-year master's degree programs.

The changes resulted from concerns about the limited length of some
teacher education–preparation programs—especially the extent of guided
clinical experience (previously set at a minimum of 40 days)—plus the
province's oversupply of trained teachers. For example, a 2008 survey of
graduates of four institutions, other teachers, and employers in 21 school
districts found that just over half of teachers felt their preparation was
"good" or "very good." Although 83% were pleased with their clinical experiences, they expressed a desire for more (Herbert et al., 2010).
The researchers noted that teachers who had graduated from programs
outside Ontario, where requirements were higher, or from 2-year post-
baccalaureate programs, generally rated their programs more highly on
integrating theory and practice and on preparing them to teach diverse
learners.

Under the new system in Ontario (Link 3-11), which took effect in
2015, teacher preparation has become at least a 2-year program, with
a practicum of at least 80 days, twice as long as the previous requirements, and many programs substantially exceed that framework. The
reforms also added an enhanced emphasis on diversity and students with
special needs, as well as an increased focus on the use of technology.
With a huge surplus of teachers in Ontario, policy makers decided that
preparing fewer teachers more thoroughly and enabling them to be more
successful from the start made sense. As in Finland and Australia, this
greater success is anticipated as a result of merging theory and practice,
focusing more on the sophisticated and targeted strategies needed for
teaching students with a wide range of needs, and learning how to enact
an "equity pedagogy" in the classroom (Banks & Banks, 1995). Lopez
noted that the changes

were not purely a response to oversupply. It is as well a response to what teachers should bring to the table as 21st century learners and 21st century educators meeting the needs of a 21st century society: Looking at issues such as the environment [and] recognizing the needs of students who learn differently, special education must be foregrounded; this kind of knowledge must be embedded in the curriculum. It is supporting teacher candidates to develop a mindset and culture of learning as learners who respond to the needs of all students. . . I think the Ministry is responding to that in the new two-year program—highlighting the importance of culturally relevant and responsive pedagogies and ensuring that we infuse Aboriginal knowledges in the curriculum and do a better job of educating students from our Aboriginal communities. I see these as important issues in the new teacher education curriculum.

Demetra Saldaris, in the Teaching Policy and Standards Branch at the Ontario Ministry of Education, agreed that the extension of the program time is intended to strengthen learning and experience rather than to emphasize longer academic study time:

I think you've heard how important a learning stance has been. Not just for the teacher, but for the system. It is not a learning stance in terms of academia; it is learning about what the students need, being open to learning at all levels of the system. The learning stance we mean is based on how society is changing; therefore, what do students need to know and to be able to do to be part of that society, and what do educators need to learn to address these needs? That's the learning stance we're talking about . . . and it's a stance we all have to take whether at the ministry, board, school, or classroom level. It's not a "study longer" stance.

In Alberta, eight of the nine approved teacher preparation institutions offer 2-year post-baccalaureate programs that result in a credential to teach. A master of education degree takes about 3 years to complete. Most institutions also offer 5-year dual or combined degree programs resulting in a bachelor of arts or science and a bachelor of education degree. Some offer 4-year undergraduate programs. Secondary education programs require a major and a minor specialization; elementary programs are broad and interdisciplinary, covering, at a minimum, English/French literature and composition, Canadian studies, mathematics, and science.

As in other jurisdictions, there is a move to extend the length of study, especially clinical training, to better prepare teachers for the wide range of student needs. The director of the ministry's Professional Standards

Branch noted that many teacher education programs are moving from an average of about 14 weeks of clinical training to a 20-week practicum.

Alberta, too, holds a strong commitment to a learning stance for teachers and an expectation for high standards. Paul MacLeod, the former director of the Professional Standards Branch, explained why Alberta believes in serious training for all teachers:

> We often talk about cardiologists. I really prefer he [complete] his program before he opens me up. I would prefer he's not learning on the job. We know there's an internship process. We know he's going to be going through that but we prefer the [degree is] in place before he actually decides to split me open. Same with teachers. We know that they're going to grow. We know that you never stop learning professionally, but you've got to have that degree and meet a certification standard.

This view has shaped Alberta's approach to the new Teach for Canada, which aims to serve First Nations students. Unlike alternative pathway initiatives in which candidates begin teaching before they have received preparation, Teach for Canada will include only individuals who have already completed an approved teacher education program, plus additional training for working with First Nations, Métis, and Inuit (FNMI) students.[4]

Singapore

Singapore revamped its teacher education programs in 2001 to increase teachers' pedagogical knowledge and skills as well as their content knowledge. Singapore has been moving toward graduate-level training of teachers, with about two-thirds now completing a 1-year postgraduate diploma education program following the undergraduate content major, and one-third completing a 4-year undergraduate program. All teachers, including those who will teach in elementary schools, must demonstrate deep mastery of at least one content area (plus study of the other subjects they will teach), and clinical training has been expanded. A school partnership model engages schools more proactively in supporting trainees during their practicum experiences.

Based on the V^{3}SK framework, the teacher education curriculum includes study of the academic subjects teachers will teach; curriculum, teaching, and assessment; information and communication technology; teaching of language and academic discourse skills; character and citizenship; service learning; and research. Students in the 4-year undergraduate program must obtain a major in an academic discipline, and those in the graduate program must have a degree in a discipline. Curriculum studies aim to equip student teachers with pedagogical methodologies for teaching specific subjects. Primary teachers are prepared to teach two or three subjects; secondary teachers are prepared to teach two.

All preservice preparation in Singapore occurs in the National Institute of Education (NIE), which is affiliated with Nanyang Technological University (NTU). At the NIE, candidates learn to teach in the same way they will be asked to teach. Every student has a laptop, and the entire campus is wireless. The library spaces and a growing number of classrooms are consciously arranged with round tables and groups of three to four chairs so that students will have places to share knowledge and collaborate. Comfortable areas with sofa-and-chair arrangements are designed for group work among teachers and principals, with access to full technology supports (e.g., DVD players, video and computer hookups, and plasma screens for projecting their work as they do it). During the course of preparation in course work and the practicum, there is a focus on teaching for problem-based and inquiry learning, developing collaboration, and addressing a range of learning styles in the classroom.

NIE's teacher education model for the 21st century (TE[21]) (Link 3-12), based on the standards previously described, aims to prepare teachers for a heterogeneous student population, enabling teachers to be thinking professionals who can perform the multiple roles of 21st-century teaching, such as knowledge organizer, motivator, facilitator, co-inquirer, facilitator, and designer of the learning processes.

Key to this vision is a focus on problem-based learning with real-world applications and a new assessment competency framework for 21st-century teaching and learning aimed at enabling NIE educators and teachers to adopt innovative assessment practices *as*, *of*, and *for* learning. This includes helping teachers learn to design appropriate assessment tasks, plan assessment as part of effective teaching and learning, provide feedback to help learners improve, and develop the capacity for self-assessment in order to build reflective and self-directed learners. Different course coordinators constantly communicate with each other in order to ensure continuity and alignment in the assessment competence coverage in different courses. In addition, preservice teachers are exposed to assessment literacies within and across content disciplines. Throughout the program, structured reflection is encouraged and facilitated.

In order to ensure that student teachers develop these reflective qualities, they are required to maintain a teaching and learning electronic portfolio (e-portfolio) to organize evidence of their learning and achievement over time. It serves to document student teachers' growth and development of their personal teaching philosophies, capacities, and competencies over the course of their preservice preparation.

There is a strong values component in teaching and teacher development in Singapore. The teacher education programs emphasize that teachers ought to have a deep understanding of learner development and diversity and be committed to bringing out the fullest potential of each child. They should be passionate about their subject and their role as a teacher and have a deep drive for high standards as well as a thirst for learning. They should be ethical, adaptable, and resilient in the challenging educational landscape and collaborative with other professionals. An early emphasis on collaborative learning and group projects in preservice programs in NIE helps to sow the seeds for professional learning and sharing when preservice teachers become beginning teachers.

In line with its strong emphasis on values, the NIE requires students to take courses in character education and to undertake a community service project. The project is conducted in groups of 20 and takes at least 20 hours, at the end of which each student prepares a tangible product. For example, a group that worked with the Retinitis Pigmentosa (RP) Society, addressing a debilitating eye disease that affects approximately 10% of Singapore's population, raised funds to purchase assistive technology that can enlarge print for RP sufferers, which the society now loans to those who need it. Teachers in Singapore are expected not only to be masters of content and pedagogy but also to be contributors to the well-being of their students, families, and communities.

Shanghai

Teacher education in China is rapidly evolving from 2-year college degrees common in rural areas to 4-year college degrees, now held by just over half of teachers nationwide. In Shanghai, nearly all teachers (95%) have college degrees, with 72% from 4-year colleges. Shanghai's teachers are largely prepared in the two normal universities—Shanghai Normal University, a provincial-run institution, and East China Normal University, a comprehensive university with national ranking.

Unlike many countries, where undergraduate teacher education takes up 2 years of the college program, following 2 years of largely disconnected academic course work, in China the full 4 years are fully packed from start to finish with focused training for teaching, which prepares teachers to be thoughtful, ethical, inquiry-oriented practitioners.

For example, at Shanghai Normal University, students typically take general education courses in their first year, comprising topics such as education history, sociology, psychology, moral principles, philosophy of education, educational research methods, education management, human resources development and management, social psychology, and family education.

In their second year of the program, students take foundational courses in their major field of study—social sciences, math and natural sciences, or performance or fine arts. Primary teachers and secondary teachers specialize in subject matter content within content domains: the social sciences, mathematics and natural science, or performing and fine arts.

In their third year, students take pedagogy and teaching practice courses, which may include age-appropriate pedagogy courses, audio-visual education, basics of computer applications, practicum in schools, and a practice teaching experience. At Shanghai Normal, they experience a 2-week teaching practice placement in each term while continuing to take content and educational courses. In their fourth and last year of their degree, along with course work, students spend 8 weeks in an internship engaging in practice teaching, typically in schools considered to be high performing so they will see best practices. The university also invites accomplished teachers of high rank to give lectures for the university students.

The curriculum for secondary teachers is similar in that it requires courses in education, content specialization courses, and an 8-week student teaching internship. Whereas primary teacher preparation is the responsibility of education faculty members, secondary teacher preparation in the content areas resides in the various academic departments of the universities, and only the pedagogical and education courses are taught by the education faculty members.

During practice teaching, the teacher candidates have a guiding teacher or mentor in the school and a mentor from the university who is typically a professor. The candidates learn how to develop lesson plans, deliver a lesson, work with children, run a class, communicate with parents, use particular pedagogies such as story time or mathematics manipulatives, and recognize the areas that they need to work on in their teaching skills.

Similar to other countries in this study, there are plans to extend clinical practice experiences further and to better connect course work and student teaching, described in China's 2020 plan. Students value the practical experiences they have and seek out their own practical teaching experience by volunteering in schools within their own community. In a focus group in our study, each participant had taken on some volunteer teaching roles, paid tutoring work, or teaching English in programs for business people in order to gain more practical experience. It seemed that the volunteer practical experience was a de facto part of the curriculum for teacher preparation.

Students at the Meng Xianchen College at East China Normal University are experiencing a new program that places more emphasis on the clinical aspects of learning to teach. The students take similar university courses, but they spend more time in practical teaching experiences. In their third year, the students spend 2 months in an internship in a school, and in their fourth year, the students work as a teaching assistant for one semester in a different school.

Induction

Although teacher education programs are designed to equip teachers with the knowledge and skills they need to be able to teach successfully, educators know that teacher learning continues beyond the program and into the classroom as they encounter a range of new experiences and challenges. Similar to doctors, who take part in internships and residencies following their medical school training, teachers need additional support to develop the broader repertoire of strategies and the reservoir of problem-solving knowledge and skills they need for their complex jobs.

According to the 2013 Teaching and Learning International Survey (TALIS), conducted by the Organization for Economic Cooperation and Development (OECD), just over half (51.7%) of middle school teachers with less than 3 years of experience reported participating in formal induction programs. The proportions were closer to two-thirds in Australia (69.3%) and Alberta (64.5%) and nearly universal in Singapore (96.9%) (OECD, 2014d, Table 4.28Web). Although formal induction programs are rare in Finland, 93% of principals reported the availability of informal mentoring supports for beginning teachers.

Most of the jurisdictions we studied have developed intensive programs of mentoring and induction for new teachers that provide helpful learning supports. These can include more frequent visits and advice from supervisors, direct coaching from an assigned mentor, seminars on key topics, shared planning time with colleagues, and a reduced teaching load to enable novices to have the time for these learning activities. Together, these supports aim to provide the scaffolding needed to enable teachers to continue learning while ensuring that students receive the instruction they need.

Perhaps the most-well-integrated models for induction occur in Shanghai and Singapore, where programs have been in existence for many years, and the career ladder system (described in Chapter 5) designates a set of teacher leaders who are formally charged with mentoring novices and have time set aside for this purpose. Teachers in both contexts have significant noninstructional time in their usual schedules (Link 3-13) for planning, grading, meeting with students and colleagues, and the additional work that comprises teaching. Novices have further release time in which they can work with their mentors, take seminars, and collaborate with colleagues.

Historically, in both jurisdictions, university preparation was heavily focused on subject matter knowledge and theories of education with relatively little supervised clinical practice. The first few years of teaching with tightly supervised induction were where teachers learned most about practice. Both have been expanding and integrating clinical practice more into preservice education in recent years; however, well-developed induction programs remain as a very strong bridge into the profession.

Induction programs are a more recent innovation in Canada and are being further refined in Australia, where some highly developed models are now emerging, especially in Ontario and New South Wales. In Finland, the very extensive preservice preparation has included so much clinical training that it accomplishes much of what occurs during the first year of practice in other jurisdictions, and novices typically receive help from their colleagues when they are hired. This peer group mentoring or co-mentoring is a collective approach distinctive from the one-on-one master-apprentice model prevalent in most countries (Geeraerts, Tynjälä, Heikkinen, Markkanen, Pennanen, & Gijbels, 2015). In recent years, Finland has also begun to pilot one-on-one mentoring in some schools.

Shanghai

Shanghai developed a formal induction program in the late 1980s. The program, created by the Shanghai Municipal Education Commission, reflects the Chinese cultural concept of *lao dai qing,* which means "the old bring along the young." Central to this notion of *lao dai qing* is the idea of connectedness:

> The old and young are connected. Their connection comes through knowledge of and skill in teaching (as well as a commitment to that practice). In this we see a glimpse of a shared collectivist orientation.

At the same time, there is an expectation of difference: that the older teachers, the *lao dai*, have something to offer the young, the *qing*. (Paine & Ma, 1993, p. 681)

Under the policy, new teachers are given a 1-year probationary period, during which time each is assigned a mentor who is selected based on experience and reputation as a highly skilled teacher. This experienced colleague works closely with the new teacher, guiding him or her through processes such as lesson planning, selecting teaching materials and methods, decisions about student assignments, and giving feedback to students. The mentoring pair works together for a minimum of 2 hours per week (International Alliance of Leading Education Institutes, 2008, p. 65). Mentors also observe new teachers and new teachers are expected to observe their mentors in order to see models of highly skilled instruction. Mentors keep records of their activities and they document the development of the beginning teachers for review by the school principal.

Given the school schedule structure, which permits most teachers to have at least 20 hours a week when they are not teaching children directly, mentors have time in their contractual day to work with beginning teachers and to make these observations possible. In addition, mentors are also evaluated through feedback from the beginning teachers and the expectations that the school leaders have for the development of the beginning teacher (Salleh & Tan, 2013). Schools generally also have a teacher serving as a professional learning coordinator who has responsibilities for structuring the mentoring pairs, organizing the teacher research meetings, and reporting to the district.

In addition to formal mentoring, beginning teachers have close contact with experienced teachers on a regular basis through teacher study and research groups. (See Chapter 4 for a description of the *jiaoyanzu*.) Teachers begin to participate in joint lesson planning sessions and are observed by peers on a regular basis, not just for the purposes of formal evaluation but also to improve lesson design and hear how experienced teachers think about instructional design and decisions. Participating in teacher working groups provides a method of socialization for new teachers into a community that shares a common body of knowledge, speaks a common language, and, most important, shares a set of expectations for student performance and how to support them toward those goals.

From an employment and evaluation perspective, the first year of teaching is a critical decision point for the hiring school and for the beginning teacher. At the end of the first year of teaching, teachers are assessed based on the observations made at the school level by the mentor and the school principal, as well as by written exams. Those who do not meet the assessment standards at the end of the first year are either not rehired or are delayed from moving to permanent status.

When rehired after their probation year, it is very rare for a teacher to be released from the job or fired later in his or her career. Most teachers are evaluated as having potential to succeed. According to a district deputy superintendent in Shanghai, about two to four teachers are dismissed from her district each year after their first year and after that, dismissal rarely occurs. The teachers who are released, Zhu says, "are usually ones who have been pressed into becoming a teacher by their families, and their heart is not in it."

Singapore

All new teachers in Singapore are immersed in a 2-year formal induction program funded and managed by the Ministry of Education (see Figure 3–3).

The program starts, in essence, with the teachers' compass ceremony before the start of preservice preparation, when prospective teachers have been hired by the Ministry of Education (MOE) and engage in ceremonies designed to reinforce the importance of the moral and ethical missions they have undertaken. This is the first opportunity the ministry has to orient and socialize teachers—who are already MOE employees—to the expectations for their role. Teacher induction picks up postgraduation with an orientation program, which helps them understand their roles and the expectations of the profession; reflect on their personal

Figure 3–3   MOE Teacher Induction Framework

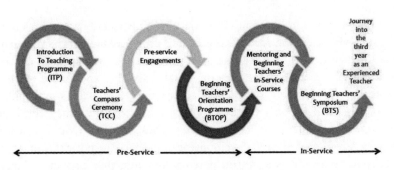

Source: Academy of Singapore Teachers (n.d.).

beliefs, values, and practices; and highlight the importance of nurturing the whole child. These expectations, beliefs, and values are articulated in the ethos and code of the teaching profession documents to guide the conduct of teachers and ensure that they meet the standards of the profession.

Within the first 2 years, while they are being mentored within their school, beginning teachers also attend in-service courses designed specifically for them, covering topics such as classroom management, parent engagement, teacher-student relationships, reflective practice, pedagogies, and assessment literacy. The 2-year journey concludes at the end of the second year of teaching with the beginning teachers' symposium. Entitled "What Matters Most: Purpose, Passion and Professionalism," the symposium calls for effective practices and strong commitment to teaching and marks the transition of the novice into the role of a professional.

School-based mentoring enables beginning teachers to gain knowledge within a community of practice with the support of more experienced peers. Mentoring arrangements—available to novices and veterans— are typically overseen by the school staff developer and teacher leaders. Although beginning teachers are assigned a formal mentor, typically in their subject area, they also receive support from others in the school, because mentoring is considered a school-wide practice. Beginning teachers are typically given about 80% of the teaching workload of an experienced teacher so as to provide the additional time and space for the beginning teachers to grow into their profession.

TALIS results indicate that among all countries in that international survey, Singapore has the highest ratio of teachers serving as mentors (39%) or who currently have an assigned mentor (40%), in sharp contrast to the TALIS averages of 14% and 13%, respectively (OECD, 2014d). Furthermore, 85% of the mentees are assigned to mentors who teach the same subject, compared to the TALIS average of 68% (OECD, 2014d).

Mentors serve in different capacities. There is usually a mentor coordinator who leads the school's mentoring program and acts as the mentor for mentors so that the mentoring goals at the school level can be achieved. Then there is the mentor, usually a more experienced teacher or teacher leader (i.e., senior or lead teacher), who serves as a pillar of professional support for beginning teachers (BTs) as they continue to hone their professional competencies. These mentors would typically have received professional development to prepare them for this mentoring role, because it is a central part of their job; they provide subject-specific pedagogical leadership, socioemotional support, professional development, resource sharing, and expertise in particular disciplines or skill areas.

Ms. Tan Hwee Pin, principal of Kranji Secondary School, described the support for beginning teachers in this way:

> We welcome our beginning teachers [or BTs] to our school as part of our Kranji family. It is important to induct them into our school's culture so that they know the role that they play and the expectations and standards required when they interact with our students. Our mentoring program is led by a team of seven senior teachers, under the advice of our vice-principal. Every BT or trainee will be given an experienced teacher as their mentor. BTs not only observe lessons of their subject areas but also teachers from other subjects; I believe that every subject teacher has different strengths and they employ different pedagogies in different disciplines. By casting the net wider, new teachers will be able to assemble a repertoire of strategies, which they can activate when they become a full-fledged teacher.

New teachers we interviewed expressed their appreciation of "all the mentors I had, all the teachers I worked with" because they were "all very supportive, quite caring. They will check constantly how are you coping, any help they need to offer." We heard that "mentors try to use [mentee's] prior knowledge . . . [to] . . . try and build on [mentee's] strengths" and help new teachers come to "know about school culture, what are the expectations, some of the 'dos and don'ts.'" In interviews, respondents felt that help was constantly available to them, "I don't even need to ask 'Can I borrow?' [Mentors] will say, 'Come and take.' So I think it's a very good environment . . . everyone is helpful."

Mentors support their mentees in going beyond the immediacy of daily practice by encouraging them to build their knowledge. As one new teacher noted,

> [Mentors] will ask you things like, "Have you heard of this concept called, say, tacit learning? No right? It's quite new you know. Maybe you should know about it. I don't really agree with it. Let me know what you think." Or maybe one might sneakily sit down next to you and say, "I'm reading this book. It's really interesting. Why don't you read a few pages and tell me what you think about it?"

In Singapore, the probationary period for BTs is 1 year. Once teachers are confirmed, they do not need to be recertified or licensed. Thus, confirmation is analogous to having tenure. Sclafani and Lim (2008) observe:

> New teachers are observed and coached by grade-level chairs, subject area chairs, and heads of departments. If a teacher is not performing

well, additional support and coaching come into play. Everyone tries to help the new teacher adjust and improve, but lack of improvement, poor attitude or lack of professionalism is not tolerated . . . The new teacher may be allowed to try another school, but if a year of working with the teacher has not improved his or her performance, the teacher may be asked to leave the profession. The system believes that it should do its best up front and counsel out those who do not make progress despite the support and assistance. Past this milestone, very few teachers are asked to leave, and then the causes may be lack of integrity, inappropriate behavior with a student, financial mismanagement, or racial insensitivity. (p. 4)

Canada

Induction opportunities for teachers vary across Canadian provinces. Although Alberta does not currently require or fund mentoring, most schools provide it: According to the 2013 TALIS survey of lower secondary teachers, formal induction programs are available for more than 80% of teachers new to teaching and informal programs are available to more than 80% of teachers new to a school (OECD, 2014d). The nature of these programs varies from school to school, however.

By contrast, in Ontario, all first-year new teachers hired to a permanent contract—and those who hold long-term occasional contracts (typically given to substitute teachers)—are expected to participate in the New Teacher Induction Program (NTIP). Established in 2006 and funded by the ministry, NTIP includes (1) an orientation to the school and school board, (2) ongoing mentoring by more experienced teachers throughout the first year, and (3) professional development and training appropriate to the needs of new teachers. According to Paul Anthony, former director in the Ontario Ministry of Education, the goal of the program is to help novices become comfortable and competent more quickly so as to serve their students more effectively:

> There's lots of evidence that the more experienced teachers can deliver a better educational experience for their student, but the core notion of the NTIP was, "how do we accelerate that experience"— everything from helping the teacher get comfortable in the physical setting and [learn] where the resources are to supporting them in terms of all the different issues they will run into with the kids and their parents and the school, etc. and how to handle those faster. The whole notion behind it was "how do we accelerate that experience so that ultimately the students are getting that improved educational experience that you get from a more experienced teacher?"

Boards of education may decide to extend NTIP supports to the second year for either permanent hires or long-term occasional teachers. Anthony noted that the extension to a second year developed in recognition that after their first year, new teachers were saying

> "I'm only just now at the end of my first year, realizing what I don't know. I only know now what I don't know." So they came to us and said, "What about a second year?" That's another one of those things that have evolved directly from the field and people being comfortable saying "I just realized what I don't know and I need more time."

Mentors are selected for their teaching and mentoring skills and are expected to be trained within their district. The NTIP provides shared release time for mentors and new teachers to collaborate. This time can be used for co-planning, classroom observation, and collaborative assessment of student work, among other areas. Schools may choose from different mentoring models such as one-to-one mentoring and large- or small-group mentoring. Mentors provide guidance that is suited to the individual needs of the teachers, which can include demonstrating teaching strategies and offering coaching or feedback, goal setting, offering tips and advice around classroom management, being a sounding board for teaching strategies, providing insight into the school climate and related politics, and offering emotional support during the first few days of schools. A major emphasis is on helping novices manage professional relationships and learn to seek out the resources they need for ongoing growth and development. As one beginning teacher explained,

> My mentor provided a lot of goal-setting support. . . So, sitting together and figuring out what were my goals for the year. They were all centered on my personal visions, but it was in the context of a school. . . Getting more familiar with how I can increase engagement, which went back to classroom management and then how I could create a broader network. . . So we sat down and we looked at professional development opportunities for classroom management and she walked with me into the Principal's Office to have a conversation and modelled how you could just create that personal relationship that you would need to broaden your network. (Tina)

Mentoring is designed to be supportive rather than evaluative. Principals conduct two performance appraisals throughout the first 12 months, and if not satisfactory, teachers are given up to 24 months to improve. Although a small number of teachers are counseled out, a major goal is to help novices become experts and keep them in the profession. With that in mind, the Toronto School Board—the largest and most diverse district in the province—has extended mentoring for an additional 2 years beyond NTIP and has organized the program to offer demonstration classroom learning: focused observations, debriefing, action planning, and co-teaching opportunities in various grades and subjects, along with professional learning for mentors.

The results have been noteworthy. The Ontario College of Teachers (2012) in its Transition to Teaching study found a retention rate of new teachers of over 95% who renewed their licenses within Ontario. (Of those nonrenewing, most have left for other provinces with greater supply needs, but more than 80% hope to return to Ontario at some point.) Even more extraordinary is that the Toronto District School Board found that of the nearly 4,000 beginning teachers hired between 2005 and 2010, the district retained 98% to 99% of first-year hires annually (Darling-Hammond, 2013). By comparison, in the United States, most studies find at least 10% of first-year teachers depart before their second year, and about 30% leave by their fifth year (Darling-Hammond, 2010).

The result is a strong start on a career in teaching. As a University of Ottawa study about NTIP concluded,

> Beginning teachers across Ontario are confident in their own abilities as teachers responsible for supporting student learning. They are satisfied with their choice of profession; they intend to remain in the teaching profession and a large majority would like to remain in the same school. (Kane, Jones, Rottman & Conner, 2010)

Australia

As in Shanghai and Ontario, induction in the Australian states of Victoria and New South Wales is tied to full certification (known as *registration* in Victoria and *accreditation* in New South Wales). New teachers are awarded a provisional certification and must show that they have met professional standards for teaching within 1 to 3 years, depending on which state and whether they are in government or nongovernment schools.

Induction is well-established, having been launched and sustained since the early 2000s. NSW Department of Education and Communities has provided a teacher mentor program since 2003. When first launched, the program employed 50 teacher mentors who worked across 90 to 100 schools that had a significant numbers of new teachers. These mentors were appointed to schools and annually supported about 60% of the total number of newly appointed teachers in government schools. The evaluation of the teacher mentor program indicates that it has provided benefit in terms of teacher quality as well as teacher retention. Other schools appointed mentors internally to support their early career teachers. Current processes in New South Wales require all early career teachers to be supported by experienced colleagues and school leaders through an induction program. Online professional learning programs are available to support in-school mentors and early career teachers.

Victoria tied induction to teacher registration in 2004, and it has become nearly universal; well over 90% of provisionally certified teachers have received mentor support each year (Victoria Institute of Teaching [VIT], 2014, p. 10).

The VIT provides training to mentors in the knowledge and skills of mentorship; the 2-day program, offered in the first semester of each year, has reached some 12,000 teachers since 2004 (interview with D. Paproth and F. Cosgrove, Victorian Institute of Teaching, May 21, 2014).

Surveys conducted by the VIT have shown that about 90% of provisionally registered teachers indicate they have made beneficial changes to their teaching through feedback from mentors or experienced teachers. Ninety-four percent indicated that working collegially in the classroom with an experienced teacher had enabled them to see what good professional practice looks like and had focused their professional reflection on engaging students and student learning. In addition to the benefits reported by mentees, over 95% of mentors agreed that they had experienced professional learning benefits from their involvement with mentoring a provisionally registered teacher (VIT, 2014).

As teaching policy has evolved in Australia, two things have enabled more productive mentoring. The first is the focus on professional standards—initially enacted by the states and then reinforced with the new national standards—which the states have attached to the registration and accreditation of teachers. As VIT director of special projects, Fran Cosgrove, explained, linking mentoring to teaching standards helped expand the view of mentorship from one of collegial friendship and emotional support to one based on professional conversations about teaching competencies and centered on student learning:

> We said, "If we're gonna do this, it has to be a professional relationship, and we have to set up that professional relationship. We have to define it through the standards and this full registration process." (Interview with D. Paproth and F. Cosgrove, Victorian Institute of Teaching, May 21, 2014)

To guide their reflection and action, teachers are encouraged to use a cycle of teacher inquiry and knowledge building (Link 3-14) as framed

Figure 3–4   Cycle of Teacher Inquiry and Knowledge Building

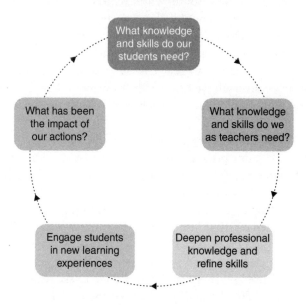

Source: VIT (2013).

in the national standards (see Figure 3–4). It asks teacher to identify students' needs, develop an area of teaching practice necessary to meet those student needs, implement the new teaching practice in an action plan over a period of 4 to 6 weeks, and assess the effectiveness of the approach. This approach helps scaffold teacher induction into a cycle of professional learning that experienced teachers use in maintaining their own registration and provides a common language for discussing practice.

Fran Cosgrove described the process as follows:

> [Beginning teachers] come up with an inquiry question. Then they're building up their capacity and knowledge around how you approach that through observation and discussion with others. That can be school-based, but they might also do professional reading [or] under-take professional development activities that are outside their school or within their school.
>
> [W]e then ask them to use that knowledge to develop an action plan of how they're going to approach their teaching practice to focus on that particular area of learning they're going to improve in their

students. We ask them to do that through interaction with their mentor [and] to implement that in their classrooms over a period of time. This is where we ask the mentors to be as involved as they can. The whole idea is that you've got a colleague at your shoulder who can see things you might not, who[m] you can talk about the implementation with.

It's then a case of looking at the artifacts of learning. What did the students produce? How do you know? What are the questions you asked? Did they learn things you didn't expect? Did some learn some things and others not? Why?

Then, it's their reflection on that. What does that mean for my practice? What does that mean for this inquiry? Does that move into another kind of an inquiry? The last thing is really what have I learned from this as a practitioner? Then you start the whole cycle again. (Interview with D. Paproth and F. Cosgrove, Victorian Institute of Teaching, May 21, 2014)

The second major change was the provision of time for collaboration. Although teachers in Australia have less time free from teaching than those in Shanghai or Singapore, recent initiatives have created more opportunity for teachers to work together. In Victoria, under a collective bargaining agreement with the educators' union, new teachers have a reduced work load of at least 5%, equivalent to 1 to 2 hours a week. Although mentor teachers do not receive additional release time under the AEU agreement, principals are required to ensure that assigned mentors are able to undertake this role within the context of a 38-hour working week.

New South Wales has recently gone further in funding an additional 2 hours each week for beginning teachers. This brings the total time each week to 4 hours for beginning teachers—and 2 hours for all other teachers. This time is provided to enable collaborative planning, lesson preparation, and assessment. Beginning teachers typically use this additional time to observe or work alongside an experienced teacher, gather evidence of their teaching practice as part of their accreditation process, engage in professional learning with their school-based mentor, or collaboratively plan, teach, and assess student learning.

As the leader of the NSW government school sector, Michele Bruniges, secretary of the Department of Education and Communities, noted (Link 3-15):

Collaboration within the profession is absolutely fundamental to teacher development and continuing learning. Supported by government, we put in release time for the first two years for our beginning teachers. We wanted certain conditions to be met within the schools for that to happen: having a mentor in place where that would be consistent over a period of time, so that we have ongoing support; link[ing] to the teacher professional standards so they have a road map there for their own professional learning and growth is incredibly important. . . That's just the . . . support for beginning teachers, but every teacher in every classroom deserves the right to be supported. It's very, very critical that we support teacher collaboration and teacher professional learning right throughout the cycle. (Interview with M. Bruniges, Secretary of NSW Department of Education and Communities, June 2014)

The importance of creating a collaborative environment for supporting and retaining beginning teachers was made clear in an NSW study that followed teacher education students through their first 4 years of teaching. When asked to identify the factors that had the greatest impact on their teaching and their desire to stay in the profession, the teachers identified nine factors. The first two—student engagement and professional challenge and satisfaction—had to do with the capacity to engage students and find joy in teaching. The next seven factors all relate to professional learning and within-school peer support: collegial support, professional collaboration, supervision and mentoring, executive support, staff culture, school climate, and pedagogical support.

The study revealed that one of the most significant factors contributing to teacher expertise is the provision of feedback on teaching practices and collegial, collaborative professional learning. It is clear that the school must become not only a place for students to learn but also for teachers to learn. This research now underpins the policies and practices for teacher professional learning and the new policies for teacher performance and development, described in Chapters 4 and 5 (McIntyre, 2012). Building on the models in place in states such as New South Wales and Victoria, new policy initiatives developed through AITSL will see nationally consistent guidelines for induction and teacher registrations extended to all states and education systems in Australia.

Lessons Learned

Looking across these jurisdictions, there are a number of common themes regarding entry into the profession of teaching. Among these are the following:

The systems are highly selective, using a broad set of criteria to select recruits. A report by McKinsey and Company (Auguste, Kihn, & Miller, 2010) attracted a great deal of attention in the United States with its finding that teacher education institutions in countries such as Finland and Singapore draw from the top 30% of students, based on their academic skills. Although it is true that both countries expect strong academic qualifications for teacher candidates, that is not the only criterion they use to select candidates. In these and other jurisdictions we studied, candidates are expected to demonstrate interest in, experience with, and commitment to children and a range of competencies and dispositions that are surfaced in selection processes that extend beyond transcripts and grades. These can include interviews and performance tasks as well as a range of references.

Selective recruitment is supported by competitive salaries and subsidized preparation. The jurisdictions we studied pay teachers comparably with other college graduates, so there are few opportunity costs for choosing teaching. In addition, preparation is free or subsidized and, in some countries, accompanied by a stipend or salary.

Preparation programs are grounded in academic content, pedagogical knowledge, and professional standards. All of the programs described here ensure that all teacher candidates have a solid grounding in disciplinary knowledge as well as pedagogy. Undergraduate programs begin with course work in the subjects candidates will teach. Graduate programs, which have become the norm in several of the countries we studied, require teachers to have a bachelor's degree in one or more academic subjects. In most jurisdictions, secondary teachers prepare deeply in two content areas, with two majors or a major and a minor they will be able to draw on in their teaching. Elementary teachers are prepared across a wide range of content areas they will teach. In Singapore and Shanghai, elementary teachers choose subject areas within which to specialize further, a practice that is also appearing in some Australian universities. In all cases, teachers study subject-specific pedagogy that enables them to learn teaching strategies unique to the content areas they teach. This work is grounded in professional standards articulating what teachers should know, be like, and be able to do—including the moral and ethical commitments of teachers as well as their technical knowledge and skills. The standards create a framework for professional practice that shapes not only preparation but also ongoing expectations and learning throughout the career.

Preparation programs are grounded in research and prepare teachers to use and conduct research. Research plays a major role in defining the profession in these countries: Research on learning, development, curriculum, assessment, effective teaching, and learning strategies for different content and for specific populations of students provides a serious grounding for program design. Teachers are expected to read research and to use it in their practice. Furthermore, they learn to conduct research on practice and are expected to do so during preparation and throughout their careers. Action research is an important and growing element of professional training and practice in all of the jurisdictions we studied. In Finland, teacher candidates are expected to conduct a study and write a research thesis as part of their master's degree for entering teaching. Across jurisdictions, the goal is to prepare teachers who are conversant with research and research methods, which will enable them to become sophisticated consumers of research and also to be able to collect and analyze data on their own students and become reflective practitioners.

Preparation includes well-mentored clinical experience. All of the countries recognize that teacher candidates learn the most about teaching when they are in actual classrooms working with expert mentors who model and coach candidates on the practices they are trying to develop. Many are emulating the model that Finland launched decades ago, in which teachers spend their student-teaching time in teacher training schools that partner with universities, offer highly skilled mentor teachers, and support research-based practices that are linked to the university's course work. At the same time, structured mentoring in the initial year or two of teaching extends clinical learning, a practice that is very highly developed in Shanghai and Singapore and has deepened across all the jurisdictions. In several jurisdictions, the induction process is tied to certification, creating a formal career continuum.

Preparation and induction are part of a system. The recruitment, preparation, and induction systems in countries such as Finland, Singapore, Australia, and Canada are aimed at making sure that teachers are ready to teach from the start of their careers. But they do not stop there. As we describe in Chapters 4 and 5, all of these countries have put in place well-structured systems to enable teachers to continue their learning during their career and to advance in their careers based on their abilities and interests.

The professional learning and career ladder systems accomplish a number of goals. They help ensure that teachers keep up with the latest research and adjust their instruction based on what is known about teaching and learning. They keep teachers active as learners so that they can model their learning for their students. And they help encourage teachers to stay in their jobs, maintaining a stable workforce.

NOTES

1. The average starting salary for US teachers in 2012–2013 was $36,128. National Education Association. 2012–2013 average starting teacher salaries by state. Retrieved from http://www.nea.org/home/2012--2013 -average-starting-teacher-salary.html
2. Known as the Department of Education and Early Childhood Development (DEECD) between 2008 and 2014.
3. http://www.oise.utoronto.ca/ite/Home
4. Teach for Canada is a Canadian initiative that is not affiliated with Teach for All.

4

DEVELOPING HIGH-QUALITY TEACHING

Every school must be a model learning organization. Teachers and principals will constantly look out for new ideas and practices, and continuously refresh their own knowledge. Teaching will itself be a learning profession, like any other knowledge-based profession of the future.
—Prime Minister Goh Chok Tong, Singapore (1997)

AS CHAPTER 3 DESCRIBED, high-performing systems place a strong emphasis on providing prospective teachers with a solid grounding in knowledge and experience to ensure that all teachers are ready to practice from the start. But they do not stop there. These systems also provide structures and opportunities to enable teachers to continually hone and improve their practice and keep learning so that they can become better and better each year. Finally, they provide teachers with opportunities to use their enhanced skills to take on new roles in schools and school systems.

These opportunities and structures take many forms. First, the systems have articulated clear statements about what constitutes high-quality teaching; these are often codified in standards of practice. These standards guide teacher education, beginning teacher mentoring and induction, professional development, assessment, and feedback.

Second, the systems provide teachers with time to work with and learn from colleagues and to conduct their own research to test and measure the effects of innovative practices. To accomplish this, schools in these countries break down classroom walls (metaphorically) to allow teachers to collaborate and observe one another's practices, and they structure the school day so that teachers have time for these activities—they are not in front of students every minute of the school day. They also encourage teachers to engage in research about practice and find ways to share, use, and celebrate what is learned.

Third, the systems view teacher evaluation as a way of providing feedback to teachers to help them improve their practice, rather than as a punitive measure aimed at weeding out the weakest performers. And some, such as Singapore, couple appraisals with opportunities for teachers to grow in the profession.

Jensen and colleagues' (2016) study of four high-performing systems—British Columbia, Hong Kong, Shanghai, and Singapore—identified a set of common policies that support professional learning in each system. These include policies for building in time for collaboration, developing teacher leadership roles that organize and support professional learning, and using school-level and individual-level evaluation and accountability systems to support learning and collaboration. When well managed, these policies result in the following:

- School improvement organized around effective professional learning
- Professional learning built into daily practice
- Recognition for the development of teacher expertise—and use of that expertise to support learning for others
- Teachers sharing responsibility for their own and other's professional learning
- District or state strategies that lead to professional learning throughout the system

These features are also apparent in the additional countries we studied and are consistent with a substantial body of literature showing that teacher professional development is more likely to be effective in improving teacher practice and student learning when it is collegial, sustained, and ongoing; connected to the work of teachers in the classroom; and coherently related to broader school reforms efforts (Darling-Hammond & Richardson, 2009; Elmore & Burney, 1997).

In this chapter we describe the practices of professional learning and growth we encountered. We note that prominent cornerstones for teacher learning include the national or state curricula in each of the jurisdictions—which offer a common foundation for joint work—and the professional standards for practice, described in Chapter 3, which guide preparation, induction, professional development, evaluation, and ongoing feedback. We also note that professional development is not something that is done unto teachers in special periodic sessions: It is part of the regular daily and weekly experience of teaching and learning, which are inextricably linked together. The chapter is organized in terms of the ways in which the jurisdictions provide for this learning through

- o Incentives and infrastructure for learning
- o Time and opportunity for collaboration
- o Curriculum development and lesson study
- o Teacher research
- o Teacher-led professional development
- o Appraisal and feedback

Incentives and Infrastructure for Learning

A key theory of action in all of these jurisdictions is that continuous professional learning for teachers and leaders is essential to school improvement. This belief manifests in a set of requirements and incentives to stimulate ongoing learning embedded in the day-to-day work of teachers in schools as well as the creation of organizations and funding streams that ensure a steady supply of good options for learning in collaborative settings—often organized using shared subject matter or other pedagogical goals—outside of school.

Many jurisdictions attach requirements for professional learning to the renewal of the teaching license. In Shanghai, Chinese regulations require all teachers to participate in ongoing professional learning opportunities for 240 hours every 5 years. Districts and higher-education institutions provide workshops for teachers, which cover topics such as education theory and practice and educational technology.

In New South Wales, 100 hours of continuing professional development are required every 5 years to maintain accreditation, and teachers must show how the learning addresses at least one standard in each of the seven domains of the national standards for teaching. Similarly, in Victoria, where teacher registration must be maintained each year, teachers elect, complete, and document 20 hours of professional learning annually. NSW pays for 5 school development days each year, when teachers can work together on school-identified professional learning. In Australia, 97% of teachers undertook professional development in 2013 compared to an average of 88% among countries participating in the TALIS surveys (OECD, 2014d).

Singapore believes in teacher-led professional learning for growth. As a guideline, Singapore offers about 100 hours of paid professional development time (over 12 days). In reality the time offered to teachers often exceeds 100 hours. At the national level, the ministry has established an Academy of Singapore Teachers (AST) and other academies and language centers to provide teacher-led professional development for teachers. These organizations work with teachers and connect to schools to provide professional opportunities "by teachers for teachers" through the extensive networks of teacher leaders who offer a wide range of professional learning courses, activities, learning communities, resources, and expertise. AST also supports professional learning communities (PLCs) within schools, offering training to professional learning team facilitators and a toolkit to help them create and sustain PLCs. Learning communities of teachers across schools—known as networked learning communities—are supported to facilitate teacher collaboration. These learning communities within and across schools are typically facilitated by teacher leaders.

In Ontario, the Ministry of Education has provided substantial funding to teacher federations to support professional learning activities, including support for release time, travel, and accommodations to create incentives for teachers to take advantage of them. School boards in Ontario also receive funding and support from the ministry to support professional learning and capacity building linked to priority strategies and needs each year; for example, in 2014–2015, the ministry supported professional learning in special education K–12, PLCs to support the development of French language, support for Aboriginal students, mathematics support, differentiated instruction, literacy, innovative practices integrating assessment and feedback, teacher inquiry, and supporting transitions for students between grades and schools.

Ontario's incentives for professional learning also include a salary structure that can reward teachers for additional qualifications (AQs) that upgrade their knowledge and enhance their practice. The more than 400 AQ courses available in 2014 were offered by Ontario faculties of education, teachers' federations, and other organizations and are accredited by the Ontario College of Teachers (OCT).

Finland has recently expanded its professional learning support in part because of evidence that the amount of learning teachers took part in varied widely. A 2007 survey, for example, found that only two-thirds of Finnish teachers had taken part in professional development activities (Piesanen, Kiviniemi, & Valkonen, 2007). In response, the Finnish government established a new program, called *Osaava* ("capable" or "skillful"), to promote professional learning. The program added 8 to 10 million euros per year to the 40 to 60 million euros annually provided by the ministry and municipalities on behalf of five strategic aims:

1. Promoting equity and leadership in teachers' lifelong learning
2. Making flexible learning paths a reality in educational institutions
3. Enhancing the adaption of innovative professional development models
4. Improving networking and collaboration among educational institutions and professional development providers
5. Mainstreaming successful professional development practices

The program also establishes a continuum of professional learning, starting with induction for new teachers and including support for professional learning for educational leaders. About 20% of the funding was specifically allocated to supporting a mentoring program for new teachers, the use of educational technology in teacher training schools, and a program of long-term professional development for educational leaders. Formal professional development in Finland is usually offered by universities, the National Board, or other organizations for specific kinds of needs, such as infusing technology or learning to support students with special needs in the newly reformed service system. This kind of professional learning is funded by the government and local schools; teachers are rarely asked to pay for learning opportunities. Teachers noted that there are a great many professional development opportunities available, and they appreciate and tap into these opportunities periodically, but their strong commitment to their students often stops them from wanting to leave the classroom or secure a substitute to attend, especially because they can have many of their learning needs met in the school.

In New South Wales, the Department of Education and Communities has provided a fully devolved system of professional learning and leadership development since 2005. Each year the full professional learning budget of AU$36 million has been distributed to all 2,250 schools, based on their size and distance from large regional centers—roughly AU$700 for each teacher generally or AU$1,000 for teachers in rural areas. Additional funding was allocated to support teachers in their first year.

The Professional Learning and Leadership Development Directorate designed professional learning programs for teachers and school leaders based on consultation with teachers and leaders and an annual survey, which sought information about professional learning priorities from each school's professional learning team. Schools selected which programs or providers could best address their priorities; the department's programs were the most popular with schools. All teachers in New South Wales are required to complete professional learning aligned to their performance management and development plan. Teachers are responsible for determining their professional learning within the context of their professional and career development needs and the priorities of their school.

The school-based professional learning system was driven by two key beliefs. These were, first, that schools were in the best position to align the learning needs of their teachers with the learning needs of students, and, second, that the professional learning that would have the greatest impact on classroom practices would be that which was closely aligned to the day-to-day work of teachers within the school. The devolution of professional learning funding to schools required the development of a system to account for the allocation and the impact of the teacher professional learning funds. This system enabled the gathering of substantial evidence from teachers and school leaders regarding the professional learning strategies that had the greatest impact on the learning of students, teachers, and school leaders. It also paved the way for longitudinal research to establish what teachers find has the greatest impact on their learning and their capacity to teach (McIntyre, 2013). Among the lessons from the 6,000 teachers who contributed to this research was the importance to their learning of collaborative preparation of lessons and teaching resources, opportunities for observing each other's lessons, as well as the collaborative assessment and evaluation of student work.

The allocation of the system's professional learning budget directly to schools enabled teachers and school leaders to structure time within schools for lesson observation and feedback and the collaborative development and evaluation of lessons. This provided a significant source of professional learning for teachers. Each year, an average of 60% of teacher professional learning funding was spent on additional time for teachers to support them in their learning. This initiative highlighted the importance of reframing activities within schools to ensure that schools are not only places for students to learn but also places for teachers to learn. As Daniel McKay, a New South Wales teacher noted (Link 4-1):

> We've talked about our school being a community of learners, seeing everyone as a learner and that we can learn off each other. Teachers learning off teachers and students off students. Teachers off students and vice versa. We thought it's a great way for teachers to learn. They're not just sitting in the classroom by themselves or going to a one-off professional learning and then coming back and trialing

something or not trialing something in the classroom. Just having that support with each other. We've looked at changing our professional learning in our school so that teachers are learning as we want the students to learn. Obviously we want students in the classroom working with each other—[engaged in] group work, supporting each other, reflecting and being critical of each other. That's what we want our teachers to be in their own teaching profession.

Time and Opportunity for Collaboration

Collaboration is at the heart of effective schools. Although many policy makers think about effective teachers as individuals who have certain traits and training and who create special oases in their classrooms, the evidence is clear that the most effective settings for learning feature considerable joint work among teachers. Collaboration among educators is critical, not just because working with other teachers is a nice thing to do and it makes school a more pleasant place to be. In fact, it turns out that high-performing schools—similar to high-performing businesses—organize people to take advantage of each other's knowledge and skills and create a set of common, coherent practices so that the whole is far greater than the sum of the parts.

In one study, economists were able to quantify the student learning gains generated by the collective expertise of teams of teachers. They found that the greatest gains were attributable to teachers who are more experienced, better qualified, and who stayed together as teams within their schools. The researchers found that peer learning among small groups of teachers was the most powerful predictor of improved student achievement over time (Jackson & Bruegmann, 2009). Another found that students achieved more in mathematics and reading when they attended schools characterized by higher levels of teacher collaboration for school improvement (Goddard, Goddard, & Tschannen-Moran, 2007). A third found that teachers become more effective over time when they work in collegial environments (Kraft & Papay, 2014).

It is not surprising, then, that teachers around the world report that their colleagues contribute to their teaching effectiveness (OECD, 2014d). Contrary to the factory model system designed for isolated teachers to work alone at different spots on the assembly line, education is a team sport. Successful schools raise achievement because they assemble the right mix of skills and abilities and enable people to work collaboratively.

The value of collaboration has been underscored in recent international studies. Analyses of the TALIS surveys found that teachers' participation in collaborative forms of professional development is associated with innovative teaching practices, such as the use of small-group work, interactive computer technology, and active teaching practices such as extended project work (OECD, 2014d, pp. 380–382). Further, TALIS analyses found that teacher professional collaboration is positively associated with teachers' confidence in their abilities and their enjoyment of teaching. In particular, frequent engagement in joint activities across classes and collaborative professional learning are positively associated with teacher self-efficacy and job satisfaction (OECD, 2014d) (see Figures 4–1 and 4–2).

Previous research has also shown that opportunities for collaboration with and learning from colleagues, such as induction and mentoring for early career teachers, are significant factors in determining teacher retention in the profession (Ingersoll & Strong, 2011). Further research has found that teachers gain in effectiveness with experience (Kini & Podolsky, 2016), and thus increased teacher retention is associated with

Figure 4–1 Teachers' Self-Efficacy Level and the Frequency of Teacher Professional Collaboration

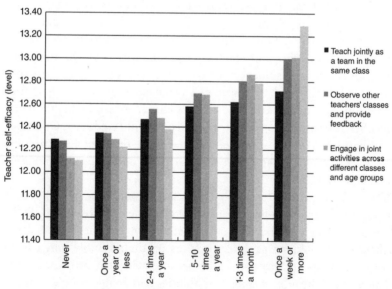

Source: OECD (2014d). Used with permission.

Figure 4–2 Teachers' Job Satisfaction Level and the
Frequency of Teacher Professional Collaboration

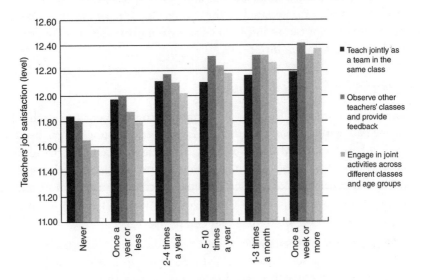

Source: OECD (2014d). Used with permission.

a more effective teaching workforce (Clotfelter, Ladd, & Vigdor, 2006; Henry, Bastian, & Fortner, 2011).

Time for Collaboration

As these examples suggest, teachers in high-performing countries spend a great deal of their learning time in collaboration with peers. This is possible because, in many of these countries, teachers spend less of their working day directly in front of students than do teachers in the United States. According to the TALIS, US teachers, for example, spend about 27 hours a week teaching students directly, about 50% more than the international average of about 19 hours. By contrast, teachers in Singapore spend about 17 hours a week teaching (OECD, 2014d). In Shanghai it is about 15 hours. As we noted in Chapter 3, the Australian Education Union has negotiated additional time for beginning teachers, and New South Wales has added to this time for novices and veterans.

In the time that teachers are not directly engaged with students they are frequently working with each other to plan lessons collaboratively or to conduct action research and analyze their practice and its outcomes.

Schools create time and structure meetings to enable teachers to take part in opportunities ranging from formal seminars offered by government agencies, teacher associations, and other teachers, providing targeted learning in areas related to the standards for teaching and school improvement priorities to informal learning opportunities that are available from colleagues in the school.

Opportunity for Collaboration

Finland, for example, features a substantial commitment to in-school sharing and learning that is organic and widespread. Jouni Kangasniemi, senior advisor in the Ministry of Education, emphasized that the ideas undergirding Osaava move from a traditional professional development notion to a conception of teacher learning as occurring within more natural, local (or national) networks and communities that enable teachers to learn from one another. He noted:

> It is essential to understand that we can use the already existing teachers' know-how and knowledge and innovations to develop others, and to see that "the wisdom" does not exist outside the schools but inside them.

The organic nature of teachers' professional learning in schools takes forms that are democratically organized. Principals described formal and informal opportunities for dialogue, feedback, collaboration, and working in professional teams within the schools themselves. For instance, Principal Heidi Honkanen in Langinskoski lower secondary school in Kotka emphasized the importance of constant professional dialogue and weekly teacher meetings as efficient ways to share new ideas, knowledge, and give peer support to and learn from colleagues. These meetings are tied directly to everyday school life and enable teachers to handle issues when they arise.

The fact that teachers share a large common space for their working area—as is also true in Shanghai—expands the possibilities for teachers to learn from each other. Indeed, Jouni Partanen, a novice history teacher in Langinkoski, noted that this enabled him to secure new ideas and useful tips for practical solutions from his colleagues even during short breaks. He explained that this kind of in-time local, personal support was crucial for him as a new teacher:

> It's very handy since if I have, for example, a practical question concerning how to organize my lessons or so I can just consult some more experienced colleague while we get coffee between the lessons. So, I'm able to get help immediately and [do] not need to wait.

Principal Anna Hirvonen in Myllypuro Primary School described organizing "demo lessons" in their school in which one teacher who has special expertise on some method or subject teaches a lesson to others, which enables teachers to enrich their teaching and informs them about new possible ways of doing things. Other opportunities are more organic and informal, such as getting help from more experienced teachers in a shared common space at the school. The orientation is local and democratic rather than focused largely on professional learning that occurs beyond the school environment.

Collaborative learning is also the rule in Victoria. Professional learning commonly takes the form of in-school collective readings, professional learning teams, joint planning, student data analysis, classroom observations, and subsequent professional conversations to identify problems and improve practice as well as to see how teachers are incorporating elements of professional learning into their classroom teaching. The use of school networks for joint workshops and activities is also common.

School boards and schools in Ontario, meanwhile, are involved in initiating and leading a range of professional learning connected to local needs. The types of activities vary widely. For example, some schools provide opportunities for teachers to visit the classrooms of other practicing teachers to observe the implementation of particular teaching and learning strategies. School-based programs also include book study groups, "lunch and learn" mini-workshops, and a variety of school-based communities of practice and professional learning groups in which teachers work on specific problems of practice or school-improvement initiatives.

In many respects, teaching is a collective activity in China, built on the premise that the pooling together of good ideas and resources will reflect well on the school and better support the students. Teaching is an open and publicly examined practice. Teachers plan together and observe each other's lessons. They conduct peer observations in their own school and in other schools, a practice referred to as *open classroom*. This openness creates a stronger collective set of ideals for which to gauge strong teaching versus weak teaching. It is still up to the individual teacher to execute lessons and manage large groups of students in tight fitting classrooms. However, the individual holds images of good teaching and the drive toward individual improvement by being immersed in an overall culture that enables him or her to see colleagues perform on a regular basis.

> Given frequent peer observation and joint preparation, Chinese teachers are well informed about the teaching quality of their colleagues in the whole school and are able to make comments on colleagues'

teaching style, subject knowledge level, capacity for managing class discipline, strength and weakness in teaching, and reputation among students. They are proud of good teachers in the school and feel sorry for some colleagues who have trouble in teaching. Outstanding teachers are respected among their colleagues for their excellent teaching rather than their personality. (Paine & Ma, 1993, p. 682)

In a national survey of teachers about their professional learning activities 57% reported that they had participated in classroom observations, teaching competitions, and other teaching research activities in the past 2 years (Gang, 2010).

As we describe in later sections, many schools organize this in-school professional learning for curriculum planning and lesson study, teacher research groups, and other joint work to solve problems of teaching practice.

Curriculum Development and Lesson Study

Much of teachers' joint work in these countries is organized for curriculum planning and lesson study with colleagues. Working from national or state curriculum guides, teachers collaborate to develop curriculum units and lessons at the school level, and they frequently develop, use, and jointly review school-based performance assessments—which include research projects, science investigations, and technology applications—to evaluate student learning. This helps teachers deeply understand the standards and curriculum goals and share their knowledge of content and students.

Curriculum and Assessment Development

This deep collaborative work in curriculum design creates an ongoing learning context for teachers. One important way high-performing systems have enabled teachers' professional learning is by involving them in curriculum planning and developing and scoring assessments. The curriculum in these countries emphasizes the ability of students to use their knowledge to think critically, solve problems, and communicate effectively, so the assessments include extended performance tasks that engage students in complex work—both within schools and in formal examination systems. This provides substantial learning opportunities for teachers. By collaboratively developing and scoring assessments, teachers develop a strong shared understanding of the standards students are expected to reach and an understanding of the instruction needed to enable students to reach those standards.

Finland is well-known in the education world for the primacy of class-room-based assessment, using no external standardized student testing until the open-ended matriculation exam that is voluntary for students in 12th grade. In Finland, the national core curriculum provides teachers with curriculum goals, recommended content, and assessment criteria for specific grades in each subject and in the overall final assessment of student progress each year. Local schools and teachers then use those guidelines to craft a more detailed curriculum and set of learning outcomes at each school as well as approaches to assessing benchmarks in the curriculum. Teachers are treated as pedagogical experts who have extensive decision-making authority in the areas of curriculum and assessment in addition to other areas of school policy and management (Finnish National Board of Education, 2007; Lavonen, 2008).

According to the Finnish National Board of Education (2007), the main purpose of assessing students is to guide and encourage students' own reflection and self-assessment. Consequently, ongoing feedback from the teacher is very important. Teachers give students formative and summative reports through verbal and narrative feedback. Finland's leaders point to its use of school-based, student-centered, open-ended tasks embedded in the curriculum as an important reason for the nation's extraordinary success on international student assessments (Lavonen, 2008).

The voluntary matriculation examinations that provide information for university admissions are based on students' abilities to apply problem-solving, analytic, and writing skills. University and high school faculty members construct the examinations—which are composed of open-ended essays and problem solutions—under the guidance of the Matriculation Exam Board ("Finnish Matriculation Examination," 2008). The board members (about 40 in number) are faculty and curriculum experts in the subject areas tested, nominated by universities and the National Board of Education. More than 300 associate members—also typically high school and college faculty members—help develop and review the tests. High school teachers grade the matriculation exams locally using official guidelines, and samples of the grades are reexamined by professional raters hired by the board (Kaftandjieva & Takala, 2002).

Currently, Finland is in the process of reviewing its national curriculum, as it does on a regular periodic basis, and teachers are playing an integral part in that process as well, providing them with another opportunity for professional learning. Because teachers have been so central to this process, as Hannele Cantell, a former teacher and faculty member at the University of Helsinki who teaches in the subject teacher education program points out, they do not express stress or concern about the curricular change—because the teachers have already seen drafts, and they have read and reviewed multiple versions. "They know what is coming," as she explained. The curriculum revision is an example of the ways in which the knowledge, expertise, and experience of teachers are placed at the center of key policy decisions and national efforts involved in education. It also reflects the strong sense of shared vision that underlies the Finnish approach (Halinen, 2014).

Victoria and New South Wales also provide substantial opportunities for teachers to develop and score assessments. High school examinations, developed by the state with teacher input, include mostly open-ended items with written, oral, and performance elements that are scored by classroom teachers in "moderation" processes offering training and calibration for consistency. In addition, classroom-based tasks that are given throughout the school year comprise at least half of the total examination score. Teachers design these required assignments and assessments—lab experiments and investigations on central topics as well as research papers and presentations—in response to syllabus expectations. The required classroom tasks ensure that students are getting the kind of learning opportunities that prepare them for the assessments they will take later, that they are getting feedback they need to improve, and that they will be prepared to succeed not only on these very challenging tests but also in college and in life (Adamson & Darling-Hammond, 2015; Darling-Hammond & Wentworth, 2014).

These tasks are graded according to criteria set out in the syllabus and count toward the examination score. The quality of the tasks assigned by teachers, the work done by students, and the appropriateness of the grades and feedback given to students are audited through an inspection system, and schools are given feedback on all of these elements. The result is a rich curriculum for students with extensive teacher participation and many opportunities for teacher growth and learning.

The Singapore assessment system is similarly designed and increasingly project-based as a function of the reforms under the "Thinking Schools, Learning Nation" initiative that began in the late 1990s. A new A-level curriculum and examination system for grades 11 and 12 include performance-based assessments that involve students in designing and conducting science investigations, engaging in collaborative project work, and completing a cross-disciplinary inquiry as part of a new subject called "Knowledge and Inquiry," which requires students to draw knowledge and skills from different disciplines and apply them to solving new problems or issues. These new assessments, such as the essay and problem-based examinations they supplement, are designed by the Singapore Examinations and Assessment Board with the help of teachers and scored by teachers, who engage in moderation processes to ensure consistency of scoring. This professional role enables teachers to better understand the standards embedded in the curriculum and to plan more effective instruction.

Lesson Study

Another key strategy is lesson study, used in Japan, China, and many parts of Asia and spreading to Australia, Canada, and the United States, among other countries. Schools in China, for example, form grade-level lesson-planning groups, or *beikezu,* that have a particular focus on lesson planning and focus on bringing the curriculum to the appropriate grade level of the student. The work of these groups reflects a more recent phenomenon of focusing on the child as learner and trying to make curriculum and instruction more learner-centered.

Lesson design is a tightly choreographed activity in Shanghai that usually involves the input from many teachers within the school. Lessons that will be used as demonstration lessons for other schools or in competitions will be taught and modified based on feedback from several teachers. In many schools the lesson plans have to be approved by the subject area lead teacher or, in smaller schools, by the principal.

The lesson plan format varies by school. Furthermore, although teachers may be working to teach the same content in a similar fashion, the objectives for the lesson may vary from one class to the next, because each class may have its own needs in terms of pacing the learning and focusing the lesson. Teachers are expected to think through their decisions and rationales for why and how they will teach the lesson in advance. This lesson analysis includes the teachers' reasoning behind what is being taught (textbook analysis), what they expect the students to learn and at what depth (knowledge and proficiency evaluation), and what they anticipate the students having difficulty with during the lesson (difficulty analysis).

Lesson Study in Shanghai

In each Shanghai school we visited, the teachers brought forward lesson plans for discussion, then one taught the lesson in her classroom while other teachers and administrators observed, and then the group debriefed the lesson to give feedback on how to improve the lesson. The feedback discussion followed a common structure. The teacher gave some opening comments about the lesson and a summary of how he or she thought the lesson went. The group leader, typically the most senior teacher, then provided a few comments on what the lesson did successfully and then gave one or two suggestions for improvement. A few other teachers would then follow suit, give a summary of what they thought went well and some suggestions for improvement. If a principal or other higher ranked person was participating, he or she gave a longer summary at the end of the conversation, inserting some broader commentary about the kind of teaching the school should be striving toward. Otherwise, the leader of the group would provide a summary of the comments. These meetings lasted the same duration as a typical school class period—about 35 minutes.

At Qilun Elementary School in Minhang District, a manufacturing area of the city, 5th-grade teacher Jiaying Zhang presented a mathematics demonstration lesson, having prepared a formal lesson plan for several observers to see in advance and for observing teachers to be able to discuss after the lesson was completed. The very detailed lesson plan (see Appendix B), typical of planning in this school, begins with an analysis of the textbook and explores the mathematical concepts that the teacher is planning to teach. Her analysis shows her deep knowledge of the mathematics and how children might understand the concepts. She raises questions about how the textbook represents the geometric concepts and introduces her own thinking about how to build understanding of polygons and their relationship to their component parts.

Jiaying then analyzes the learning objectives through the lens of student learning. She is aware of what the students have learned about polygons prior to this lesson, the challenges the students might face in exploring new ideas about angles within polygons, and considers how she might help them make stronger connections between what they already know and the new concepts she is introducing in the lesson. Her analysis illustrates her knowledge of the mathematical concepts as well as her knowledge of how the students will engage with the ideas. The planned teaching and learning strategies include teacher questioning, the use of hands-on manipulatives, student hypothesizing, and students sharing their ideas in pairs. There is a lot of activity packed into the 35-minute lesson period, making the pace of the lesson fast-paced and nonstop.

The analysis in the lesson plan concludes with a question—"How to make students think further about the connections in addition to an understanding?"—which illustrates the research mind-set of Shanghai teachers. Instruction is a place to ask questions and learn more about how students are learning in order to continually refine teaching practices.

During the actual lesson, Jiaying stayed true to the lesson plan and the students were engaged from the moment she entered the room until she dismissed them. In the post-lesson debrief, the observers made several suggestions for improving the lesson. One teacher suggested having the students actively work through the process of making a hypothesis about the structure of the parallelogram before exploring with the materials and then drawing conclusions about what they find through their exploration. Another teacher suggested making the materials for the activity more challenging by having different lengths of sticks for building the polygons to allow the students more freedom to explore a wider variety of relationships. A principal commented that the questions a teacher asks of the students should be "bigger" questions that will allow the students to find relationships by themselves, rather than the direct teacher question and student response that he observed during the lesson. All of these suggestions support an approach to teaching that is driven by more student thinking and engagement with the learning process, envisioning the teacher's role as that of a designer of materials and activities enabling student exploration and the ability to draw their own conclusions from what they discover.

In Singapore, teachers can learn or refine their lesson study practice (Link 4-2) with help from their teacher leaders in schools (i.e., senior and lead teachers) and master teachers at the AST.

Principal master teachers, Ms. Irene Tan and Ms. Cynthia Seto together described how teachers are supported to learn lesson study through workshops and networked learning communities:

> For lesson study [workshops], we require the schools to send a group of at least three teachers so that they have each other's support in the journey. There are four sessions. . . Before they come for our first lesson study, we will send them some reading material so that they have some idea of what lesson study is. This year, part of the learning [is done] in an online module so they will have some interactions in the online environment first.

Figure 4–3 Teacher Study Group Conducting a Post-Lesson Discussion with Professors from East China Normal University, Pujian No. 2 Elementary School, Shanghai

The first session is face-to-face, where we talk about what lesson study is and how the lesson is designed. In the second one, they will go into the lesson design and be critiqued to give each other feedback on their design [and] any of their perspectives about how [their] lesson has been designed. Then they refine the lesson [after it is taught in the school], so that we all have this experience of what is it like to facilitate a lesson observation as well as a post-lesson discussion. That will happen in the third session. In the fourth one, everyone will come and report. "What have you done, and moving forward, what you are going to do with your learning?"

We do not stop there. We encourage them to say, "Okay, we also have a lesson study networked learning community. If you want to continue this journey with us, you could participate. Bring your team." The network [offers] a more fluid approach in the sense that the members will direct what they want to do. If someone was to say, "Okay, let's look at how we could use technology to promote effective learning," then we can work on a lesson together. Again, we observe the lesson and see how we can improve from there.

The AST emphasizes a discipline-specific approach that develops pedagogical content knowledge:

> More often than not, the teachers will continue with lesson study
> . . . in their own department. One of the reasons I see this [is that] our

lesson study approach has not been done in a generic manner. When we conduct these series of workshops, we do it by subject. For example, if I do a lesson study workshop, it's for chemistry teachers only. Cynthia would do [a workshop] for elementary maths teachers. The conversation is very rich in terms of content. [We rely on] the signature pedagogy that comes with this particular subject: Maths has a way to teach mathematics. Science: there's a way to teach science. . . For us in AST, we have the luxury of a few of us all doing lesson study. Then we can really tailor the discussion to the subject.

Teacher Research

A major emphasis of professional learning in high-performing systems is research. As noted in Chapter 3, teachers gain a solid grounding of research methods in their preparation programs and are expected to be able to conduct their own inquiries and draw conclusions based on evidence. This focus carries through in their careers as well.

In Singapore, almost all teachers are involved in research and innovation (Link 4-3) projects examining their teaching and learning to better meet the needs of students. Every school has a PLC, and there are learning teams organized by subject, grade level, and special interest. Schools provide structured time for teachers to come together as a group to discuss and implement their projects. The PLCs may choose to use a variety of teacher inquiry approaches—action research, lesson study, learning study, and learning circle—to investigate their practices. The PLCs meet weekly; they select a key issue concerning student learning, collect and analyze data, develop and try out instructional solutions, and assess the impact of these solutions. A vice principal of a primary school described how the PLCs operated:

> Individual teachers introduced changes in their own classes, collected evidence from class discussions and student work on what the students understood and have done. Teachers . . . would observe the lessons and discuss what had worked well and what are the areas for refinement. (Jensen et al., 2016, p. 35)

To facilitate teachers' development of research competence, they may receive support from teacher leaders within the school, who have typically had opportunities for action research training, and they may take seminars or workshop series at NIE or the AST. Research findings are also shared at various platforms at the departmental and school levels, other local schools, and at local and international conferences.

Jiaoyanzu *in Shanghai*

The emphasis on research and inquiry is particularly well-developed in Shanghai. There, the *jiaoyanzu*, or teacher research groups, spend much of their time developing hypotheses, collecting evidence, analyzing the evidence, and developing conclusions. The goal of the *jiaoyanzu* is the improvement of educational practices for individual teachers as well as the school. To accomplish this goal, the *jiaoyanzu* members meet weekly and engage in a variety of activities, including examining curriculum together, designing lessons, observing each other teach and discussing the lesson together, writing tests, coordinating teacher professional development such as lectures and visit to other schools, working with student teachers from preparation programs, soliciting input from students on the quality of teaching they are experiencing, and looking at student work.

Jiaoyanzu are led by a teacher who is recognized in the school as high-performing. The leader can be higher on the teaching ladder or a promising young teacher. The school principal works closely with the heads of the *jiaoyanzu*, who serve as an informal council or cabinet offering advice.

Teachers are taught in their preparation programs about research methods and how to think through a research problem, and throughout their careers, they conduct research on their teaching and their schools. Teachers also do their own research individually (Liang, Glaz, DeFranco, Vinsonhaler, Grenier, & Cardetti, 2012), and about 75% have published at least one study (Gang, 2010). Schools annually file some of their research reports with their district office, and much teacher research is published in books and teaching magazines.

Some teachers hold the title of *researching teacher* and have positions in the district offices. These teachers help coordinate and monitor the research happening in schools. Topics of research range from pedagogical issues, subject matter–specific questions, administration processes, and educational policies. Teachers give most attention to subject matter–specific questions.

The Alberta Initiative for School Improvement

One of the most ambitious teacher research initiatives was the Alberta Initiative for School Improvement (AISI)—launched in 2000–2001 as a project bringing together government, universities, the union, superintendents, and school boards—to encourage teachers and local communities to develop collaborative, school-based action projects aimed at improving student learning across the province. With a CA\$75 million budget per year, the AISI was able to support more than 1,800 projects engaging 95% of the provinces' schools. Sahlberg (2009, p. 87) observed that it is "difficult to find anywhere a comparable change effort that would be of the scale and overall magnitude of AISI."

Teachers were responsible for all aspects of their projects, including design, collection and analysis of data, sharing of findings, and fiscal accountability. The project operated in 3-year cycles, with each one building on the learning in the previous cycle, ultimately enabling leadership capacity building and the networking of schools and projects across the province.

Projects developed under AISI used student learning as one of the measurable outcomes, and evaluators concluded that their positive outcomes accrued to make a difference in achievement province-wide (Crocker, 2009; Parsons & Beauchamp, 2012). Although numerous individual school strategies for improved teaching were developed throughout the various projects, the growth and success of two approaches, problem-based learning (PBL) and PLCs, were especially pronounced. The teaching community in Alberta realized the value of PBL, and many of the projects throughout the four 3-year cycles focused on combining technology and PBL strategies to improve student learning. The goal of PBL is for students to have an authentic experience with the problem or issue being examined and to work in groups to collaboratively discuss to develop a deeper understanding. Students take the lead in the PBL model with teachers acting as facilitators throughout the process. Through AISI projects, the province experienced particularly successful changes in how math and science were taught. Through the increased use of technology, Alberta's math and science teachers were able to create PBL lessons and units that students and teachers identified as more engaging than past pencil-and-paper activities, which facilitated their spread (Parsons, McRae, & Taylor, 2006).

Early in cycles 1 and 2, those participating in AISI projects began to recognize the role that PLCss could have in changing how curriculum was taught in Alberta. PLCss encouraged greater collaboration among stakeholders such as teachers and administration to address specific goals and issues in their schools and districts. Many of the AISI projects identified community building among school staff members as a key outcome in their proposals. Consider the following from a final report of an AISI project: "Teachers morale, skills, and sense of professionalism improved as they worked in teams to plan lessons, integrate technology into curriculum, develop assessment tools, share teaching strategies, and implement school improvement initiatives" (University of Alberta, 2004, p. 12).

Assessments of AISI concluded that by the end of its 12 years of operation, the culture of teaching in Alberta had changed. These changes included teachers' access to the wealth of curriculum resources teachers created and made available through the Internet, changes in the use of technology, the role of PBL and student-driven knowledge creation, and of course the importance of action research in classrooms and schools, as well as the emergence of teachers as leaders in Alberta's education system (Alberta Education, 2010; Gunn, Pomahac, Striker, & Tailfeathers, 2011; Hargreaves et al., 2009; Parsons et al., 2006; Parsons & Beauchamp, 2012). In combination, these results of teacher action research changed thinking about pedagogy and professional development in Alberta (Alberta Education, 2012).

Funding from AISI went into the general budget to be controlled by schools, which are now responsible for continuing the work. Meanwhile, professional development for Alberta's teachers incorporates many lessons learned over the four cycles of AISI. Teachers are now recognized as leaders and experts in their field and are now asked to deliver professional development to their colleagues—a shift from the previous practice of bringing in external experts. Schools support collaborative sharing and knowledge building through PLCs.

The Alberta Teachers' Association (ATA, 2010) has developed a framework for professional development (Link 4-4) that acknowledges the insights gained from AISI:

1. *Process:* Professional development should encourage teachers to explore, reflect critically on their practice, and take risks in the planning and delivery of curriculum.

2. *Content:* Use current research highlighting effective teaching and learning strategies.

3. *Context:* Regardless of the professional development activity, teachers' professionalism is recognized as well as their judgment in determining their needs.

To achieve these goals, professional development in Alberta takes many forms: the continued growth of PLCs, a structured approach to coaching, training and mentoring of teachers in Alberta, as well as traditional professional development events such as conferences and workshops. Critical to the success of professional development in Alberta is the follow-up after the session. Teachers are expected to initially apply what was learned in conjunction with professional reflection and sharing with their peers. After this, the teacher adjusts the strategy and uses it in the classroom not only based on his or her reflection and peer feedback but also on student performance (ATA, 2010). The goal is to ensure that theory, reflection, and practice work together to improve student learning.

Teacher-Led Professional Development

Teachers lead professional learning within school-based contexts and in more formal settings outside the school. We discuss these opportunities in the following sections.

Developing Teachers' Skills for Leading Professional Learning Within Schools

In Singapore, a series of system-wide strategies was established to attain the vision of teacher-led professional learning. First, platforms for teacher leaders to lead professional learning were created via subject chapters, professional networks, professional focus groups, and PLCs. Second, strong organizational structures for professional learning were developed, among which are training entitlements for teachers, funding for MOE-organized courses, protected in-school time for teachers to engage in lesson planning, reflection and professional development activities, and an online portal providing one-stop access to learning, collaboration, and resources for all MOE staff. Third, awards and recognition for teachers were established to recognize role models in education.

The establishment of the AST and other academies and language centers was explicitly to support teacher-led professional learning. These academies and language centers support

> the professional learning and development of teachers by drawing out pedagogical leadership from the fraternity, infusing expertise into the system, imbuing a sense of pride, identity and ownership among teachers, strengthening content mastery, building instructional capacity, raising the standards of practice, driving pedagogical innovations and change, advancing continuous learning. (Tan & Wong, 2012, pp. 452–453)

Because Singapore has institutionalized the practice of embedded professional learning within schools, the ministry and NIE provide professional development to department heads and teacher leaders to enable these in-school practices. Each school has a school staff developer and a team of senior or lead teachers who are responsible for professional learning in the school. Based on school objectives, the school staff developer sets a school learning plan and works with department heads to determine teacher development needs. In addition, each teacher has an individual learning plan.

The idea of pedagogical leadership brings the skill and knowledge of senior, lead, and master teachers to bear on reform and improvement across the Singapore school system. The AST mantra, "for teachers, by teachers . . . epitomizes the Academy's commitment and dedication to teacher professionalism, professional identity and to the growth and lifelong learning of teachers" (Tan & Wong, 2012, p. 452). The academies and language centers support teachers in learning communities and sponsors numerous teacher networks developed to address mutual interest, needs, or disciplines.

Singapore's cluster system (each cluster is a network of about 10 to 13 schools) provides another professional learning platform for teacher leaders to help build their teacher leadership capacity so that they can, in turn, build the capacity of teachers in their schools. Teacher leaders provide and receive professional development in how to lead and facilitate learning communities, action research projects, lesson study, and other aspects of in-school professional learning.

Shanghai has also created a career ladder that includes roles for teachers to support professional learning throughout the system. Within schools, a subject mentor provides support for beginning teachers, a district subject leader develops professional learning across a district, a master teacher develops school subject teachers and school professional learning, and a municipal subject leader sets curriculum and broad pedagogical objectives (Jensen et al., 2016). All of these are veteran expert teachers who have advanced in the system.

Teacher-Led Learning Beyond the School Walls

Although job-embedded professional development is important, it is also important for teachers to get beyond their local venues to learn practices they would not encounter in their home sites and to work closely with other teachers, often within their specialty areas, who have valued ideas and techniques to offer. In any area of practice, some schools have gone further than others in developing more sophisticated approaches, and these advances need to be made accessible. This is critical in jurisdictions that seek to share promising practices and profession-wide learning broadly across the system.

In many cases, teacher-led professional development is sponsored by teachers' unions. In the jurisdictions we studied, teachers' unions play an important role as professional associations, setting the standards for the profession, holding their members to that high standard, and organizing learning experiences for their members to improve their practice.

In Ontario, for example, the teachers' federations play a significant role in the provision of professional learning, with thousands of teachers participating annually in activities, developed "by teachers, for teachers." Opportunities throughout the school year include short-term experiences such as 1- to 3-day workshops as well as longer-term experiences on a variety of topics, including leadership skills, curriculum delivery, and equity mindedness. Teacher organizations also partner with subject matter associations, the Ministry of Education, and other appropriate organizations to deliver a range of professional learning resources and activities during the school year and over the summer months. As we describe in Chapter 5, some of these teacher-led learning experiences derive from a province-wide program to develop teacher leadership.

Unions play an important role in Australia as well, offering workshops for beginning teachers and sponsoring the Teacher Learning Network, (Link 4-5) co-owned by AEU and the Independent Education Union, which provides professional learning workshops, courses, and resources free or at reduced cost to its members. The organization references each of its professional learning activities against the national professional teaching standards, helping to facilitate its members' registration renewal processes.

School networks have been a vehicle for teacher-led professional learning as well. Victoria once funded and organized such networks through its department regional offices, and schools found them so valuable, they continued after the funding was devolved to the school sites. A newly elected government has indicated it will again increase resources to support school and leadership networks. Teacher Seona Aulich explains how the school networks function to provide professional learning:

> Across our networks, once a term we have network meetings. I'm a grade five/six teacher. All the grade five/six teachers will get together from the schools within our cluster. The idea is to share best practice. Last week we had a network professional development where there were 12 sessions running. These sessions were run by classroom teachers who are doing something particularly well in their classrooms. [For example] I went to a literacy session for middle years' literacy at a different school. You're seeing something new that you

haven't seen before, but there's no cost at all to the school. We're trying to continually do that sharing of best practice, not just within the
school, but within network schools.

Interestingly, in a survey of 750 highly regarded teachers in Australia, the respondents cited many ways that collaboration improved their
practice. They also noted that the act of leading the professional learning
of other teachers influenced their own learning and practice (McIntyre,
2013). This insight has emerged from a number of studies of teacher
leaders who are involved in mentoring or supporting other teachers: they
find they learn from supporting others (see, for example, Darling-Hammond, 2006).

Teaching Competitions

Whereas many countries spend considerable energy on sports con-
tests and competitions in everything from cooking to fashion designing to Ninja warrioring, China offers incentives for teacher learning by
sponsoring teaching competitions. The teaching competitions require a
teacher to conduct a lesson in front of a panel of judges and receive a
rating on an observation protocol. The lesson plan for that lesson is
also made available to the judges so that they can see how the teacher
reasoned about their selection of teaching strategies and student engagement strategies. Teaching competitions and demonstrations at provincial
and national levels are open events with many observers and do not necessarily take place in a classroom. In Figure 4–4, a classroom has been
set up in an auditorium to enable judges and observers to participate. In
school settings, open classroom sessions look similar with several adult
observers pressed against the walls of the classroom while the teacher
conducts a lesson.

Winners of competitions are celebrated in their schools, and their
pictures are often on display on school walls. More than that, the standards for the competitions incorporate the country's standards for
teaching toward 21st-century competencies, and winners are looked
at as exemplars and teachers of teaching. Thus, these competitions
serve broader purposes of education reform and professional learning. The evaluation form for the competitions (Link 4-6) (see example
in Appendix C) articulates the aspects of valued teaching reflected in
the teaching standards; these illustrate a student-centered approach to
inquiry-oriented teaching and learning. These criteria include respecting, motivating, and appreciating students; differentiating instruction
for individuals; caring for struggling students and using various ways

Figure 4–4 Teaching Competition Photo Posted by a
Teacher on WeChat, a Social Networking Platform
in China

to involve them in learning; challenging students "responsively and appropriately"; giving timely feedback; engaging students with diversified ways of learning that involve "independent, explorative, and cooperative learning;" ensuring that students have a good grasp of the learning content, make progress in challenging areas, and have successful learning experiences.

The evaluation form also indicates that award-winning teaching in Shanghai is focused on meaningful content that is appropriate for the teaching context. The lesson should show students engaging in learning activities prior to the teachers engaging in instruction, encouraging students to think and participate in the lesson activity. The teachers' role is to encourage and motivate, to guide, prompt, and inspire the students to engage in active learning during the lesson. At least 80% of the lesson should focus on exploration, cooperation, presentation, and communication. Broad-based student engagement is expected, with attention to all the students regardless of their performance standing in the class so that students meet the learning goals.

These standards stressed in the teaching competitions are also emphasized in daily practice. For example, in line with the evaluation form in Appendix C just described, we saw in our observations for this study that teachers used a variety of tracking techniques during lessons to help them know how many and which students participated in the lesson. Lessons had a high degree of interaction between the teacher and the students through questioning, call and response with the whole class, paired conversations between the students, student's demonstrating their work on chalkboards, and students showing their work with math manipulatives and demonstration materials they brought from home. Thus, the standards are illustrated in practice and teachers learn by engaging in these demonstrations as well as observing and critiquing them.

Feedback and Appraisal

Because of the strong emphasis in high-performing systems on teacher learning, feedback on teaching is frequent, and evaluation in these systems tends to take on a developmental quality. That is, the goal of teacher appraisal systems tends to be to provide information to help teachers improve their performance, rather than to identify and sanction low performers. As we described in Chapter 3, with careful selection and preparation, along with the closely mentored work teachers do in their probationary period, these systems, by and large, do not expect to fire teachers later.

With continuous improvement in mind, the appraisals are based on the standards for teaching described in Chapter 3 and are tied to professional learning opportunities. In some cases, such as in Singapore and Shanghai, the appraisals are tied directly to opportunities for teachers to advance in their careers as well as in salaries. (For more on the career ladders and how they operate, see Chapter 5.)

And the appraisal systems provide an opportunity for feedback. Whereas in some countries, the principal is the primary source of feedback to teachers on their performance, in many countries, teachers provide feedback to their peers. Quite often, feedback from teaching colleagues is especially relevant to the specific curriculum and students being taught, especially if it is from colleagues in the same content area or teaching field within the school. According to TALIS, 42% of teachers across the countries surveyed report that they receive feedback from their peers on their teaching (OECD, 2014d). In Finland, Singapore, and Australia, the proportions were even higher (ranging from 43% to 51%) and much higher than the rate in the United States (27%).

In the jurisdictions we studied where appraisal practices are most frequent (Australia, Singapore, and Shanghai), a substantial share of the observation and feedback process involves teachers working with other teachers. Teachers learning from teachers is a strong norm in these countries. It is also often the most highly valued form of learning by teachers. In a national survey of Chinese teachers about their professional learning activities, teachers reported that experienced teachers, colleagues teaching the same grade level, and colleagues teaching the same subject had a larger impact on their professional learning than school leaders, experts outside of the school, or students did (Gang, 2010, p. 201). Furthermore, TALIS analyses found that teachers' job satisfaction was higher when the appraisal and feedback they received impacted their classroom teaching (OECD, 2014d).

Approaches to Appraisal

In some of the jurisdictions we studied, such as Finland and Canada, formal appraisal is not a major element of the teacher development system, unless a teacher is having difficulty. In the others it is an annual event for all teachers, with varying degrees of organizational investment in the process. In all, however, there is yearly attention to teacher development in the form of an annual learning plan or goal setting tied to teachers' plans for improvement. These plans, similar to the evaluation processes themselves, are tied to the professional teaching standards we described in Chapter 3.

Canada

The Ontario teacher performance appraisal (TPA) is designed to foster teacher development and identify opportunities for additional support when required. Once they have successfully completed their induction process, teachers are evaluated by the principal or his or her designee once every 5 years (unless there is a performance concern) in a traditional format: a pre-observation meeting, classroom observation, a post-observation meeting, and a summative report. The appraisals are based on 16 competencies that reflect the standards of practice set out by the OCT. New teachers are evaluated on 8 of the 16 competencies; experienced teachers are appraised on all 16.

In addition to the TPA, each year experienced teachers must also complete an annual learning plan (ALP), which outlines their plan for professional growth. In collaboration with their principals, teachers set growth goals, along with a rationale, a set of strategies, and an action plan for achieving them. In doing this they reflect on their previous performance appraisal, the prior year's professional learning, and input from parents and students.

Similarly, although formal teacher evaluation in Alberta is rare (occurring only when teachers apply for certification or a leadership position and when they request one from their principal), teachers prepare an annual professional growth plan. The plan (1) reflects goals and objectives based on an assessment of learning needs by the individual teacher, (2) shows a demonstrable relationship to the Teaching Quality Standards, and (3) takes into consideration the education plans of the school, the school authority, and the government. This is reviewed and approved either by the principal or by a group of teachers delegated by the principal.

Finland

Much of the appraisal function in Finland is integrated into the ongoing work of teachers with their principal, and personnel evaluation occurs informally. Indeed, according to the TALIS surveys, almost 26% of teachers in Finland teach in a school where the principal reports that teachers are not formally appraised (OECD, 2014d). Much of the appraisal function is integrated into the ongoing work of teachers with their principal. In general, evaluation involves a one-on-one private conversation that may focus on issues such as individual growth, participation in professional development, contributions to the school, and personal professional goals. The focus is more on steering than on accounting for teacher's work (Hatch, 2013).

In Helsinki, principals do use a common form to guide the conversation with teachers about how they have fulfilled the objectives the teacher set for the year. This form focuses on some key features of teaching that are considered important: "personal performance," "versatility," "initiative," and "ability to cooperate." In addition to the teacher's general classroom practice, the "versatility" of the teacher refers to whether she or he uses or has mastered "good pedagogical skills," can "acknowledge and meet diverse students in different circumstances," and can "acknowledge diverse learning needs." The form (Link 4-7) asks teachers and principals to consider the degree to which the teacher demonstrates "initiative" (which includes, for instance, "using new and meaningful working methods and practices" and "active participation in in-service training, [within-school] work groups, development initiatives, district workgroups"). As described by Anna Hirvonen, principal of Myllypuro Primary School in Helsinki, the process relies on many interactions with teachers over a sustained period of time:

> I have, every year, a discussion . . . with every teacher in which I evaluate how [a teacher's] personal objectives have been reached in terms of ability to cooperate, versatility, initiative, and performance. . . . Every teacher told me how they see things going, and then I brought out my viewpoints of their work; how they have reached every objective. If we agreed on things it was easy, but we did not always agree, and that was rough. Before the first evaluation round, I arranged my schedules and was able to go around the school and visit classes while teachers were teaching. It was not a short visit; I spent time there. And I see teachers engaged in many different situations in school: with students, in the hallways, and if we have to solve out some challenges together. In addition, I observe how teachers participate in school life in general, how they bring in their knowledge for the whole school community's use, how they develop themselves, how they participate in development processes, and so on.

This conversation results in the teacher setting goals for the following year and, sometimes, in identification of learning opportunities within or outside the school.

The communal notion that teachers are evaluated in part on how they contribute to the welfare of the school and share their knowledge "for the whole school community's use," as Anna put it, is a common thread across the jurisdictions. Teacher appraisal is not about ranking teacher's individual competence or effectiveness against that of other teachers. It is about building a thoughtful and effective teaching team that collaborates and continues to learn and improve. This notion was central in every jurisdiction.

Appraisal is more frequent and formal in Australia, Singapore, and Shanghai, where teacher evaluation is an annual event, closely tied to the professional teaching standards and individual teacher performance goals that are annually established in relation to growth needs.

Australia

In New South Wales, for example, the annual Performance and Development Plan (Link 4-8) documents a concise set of three to five professional goals that are explicitly linked to teachers' performance and development needs and the professional standards. There is an expectation that the goals should align to the school plan (Link 4-9) and systemic strategic directions. There is also an expectation that the goals establish a personalized pathway for each teacher through the alignment to standards by recognizing existing expertise while also identifying areas for professional growth. Principals or their designees are responsible for conferencing with the teacher and observing and documenting performance.

In Victoria, teacher evaluation, known as performance and development, is intended to connect teachers' performance against specified standards and goals with their development through professional learning opportunities and feedback on their work, to be underpinned by principles of collective efficacy, peer collaboration, and professional accountability (DEECD, 2014a). The Department of Education and Training has sought to build collective capacity by fostering a visible culture of instructional practice (City, Elmore, Fiarman, & Teitel, 2009) with schools viewed as the sites for PLCs (DuFour & Marzano, 2011).

In Australia, teacher performance is linked to school improvement and student learning in several ways. First, teachers' individual performance and development plans are closely aligned to school goals and, in Victoria, three broad categories: student learning, student engagement and well-being, and student pathways and transitions. Among these, student learning goals are the most tangible, and outcomes on a variety of assessments feed into teachers' plans. Senior teacher Seona Aulich explains:

> As a staff, we look at whole-school data a lot, and we look at trends. Collectively, we're accountable as a school. We set new goals for our strategic plan and our annual implementation plan from looking at the previous year's data. What realistically can we improve for the following year? That's where our [performance and development plan] goals are coming from.

Second, the evaluation process is tied to state, and now national, teaching standards. Beginning in 2014, Victoria has used a balanced scorecard approach in which teachers are assessed against their performance in four domains. The first three are directly connected to the domains of the national professional teaching standards—professional knowledge, professional practice, and professional engagement—and the fourth is student outcomes. Teachers and principals together discuss and set goals in each of the four domains using the level of the national standards appropriate for their career stage and job classification. Schools have considerable flexibility in the use of school-based professional learning and the use of portfolios as evidence of performance, and they have discretion in the relative weighting of each of the four domains in assessing individual teacher performance.

Figure 4–5 Example of a Balanced Scorecard Approach

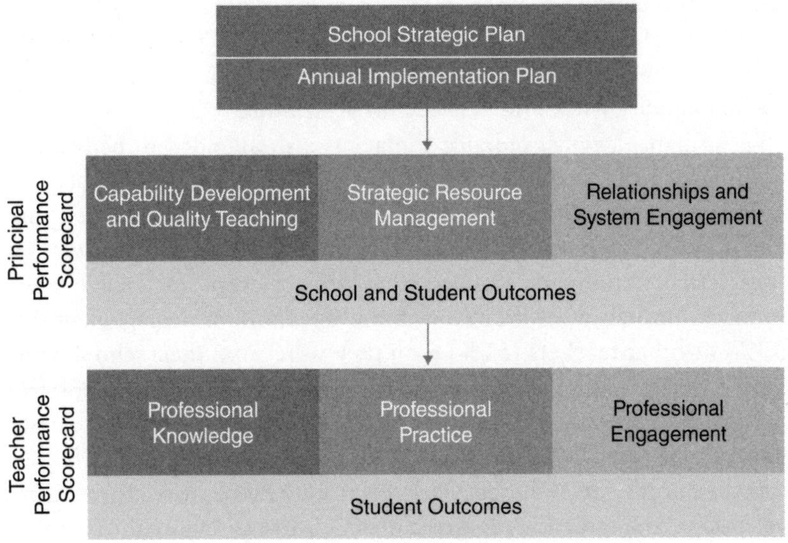

Source: Reproduced from DEECD (2013b, p. 15).

Embedded in the process are two mechanisms that direct the focus of evaluation toward teacher professional development and student learning outcomes. Under Victoria's performance and development culture framework, teachers' individual performance plans, which can include team goals—typically a grade-level team—are connected to those of the school. This is intended to promote collective accountability: teachers are accountable to each other by furthering team goals, and teachers are accountable to the community through school strategic plans. Moreover, by situating individual goals in the context of team goals, the process is intended to contribute to fostering collaborative practices within the school.

By tying the process to national teaching standards, teacher evaluation also becomes connected to professional learning and the annual registration and accreditation process in New South Wales and Victoria. Evidence of professional learning in practice may become evidence for renewal of registration and for evaluation. It connects a school-based process to state policy, national professional standards, and a common language for discussing what quality teaching looks like.

Teachers and principals are expected to undertake professional conversations based on teaching standards and continual improvement—what their students need to progress, what teachers need to learn to engage their students, and evaluating teachers' impact on student learning. In this way, the performance and development process provides another mechanism for teachers to be reflective about the practice of the school and about their own teaching practice. This process has further embedded the national standards as a common language for articulating teaching quality within the school and profession.

Performance against individual plans is also intended to be based on multiple forms of feedback. This typically includes feedback on observed classes by peers within the school, including leading teachers or those with a role in school management. Recent international survey data showed that, nationwide, teachers in Australia were more likely to receive feedback on their work from members of the school management team (57%) or other teachers (51%) than they were from their school principal (27%) (OECD, 2014d). Feedback may also include information from student and parent surveys or structured observations (DEECD, 2014a). Plans may incorporate team goals as well as individual goals.

For example, at Willmott Park Primary School in Victoria, teachers' performance plans are agreed through discussion with the school principal, incorporating individual goals and team goals for each grade level. Teachers select six improvement goals, two from each of the three domains—professional knowledge, professional practice, and professional engagement—then use these together with evidence from student achievement data to create S.M.A.R.T. goals (specific, measurable, agreed, realistic, and time-based) that include specific targets. Structured feedback is based on periodic lesson observation throughout the year, primarily from one of the professional learning leaders and supplemented by occasional informal walk-throughs by the assistant principals and principal.

Shanghai

Shanghai's teacher evaluation system also seeks many forms of input and feedback for teachers, including from other teachers and students. Although the principal plays a role in the evaluation and makes final ratings determinations, the actual appraisal and feedback process is substantially teacher-to-teacher. As a Shanghai teacher explained:

> Teachers are required to write a summary about their work, and the principal and the other teachers evaluate [their] work according to the summary. In most schools, teachers are also evaluated according to their teaching. His or her lessons are observed by the *jiaoyanzu zhang* [leader of teaching and research team] and other teachers and

> the students are required to fill in some evaluation forms. The result will be fed back to the teacher and sent to the principal, but not the district office. It does not make a huge difference in the salary, but helps the principle to decide which teachers can shoulder more important responsibility.

As this quote suggests, student feedback is a routine part of the evaluation process for teachers. Schools and the district administer surveys to students and parents as part of the school evaluation process and questions about the teacher and classroom operations are reviewed by the principal. As in Australia and Singapore, there is a cycle of goal setting, mid-year review, and end-of-year review. And, as we describe further in Chapter 5, evaluation in Shanghai also ultimately fits into a career ladder scheme by which teachers can be promoted in rank.

Singapore

Singapore's appraisal system is one part of its teacher development strategy. To appraise and develop teachers, the MOE uses a system known as the Enhanced Performance Management System (EPMS). The EPMS is designed to be holistic in nature and customized to the role each teacher plays on the career path she or he has selected. Essentially, EPMS lays out a range of professional competencies as the basis for teacher appraisal and development; these specify teachers' performance in three key result areas (KRAs): (1) student outcomes (quality learning of students, character development of students); (2) professional outcomes (professional development of self, professional development of others); and (3) organizational outcomes (contributions to projects and committee work). With these areas, competency is divided into individual attributes (e.g., professional values and ethics); professional mastery (e.g., student-centric, values-driven practice); organizational excellence (e.g., visioning and planning); and effective collaboration (e.g., interpersonal relationships and skills). Teachers are appraised not only on their own teaching but also on how they contribute to the professional learning of the other teachers in the school, cluster, or fraternity. The KRAs are open-ended with no rating scale.

As an appraisal and development tool, the EPMS functions as a formative and summative review of teachers' work. It is used as a self-evaluation tool for teachers. It can help teachers identify areas of strength, assess their own ability to nurture the whole child, track their students' results, review teaching competencies, develop personal training and development plans, and articulate innovations and other contributions to school development. Second, EPMS forms a basis for coaching and mentoring. The work review cycle begins with one-on-one target setting at the start of the year conducted with the teacher's immediate supervisor, followed by a mid-year and end-of-year work review. The review cycle helps specify areas for improvement and enables developmental and career pathways to be mapped.

In Singapore, teachers receive important feedback on their practice through the formal appraisal and development process that is married with a less formal but an equally important mentoring process in the schools. The conversations between teachers and their senior colleagues cover what the teachers have done well, along with areas for development. The Teacher Growth Model (TGM) (Link 4-10), with its comprehensive set of necessary competencies for teacher growth, often guides these developmental conversations. Azahar Bin Mohamed Noor, a teacher specialist at Raffles Girls School, explains the nature of the feedback and follow-up:

> Assessment is both evaluative and developmental. The conversation is done in a very developmental way. We have our own tools such as a classroom observation tool to assess teaching competency. We also use the EPMS, where we have two conversations a year with our reporting officer [RO]. The EPMS document is to document what are our plans for the year, what we have done and the impact it has on the school or the students. It also records teachers' training needs.

Tan Hwee Pin, the principal of Kranji Secondary School, explained:

> We want to emphasize to the teachers that this is a developmental process. It is a journey and we want them to have ownership of this journey. Our HODs [heads of department] work with the teachers very closely and they provide feedback on a regular basis. This ongoing conversation enables teachers to chart their progress and develop their plans throughout the year.

Links to Professional Learning

In high-performing jurisdictions, the links among appraisal, feedback, and professional learning are well developed. The NSW Department of Education and Communities makes these connections explicit:

> All teachers have a right to be supported in their professional learning as well as a responsibility to be involved in performance and development processes that facilitate their professional growth for the provision of quality teaching and learning. The overarching purpose of

the performance and development process is to support the ongoing improvement of student outcomes through continuous development of a skilled and effective teaching workforce.

NSW teachers and school leaders are required to work with colleagues and their supervisor to document appropriate strategies and professional learning to support the achievement of their goals. Throughout the implementation of the plan, teachers are required to collect evidence, sourced from their everyday work, that when considered holistically will demonstrate their progress toward their goals. The evidence that is required must include data on student learning and outcomes, feedback from peer observations of teaching practice, and the results of collaborative practice with colleagues.

According to a survey of 750 highly respected teachers in New South Wales, all of these are sources of professional learning. The teachers reported that, in addition to collaborative planning and peer observations, the most useful feedback for them came from evidence of assessment from student work and feedback from their students. The second most useful source of feedback was feedback from other teachers and their supervisors. Data from external testing were less highly rated than evidence from student work samples (McIntyre, 2013). The teachers' responses suggested that a key driver of teacher learning is formative assessment based on rich evidence of learning conducted during the teaching process. This assessment is most closely connected to the classroom and creates a cycle of continuous feedback for teachers to monitor the impact of their teaching as well as for students to chart the progress of their learning. These highly accomplished teachers were constantly evaluating the difference they make and how they made it. When asked what types of feedback they sought more often, the teachers identified feedback from other teachers.

In Singapore, professional learning connections are made in the conversation between teachers and their reporting officers and in mentoring conversations between teachers and their mentors. These conversations, often guided by the TGM, cover what the teacher has done well and where there are areas for development. After the conversation with the reporting officer, teachers compose their own evaluation where they write down their thoughts and plans for the future, addressing questions such as, In what ways have you improved? How you are going to improve yourself further? What professional learning activities would you like to take on? The teacher and the reporting officer identify in- and out-of-school learning opportunities that will help the teacher pursue these goals. The same process occurs in the systems in Canada and Australia whereby an annual learning plan is developed from the teachers' goals.

In Singapore, the appraisal may also launch professional learning tied to teachers' career options. For example, Rosmiliah Bte Kasmin of Kranji Secondary School described how her appraisal (Link 4-11) helped her specifically to refocus her professional development plans when she decided to shift from the leadership track to the teaching track (interview with senior teacher, Rosimiliah Bte Kasmin, 2014):

> At the beginning of every year, you discuss with the Head your career options for the next 3 to 5 years, taking into consideration the teacher's performance in the previous year. That particular conversation will help you see which direction you would like to go. For example, if you intend to take up the leadership track as the Head of Department, probably the school needs to expose you a bit more to different projects and responsibilities in the school. If you choose the teaching track, there are certain projects and things that you need to complete, or certain skills that you need to have before you can get to be promoted to the Senior Teacher position.
>
> When I was on the leadership track, I was doing more of activity organization for the students at the departmental level and was not very involved in mentoring teachers directly. So with the evaluation, I could narrow down the kind of skills that I need to mentor the teachers and exactly how I can improve on my mentoring of the teachers.

The ministry then provides these learning opportunities through NIE, the academies, and language centers, or direct mentoring is coupled with leadership opportunities on-site or in one of the many venues where teacher leaders are working.

Links to Compensation

Several countries, including Singapore, China, and Australia, have also sought to link evaluation to compensation. The nature of the compensation strategy appears to have an influence on how successful these efforts have been. As described, the career ladder systems in Singapore and Shanghai are of long-standing and appear well accepted, and teachers see benefits in the opportunity to grow and be recognized for their levels of teaching accomplishment and take on additional responsibilities that share their expertise. More junior colleagues are grateful to be mentored by more senior colleagues who have progressed into and received training and time to enact these roles.

In Australia, the initial federal government merit pay reform proposed annual salary increments awarded by the principal based on teacher performance. The proposal suggested that evidence of teacher performance would include student assessment outcomes and evidence of practice against the professional teaching standards. There were significant differences in the approach in New South Wales to that in Victoria. In New South Wales, the government supported the assessment of teaching practices as defined by the professional teaching standards. This approach was supported by the profession. In Victoria, the short-lived Liberal-National coalition government in power from 2010–2014 sought to introduce a form of merit pay by requiring that principals provide an annual salary increment only to those teachers deemed to have adequately met the goals articulated in their plans. There was also some effort to encourage principals to link these merit pay decisions to student test scores.

This approach to merit pay caused significant pushback from teachers and school leaders. The new government does not appear to be emphasizing this approach. Principals largely ignored the guidance, and salary increments were awarded for virtually all teachers. Senior teacher Seona Aulich described the notion as antithetical to the culture of teaching in Victoria:

> People are not interested in the whole performance pay concept at all. Teachers are fairly irate about it. Teachers are groups of people that work very closely together and care about one another and there are no secrets in a school. If [a teacher] fails, then everyone knows about it. . . Then you start to break down the culture of the school. . . . Particularly in a primary school, you've got all these roles that may not necessarily contribute to the academic success of the student or a school but are really important in the running of the school. . . It's this holistic view of what a teacher is. Maybe you've got children in your grade who perhaps have been incredibly shy. I'm the teacher this year who managed to get the student to open up. Now his or her school attendance has greatly improved, and s/he is actually smiling. All that sort of stuff. How do you measure that?

The educators' union opposed the government's desire to introduce performance pay, arguing that the idea would damage schools. As AEU Victoria deputy vice president Justin Mullaly stated:

> It was something that was very much the antithesis of what we wanted to see in our schools, largely around the impact it would have on collegiality [and] on the benefit that comes from teachers being able to freely and fairly work with each other, on the basis that it's

through that kind of collaboration that ideas get shared and that students are in the best place to be—having teachers [who] have well-resolved and developed teaching and learning plans that're going on into the classroom.

Although the allocation of annual salary awards by principals was not accepted by the education community, the idea of a career ladder tied to the new professional teaching standards, with a well-developed externally administered process of appraisal used for advancing through the ladder, has been embraced by the union and by educators generally. Those advances to teacher leadership roles also have salary implications, but these seem more acceptable because the standards are clear and the process of appraisal by outside experts using a common, rigorous process is credible to teachers. In addition, the awards are open to all teachers who meet the standards, and teachers are not ranked against each other in a context in which one teacher's gain comes as another teacher's loss. Finally, the career ladder is intended to expand the expertise of the profession as a whole because the advances are associated with roles that enlist teachers in helping others. Thus, the result is not an individualized bonus but a collective step forward toward ever more effective teaching. We describe that approach in Chapter 5.

Shanghai's and Singapore's well-accepted career ladders—which recognize expertise as teachers are rewarded with greater rank, responsibility, and compensation (described in Chapter 5)—also award salary allocations to recognize performance each year. The annual salary determinations did not occasion much comment in Singapore, but the career ladder was highly salient to teachers and to the functioning of schools' professional learning systems. In Shanghai, we learned that China's recently added merit pay requirements, enacted as part of an overall increase in salaries in 2009, are viewed by some school leaders as counterproductive and less helpful to the support of expert teaching than the career ladder itself.

The Shanghai merit pay rules call for annual differentiation of 30% of salary based on performance. Base pay (70% of the total) is distributed to teachers primarily based on the number of classes they teach as well as the additional tasks and responsibilities that the teacher takes on, such as being the *banzhuren* (advisor) for a class, being the head of the *jiaoyanzu* (teacher research group), or conducting demonstration lessons for colleagues in the school or at other schools.

The merit determination process varies from school to school. There are no specific metrics or weighted formulas used to determine the merit salary allocation for individual teachers. Principals rely on many different sources of information and indicators of success, including performance of the teacher's students and professional advancements that the teacher makes. The introduction of merit pay appears to have made the evaluation process more frustrating for some principals. One principal, for example, described how the evaluation approach is not specific enough to administer based on detailed differences among his teachers, so he relies on his knowledge of teachers' skill to group teachers in three big categories to make the salary system merit based.

> It is the toughest when it comes to performance incentives . . . The rationales behind these evaluations are not of high quality in particular situations when some teachers' performances are close in evaluation. For example, Teacher Li is outstanding, whereas the performance evaluation for you and me is close. But there should be some differences between our performance evaluations. This is the toughest part of the work, right? So the key issue is designing an evaluation system to the greatest details [and that] takes time and effort, which we don't have; the evaluation system that is broad and general fails to capture differences between teachers . . . What is your decision based on? . . . We cannot afford the time and effort to designing an evaluation system to the greatest details; we won't be able to have a solid base for incentives if the evaluation system is broad and general. So what we do now is global evaluation. In Chinese language arts, for example, we first determine who are the best teachers and then the worst. What is left is pretty much those in the middle. This way is efficient and it sounds fair. You are placed in the top/first rank whereas I am in the second as I should be. If one's teaching performance is apparently worse than others, or one breaks some minor regulation, they are downgraded.

To provide information that will allow teachers to be ranked for these purposes, schools and the district administer surveys to students (Link 4-12) and parents as part of the school evaluation process. The following are some questions on one school's annual student survey:

o Who is your favorite male teacher? And/or who is your favorite female teacher?

o Who is full of goodwill among your teachers?

o Which subject do you like best in your curriculum? Who teaches (taught) this subject?

o If you face difficulties in life or study, who will you seek for help?

- o Up till now, which teacher do you think helps you a lot in life or study?
- o In addition to those academic lessons, such as Chinese, math, and English, which subject do you like most? Who is the teacher?

Although there is some discomfort with this approach, these survey results are often used as the principal judgment when making evaluation and merit pay decisions about a teacher. A study conducted in Beijing after the merit pay system was implemented found that, overall, the system was not a motivating program for teachers to perform differently than they had in the past (Niu & Liu, 2012). Our research suggests that the career ladder and other recognitions of and roles for teachers appear to have more substantial motivational effects.

Lessons Learned

Professional learning in high-performing jurisdictions is part and parcel of their systems for developing a high-quality educator workforce. It builds on their efforts to recruit and prepare effective teachers; once teachers have been hired and mentored, they are expected to continue their learning, hone their craft, and become better and better each year. Feedback and evaluation is a key element: Teachers receive feedback that guides them through additional learning opportunities.

The professional learning in these countries is costly, but the costs are different from those in the United States. Rather than spend funds on nationally recognized speakers or hotel ballrooms, schools in high-performing nations spend funds by providing teachers with time in the school day to continue their learning.

The policies and practices described here differ from one jurisdiction to the next, but they share some common themes:

Teacher professional learning is continual and developmental. The standards for teaching in these jurisdictions spell out a clear set of expectations for the knowledge and skills all teachers are expected to develop and demonstrate. But they make clear that beginning teachers are not expected to be at the same level as veterans, and most veterans are not expected to be at the same level as master teachers. The standards and the systems for evaluation and career advancement imply levels of expertise to which teachers can aspire and work toward.

Professional learning is collaborative. Schools in high-performing systems have learning plans for individual teachers and school-wide learning plans. Teachers pursue learning opportunities to fulfill their own goals as well as those of the school. But in many cases the activities teachers undertake for both sets of goals involve working with other teachers. They meet regularly in groups to review student work, lesson plans, and research, and they conduct action research and report back to the group on the results. They regularly visit other classrooms and schools to observe different approaches to instruction. And evaluation provides feedback to teachers on their practice.

Teachers lead learning for their colleagues. In Australia and Canada, for example, professional teachers' associations are key providers of professional development, offering workshops and other learning opportunities "by teachers, for teachers." This arrangement also underscores the collaborative nature of professional learning in these countries. Singapore's AST performs a similar function. There and in Shanghai teachers also engage in lesson study, action research groups, and PLCs lead by teachers. And in Finland the notion of peer mentoring and co-mentoring are part of the shared learning commitment teachers make to each other and their school.

Teachers are researchers. The emphasis on research that is a hallmark of teacher education in high-performing jurisdictions continues as teachers are in the classroom. Teachers not only are expected to stay well-versed in the current literature but also they are expected to conduct their own practice-based research. This research informs their practice and that of their colleagues. And, in many cases, the research informs the field; teachers regularly publish in professional journals.

Evaluation is organized to support teacher development and growth. The purpose of teacher evaluation in high-performing countries is not primarily to reward high performers and identify and eventually get rid of low performers. Rather, it is to create goals for learning and improvement, provide feedback on performance, enable teachers to see how they are meeting their goals for improvement, and suggest what they can do to strengthen their practice. The process is linked to professional learning opportunities so that teachers have help in making progress on their own and their schools' objectives.

Professional learning in high-performing systems is, at its heart, *professional.* Countries and provinces define a body of knowledge and skills for the profession, prepare teachers to develop those competencies, and provide them with the responsibility to continue to develop them throughout their career. In that respect, teaching is, in these jurisdictions, similar to law, medicine, engineering, and other respected professions.

Teachers are also expected to remain in the profession; turnover is very low compared to the United States. But these countries also provide structures and opportunities for teachers to advance in responsibility, find new avenues for sharing their expertise, and experience greater compensation for taking on these roles. Chapter 5 discusses the ways in which these countries create teaching careers and pathways to leadership.

5

THE TEACHING CAREER
AND LEADERSHIP FOR
THE PROFESSION

I felt that after so many years of teaching and affecting students' lives, hopefully in a positive way, I wanted to go beyond the classroom walls. I found [that] as a teacher, I was very much into helping other teachers, too. I became a department head, and so the opportunity was there to help teachers within the department with resources that I had or other connections where they will be able to find resources. That gave me satisfaction in helping a wider range of teachers being in a department. Having done all of that, I wanted to go beyond the classroom walls and affect more teachers and more students on a larger scale.

—Ontario school principal

I don't have a [formal] leadership position within my school community. I'm not a chairperson, I'm not a vice principal; I'm a teacher . . . I felt that [the Teacher Learning and Leadership Program] was a way for me to become a specialist in a particular area in a short period of time. There is this extra amount of work on top of your regular job; [however], the connection, the collaboration, the brainstorming, and the creative outlet was rejuvenating for us. It was rewarding, enriching, inspiring, invigorating, captivating. The three of us on the core team would just sort of feed off one another and dream big thoughts that normally we would never have the time to do, nor offered the opportunity.

—Ontario participant in the Teacher Learning and Leadership Program

THE STRONG PREPARATION and continued support teachers in high-performing systems receive, described in Chapters 3 and 4, go a long way toward ensuring that all students in these systems have access every day to highly effective, caring teachers who know how to teach and who are working to continually improve their practice. But in these systems, teaching is more than a set of skills teachers develop. Teaching is a profession, one that highly capable individuals enter and remain in throughout their careers and that provides them with the kind of satisfaction and rewards that other professionals, such as lawyers and engineers, enjoy.

The systems do this in several ways. First, they create structures that enable teachers to take on new responsibilities based on their interests and skills. Teachers have opportunities to develop curricula, write assessments, mentor younger teachers, oversee professional development, and much more. They do not have to leave teaching and move into administration in order to advance in their careers.

Second, the systems have structures for identifying promising leadership candidates and supporting them so that they can grow into their new positions. Most of these jurisdictions have developed proactive methods for reaching out and finding teachers who are successful in helping their colleagues learn and encouraging them to become teacher leaders and school leaders. They do not wait for prospective leaders to apply for their positions but instead recruit them actively and provide them with learning opportunities.

Third, the systems use the appraisal processes described in Chapter 4 to identify talent and accomplishment. One major goal of the process is to enable schools and school systems to find teachers with particular skills and to enable teachers to demonstrate their competencies so that they can make a case for advancement.

The effects of these policies are substantial. They make teaching an attractive and rewarding profession, one that highly capable individuals are eager to join. That, in turn, enables preparation programs to be even more selective in choosing candidates. The policies also strengthen teaching overall by enabling veteran and well-qualified teachers to use their experience and knowledge to support less-experienced colleagues. And the policies encourage teachers to remain in the profession throughout their careers, reducing the costs and disruption caused by rapid turnover.

This chapter examines the career paths and leadership development practices in high-performing countries. We discuss career pathways, opportunities for teachers to lead learning opportunities with their colleagues, and strategies for recruiting and developing school principals and other administrative leaders.

Career Pathways

In some systems, such as in many states in the United States, the job description of a teacher is static. That is, a teacher's work is basically the same after 30 years on the job as it was on her first day. Her salary will have increased because of seniority and advanced degrees, but her responsibilities remain basically the same: spending almost the entire day in a classroom with 20 to 30 children. If she wants additional responsibilities, she can leave teaching and apply to become an administrator.

Other systems, though, have created structures that enable teachers to take on new roles without leaving teaching. Teachers can, for example, teach for part of the day and also lead other teachers in professional development; they can be responsible for curriculum and assessment; they can spend time in a ministry advising on policy. In these and other ways, teachers can become leaders in their schools and school systems.

The policies that establish these structures make use of appraisal systems that assess teachers' strengths and areas of need. They can help teachers identify their competencies and draw attention to them. They can help ensure that the most capable teachers lead other teachers.

One of the most fully developed career ladder structures is Singapore's. Shanghai also has a formal advancement structure, and Australia has recently developed a career ladder concept tied to the new national teaching standards that are being implemented in various ways by its states.

Ontario has developed a variety of teacher leadership roles and training opportunities as well, although it operates more like a career lattice than a ladder, with many opportunities for leadership possible from any level of the system without relying on highly developed hierarchical structures. In Finland, teachers take on a wide variety of leadership functions inside the school, but these are embedded in the work and not formally designated. These countries offer teachers different routes for advancement and leadership as they demonstrate accomplishment in the classroom and skills in supporting their peers. Although the traditional role of the principal as the main school leader still predominates, leadership in these systems has become much more shared, and tasks— such as coaching, curriculum development, and school improvement activities—are distributed across multiple roles and individuals within the school (Spillane, Sherer, & Codren, 2005).

Singapore's Career Ladder System

The Singapore model includes three leadership trajectories teachers can follow: the teaching track, the leadership track, and the senior specialist track (see Figure 5–1).

The teacher performance appraisal process feeds into the career ladders by highlighting teachers' abilities to collaborate with each other, their emerging leadership skills, and their teaching skills as part of the

Figure 5–1 Career Tracks for Teachers in Singapore

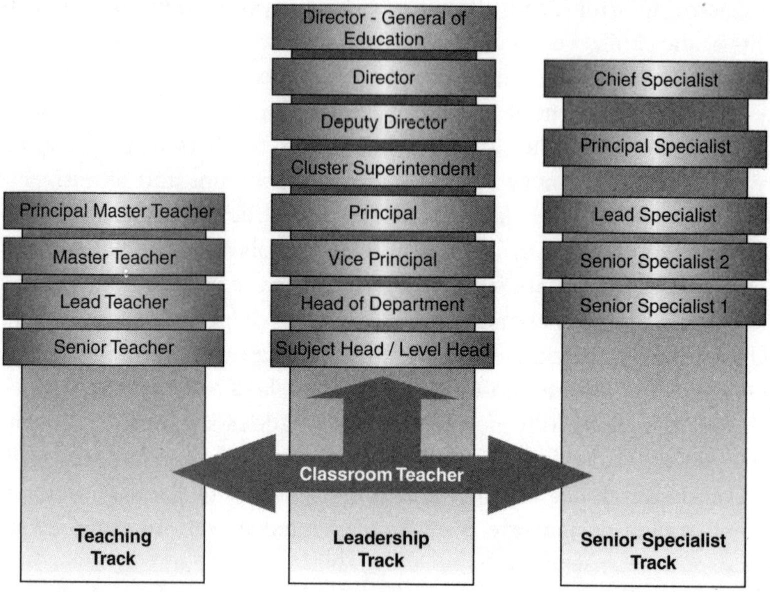

Teaching Track	Leadership Track	Senior Specialist Track
Principal Master Teacher	Director - General of Education	Chief Specialist
Master Teacher	Director	Principal Specialist
Lead Teacher	Deputy Director	Lead Specialist
Senior Teacher	Cluster Superintendent	Senior Specialist 2
	Principal	Senior Specialist 1
	Vice Principal	
	Head of Department	
	Subject Head / Level Head	

Classroom Teacher

Source: Singapore Ministry of Education (n.d.).

regular evaluation system. The school leaders and heads of departments who conduct these appraisals have been coached on how to look for and spot potential, how to cultivate it by giving various kinds of leadership opportunities to teachers, as well as how to encourage them to think about how they would like to develop their skills and apply for the training and appraisal that accompanies each of the tracks. Cluster leaders and senior management in the ministry pay attention to the teachers who are flagged as having leadership potential and help support opportunities for them to take on new challenges and access various kinds of professional learning opportunities.

The Teaching Track

Once a teacher embarks on this journey, each of the three tracks has its own set of performance standards. For the teaching track, these standards are assessed through a professional portfolio (Link 5-1) the teacher puts together, which includes a personal statement on why he or she wants to take up the higher appointment, a summary of evidence satisfying each accreditation standard, and supporting data to substantiate the evidence (e.g., lesson plans, presentations, and the like). The teaching track standards build on teaching evaluation criteria such as holistic development of pupils through quality learning, pastoral care and well-being, and cocurricular activities, and the criteria gets broader as the teacher advances to the next level. These include contributions to the school, cluster, zone, and nation; collaboration and networking; and contributions to a culture of professionalism, ethos, and standards. It is important to note that a principal master teacher or a lead specialist earns as much as a principal, so there are strong incentives for expert teachers to choose any of the three tracks, based on their interests and talents.

Through the teaching track, teachers can aspire first to be senior teachers, then they can move on to become lead teachers, and then progress further to the level of master teachers. As they advance up the teaching track, they assume teacher leadership roles within their school or the larger teaching fraternity, serving as pedagogical leaders, instructional mentors, and professional learning leaders to newer teachers or teachers in need of assistance. Master teachers move to the respective academies and are not situated in schools. These academies, such as the Academy of Singapore Teachers (AST), were established by the Ministry of Education to enable teachers to lead professional learning for other teachers.

Cynthia Seto, a principal master teacher for mathematics currently assigned to the AST, describes how this career progression operated for her:

> I was a teacher leader. I moved from a classroom teacher to become a senior teacher. [As a] senior teacher, you have teaching periods, just like any teachers, except that you may have one, two, or three periods fewer than the average teacher so that you have time for mentoring. Most of the work for a senior teacher is to help the beginning teachers, as well as some aspiring teachers who lack certain skills, for example, ICT integration in mathematics.
>
> Then from a senior teacher, I moved on to become a master teacher. When we are nominated by the principal, we are invited to write our portfolio. In our portfolio, we are assessed under five standards, which cover our engagement in professional development, quality learning of students, attention to students' pastoral care and well-being, how you work in communities, and so forth. When I decided to send my portfolio for appointment to be master teacher, I was very clear that my passion now was to build teachers' capacity.

At AST, Cynthia designs and supports professional development for other teachers and teacher leaders. The AST and the other subject-specific academies and language centers support the professional learning and development of teachers by drawing out pedagogical leadership from the fraternity, infusing expertise into the system, imbuing a sense of pride, identity and ownership among teachers, strengthening content mastery, building instructional capacity, raising the standards of practice, driving pedagogical innovations and change, advancing continuous learning. (Tan & Wong, 2012, pp. 452–453)

Teacher leaders also support the work of their schools and clusters. In all of these ways, teaching in Singapore is an exciting career in which educators have many opportunities to continue learning, take on new challenges, and share their expertise without having to become administrators. As Cynthia Seto and Irene Tan said, "For the longest time, the term *teacher leader* usually referred to heads of department and vice principals who are in-school leaders. [Senior teachers] see themselves as teacher leaders now."

The Leadership Track

The leadership track in Singapore, meanwhile, is for teachers who have the aptitude and capabilities to take on school administration roles and is a pathway that takes them into leadership positions in schools and could continue into leadership roles in the Ministry of Education. Because leadership is seen as a key enabler for effective schools, much attention and resources are given to identify and groom school leaders. All principals and department heads are fully trained at government expense before they take on their posts. There is a comprehensive suite of leadership development programs planned centrally by the ministry and customized suitably for new and experienced department heads, vice principals, and principals. At appropriate junctures in their careers, leaders are also assigned mentors to guide and coach them in their leadership roles.

Leaders are identified, cultivated, and recruited from among teachers who demonstrate potential to take on school leadership roles. Each year, teachers are evaluated on their leadership skills as well as their teaching skills in a multifaceted, competency-based process, and the ministry keeps tabs on up-and-coming potential leaders, reviewing evaluations and checking in regularly with principals about which faculty members are ready for additional challenges and learning opportunities. When potential principals are identified, they are given opportunities to take on new responsibilities and to engage in various kinds of training to further develop their leadership and management competencies. Officers undergo a rigorous selection process, after which they are appointed to school leadership positions when deemed suitable by a panel of appraisers.

Leadership development is supported in many ways. Educators on the leadership track can develop their knowledge and skills through additional preparation and course work at the postgraduate level. For example, in July 2007, the National Institute of Education (NIE) launched the Management and Leadership in Schools (MLS) program. It is designed as a full-time, 17-week, in-service program aimed especially at middle-level leaders who are already heads of departments. The selection of these leaders is made by the school principal and cluster superintendent; participants have their fees fully borne by the Ministry of Education and still continue to receive their monthly salaries.

Aimed at middle-level leaders who are already engaged in school-based reform in their schools, MLS is distinguished by a deliberate integration of theory and practice, as well as attention to "glocal" issues—that is, issues that are simultaneously global and local. Alongside a rigorous academic component, participants undertake a project that engages them in authentic learning experiences and enables them to put into practice what they have learned in the theoretical components of their leadership modules.

A key feature of the program is overseas and industrial trips. Participants are given an opportunity to visit a country within the Asia-Pacific region in order to study its education system. While there, they also visit the local industries of that country and are provided with the opportunity to observe the operational workings of the chosen organizations. The visits offer participants an alternative exposure to education systems and the running of different organizations.

The ministry is invested in expanding leadership opportunities for teachers at the system level and has announced that additional leadership positions will be created within the MOE. These positions will ensure that teachers on the leadership track have a voice in policy and program development, as well as practice, and are engaged in reform efforts across schools, not just their own setting. Teachers can apply for these positions and try them on for size in 2- or 4-year stints. The positions are available at the ministry and at the NIE, thus affording teachers the opportunity to affect the next generation of teachers as university instructors in preservice teacher preparation. After testing these particular leadership waters, if teachers decide against these pathways, they are welcome back into the classroom having expanded their perspectives and knowledge through engagement in diverse settings and activities.

The Specialist Track

The senior specialist track is for those teachers who are steeped in their discipline and choose this route to become a "strong core of specialists with deep knowledge and skills in specific areas in education (such as curriculum, planning, educational programs, and educational technology) that will break new ground and keep Singapore at the leading edge" (Teo, 2001, cited in Lee & Tan, 2010, p. 3). Their leadership role often takes them beyond the school to ministry headquarters, where they may be engaged with curriculum, applied psychology in education, and educational research, evaluation, and measurement. The ministry also sponsors postgraduate studies in these areas.

Shanghai's Career Ladder

Shanghai also has a well-developed career ladder. Teachers in China are formally classified into four grades or ranks: probationary status, second level, first level, and senior teacher. They progress from one grade to the next based on their professional competence and status among their peers. To be promoted on the rank scale, teachers are required to write a summary about their work in the previous few years, take written tests to show their language competence, write research papers on teaching, participate in an interview held by the district, and be observed by experienced teachers. Moving up the rank ladder for a teacher brings about a sense of professional accomplishment and pride. Teachers in a school readily know the grade category of other teachers and think of higher-ranked teachers as mentors and school leaders. For example, the head of a *jiaoyanzu* (teacher research group) will frequently be an experienced and accomplished teacher of a higher rank. Lower-rank teachers are typically beginning their careers.

To advance from one rank to the next, teachers submit an application at the district level. Applications typically include the teachers' current rank and all degrees they hold, an overview of school-based research work in which they are currently engaged, a list of awards and prizes, recognition of students' accomplishments, and a list of published research and papers. The school must approve the application first, which typically means the principal is in agreement that the teacher has the qualifications to apply. At the district level, a committee of experts—typically subject area coordinators or teacher professional development staff members who themselves have been recognized for their accomplished teaching—review the applications and make the decision about rank advancement.

The highest rank is a very rare honor: Just under 7% of teachers had achieved that level as reported in a 2010 study (Gang, 2010, p. 14). Between 40% and 50% of teachers had achieved each of the previous two ranks (first- and second-level teachers). The small remainder (less than 5%) were probationary teachers.

It might be surprising to many outsiders to see the amount of reliance on teacher research used in the promotions process. Yet, as discussed in Chapter 4, teachers' research on practice is a routine occurrence. During interviews for this study, teachers made reference to their research and what they had learned. In a national survey of more than 11,000 teachers, about 75% of the respondents reported having at least one publication of their own research, 30% had published four or more pieces of research, and 8% had published nine or more studies (Gang, 2010, p. 148). Some teachers hold the title of researching teacher and have positions in the district offices. Their job is to help coordinate and monitor the research happening in schools.

Highly ranked teachers are called on to support and guide veteran teachers who have not moved up in rank to assist in their improvement process. Professional learning opportunities for teachers are also structured for the different teacher rank levels to support them in moving up a career ladder. The principal of the Jiansulu Primary School in Shanghai described these opportunities as occurring at the school level, the district level, and then the municipal level:

> First, it sets up a platform for the school, which means offering opportunities for the teachers to grow, to have space. For instance, if you have several years of teaching experiences in the school and you are accomplished, then you have the opportunity to participate in district-level professional trainings for lead teachers. In the training, you could learn more through research projects and with guidance from experts of all sorts. Next, you will have the opportunity to attend trainings at the municipal level. At this level, there is a dual-prestige studio, or prestigious teachers and prestigious school studio, where you could obtain a more professional and focused support in learning. Such a space for growth actually is a strong incentive for teachers, who see the possibility of being promoted step by step. Besides the regular award system like senior instructor system in elementary and secondary schools, this serves as a great platform for teachers.

In addition to the formal career ladder within teaching, accomplished teachers, such as those who have won teaching competitions (see Chapter 4) or who are widely known for their research or mentoring, are often rewarded and publicly recognized for their knowledge, skills, and accomplishments. Teachers' awards and recognitions of accomplishment are frequent and are regularly communicated to the school community. Photos and accomplishments of teachers are routinely posted in

Figure 5–2 Award-Winning Teachers in School
Display at Pujian No. 2 Elementary School, Shanghai

the school hallways and on marquees that stand outside of the school buildings (see, for example, Figure 5–2). These awards are viewed as adding prestige to the whole school community. September 10 is, by law, national Teachers' Day, when teachers are celebrated across the nation and many award ceremonies are held to recognize accomplished teachers.

Australia's Teaching Career Stages

The teaching career in Australia is increasingly framed by the national professional standards for teachers, given their role in structuring initial teacher education, professional development, and its adoption into balanced scorecards for teacher evaluation. The national standards set out four career stages—graduate, proficient, highly accomplished, and lead—which most states are now using to construct career ladders with associated progression in salaries and, in some cases, reconfigured responsibilities.

By establishing the first of the four levels as that of graduate teacher, the standards connect expectations in teacher knowledge, practice, and engagement for new graduates with that of the profession. The establishment of proficient teachers as the second level, at which teachers move from provisional to full registration, lays the foundation for standards-based induction and mentoring for early-career teachers. The higher levels offer a pathway for teachers to continue developing their expertise and advance their career while remaining in the classroom. Highly accomplished teachers are those who demonstrate a high level of proficiency in the standards, and lead teachers are those who demonstrate these capabilities individually and show leadership across the school through highly effective teaching. As Tony Mackay, former chair of AITSL, explained (Link 5-2), the search is for a coherent system that can support learning:

> If you don't get a system of teacher quality and leadership quality thinking about all of the dimensions of [initial teacher education, pedagogy, leadership development], it's very hard to be able to drive forward an agenda that really is going to have some leverage over quality learning for all young people.

The federal government created a Rewards for Great Teachers program to support uptake of the standards and to provide financial rewards to accomplished teachers (COAG, 2012). The policy provides funds to participating states, territories, and system authorities that implement the Australian Teacher Performance and Development (ATPD) framework from 2013 and certify teachers against the benchmarks for highly accomplished and lead teachers under the Australian Professional Standards for Teachers framework (COAG, 2012). Participating states are required to have established a system for assessing and certifying these teacher levels and for establishing a performance and development cycle against the ATPD framework.

Although AITSL sets guidelines and provides templates for evidence gathering, assessment of whether teachers meet the requirements of the standards are determined by the state-based certifying authorities. (Illustrations of professional practice at each career stage, can be found at http://aitsl.edu.au/australian-professional-standards-for-teachers/ illustrations-of-practice/find-by-career-stage.) New South Wales, for example, has developed career pathways to enable teachers who demonstrate excellent performance to remain teaching and support the development of other teachers. These teachers are rewarded financially and professionally and have responsibility for providing leadership for professional learning. They engage in mentoring, school curriculum leadership, collaborative lesson preparation, evaluation, and teaching and are well positioned to observe practice and its effects so as to provide feedback to enable teacher professional learning within and across schools. They may lead pedagogical change efforts or professional learning initiatives.

New South Wales has revised its salary structure to tie remuneration to higher levels of professional accreditation based on the standards. Teachers receive significant increases in pay when they are accredited at the proficient standard, and they are paid a salary in excess of AU$100,000 when they achieve the highly accomplished and lead standard. (At the time of our research, the Australian dollar was roughly equivalent to the US dollar.) This reform has been undertaken with the full backing of the teachers' union, which is strongly supportive of more rigorous professional standards at entry and a system of advancement tied to standards throughout the career. As one union leader explained:

> We envisage that career restructuring with the highly accomplished and lead [categories] as enhancing the career structure, not destroying the salary scale. For those who want to stay in the classroom, you get to the top of the teaching scale and then you hit a ceiling. You don't want to go for a promotion, an administrative position, but you want to get some reward for the fact that you're mentoring young people. [So] you volunteer to be assessed against the standards [for an accomplished teacher]. If you meet the standards, you're deemed so, and then you attract further remuneration. You've got to keep meeting the standards, and you've got to be reassessed for continuation, i.e., reaccreditation, after five years. We signed up to all of that.

The system itself differs from state to state. Victoria has yet to adopt teacher certification at the two higher levels of the standards, and use of these designations is decided locally within individual schools. But in New South Wales, which has created a robust evidence-based system, candidates prepare a portfolio that shows evidence of how they have met each of the standards in their teaching, curriculum planning, and student learning. The nature of the evidence is geared to specific career stage they are in and seeking. For the highest level, the nature of the evidence changes from a classroom focus to a broader school focus, including the development of other teachers. Two external reviewers, trained to be able to assess in a reliable fashion, come to the candidate's school to see him or her teach and probe his or her knowledge of his or her students and pedagogical strategies. The review also includes an examination of the teacher's professional portfolio of evidence and references from school leadership. The system uses common standards, commonly administered in the portfolio requirements, and the observations of trained evaluators to determine promotions.

The union in Australia represents principals and teachers, and union leaders envision that over time these standards can apply to advancement into administrative roles as a means of creating a unified continuum in the profession and strengthening the quality of the work in schools. Although high-quality teaching is a critical element of effective school leadership, there is also widespread acknowledgment that the school leadership role requires expertise in a broad range of professional practices as articulated in the APSP. As one said:

> My view is that as a precondition to any promotion, I want you to at least satisfy the highly accomplished [standard]. You want to become a head of faculty or a deputy principal? At the very least, go through that validation process, which includes a component of external assessment. Put in your portfolios. Have the interviews. Be assessed. You want to become a principal? At the very least, be deemed that you're a lead teacher in terms of meeting these standards. Build in a quality control mechanism that has incredible additional positive effects.
>
> I think what we're going to be arguing is that there ought to be a system developed for promotion that brings those standards into play. For principals, we want to actually see if that person can teach children. We want to actually have someone go into the classroom and sit for a couple of hours and watch them: how they do it and respond to kids' needs and teach 30 children, not one class of 30, but 30 individuals, and how they program for all the different capacities of the kids. I passionately believe that you cannot be a good principal unless you are a good teacher. You just cannot be. You may be the best person at budgeting. You may be able to do the paperwork, the administration, everything that's required of you. You can talk the talk, but at the end of the day, you will fall short [if you cannot] teach children. If you can show as a principal that you can, [the staff members] will follow you to the ends of the earth.

This vision of a profession unified over growing expertise and common commitment to children characterizes the aspirations of many educators for the emerging career ladder structures in Australia.

Ontario's Support for Teacher Leadership

Ontario's career advancement opportunities for teachers are plentiful but less hierarchical. Teachers can advance through their career through a combination of experience, expertise, further training such as additional qualifications (AQs), and changes in assignments. Teachers can aim to move into a range of positions at school, board, and provincial levels, such as being an associate teacher to support teacher candidates in their practicum schools, becoming a mentor for newly qualified teachers, developing teacher leadership opportunities, participating in teacher federation or provincial organizations, and moving into school or board leadership positions. Boards also fund positions of additional responsibility, such as teacher coaches, board consultants, and department heads. In addition, there are new teacher opportunities linked to the ministry's student achievement initiatives, such as the Student Success Strategy (see Chapter 6).

The AQ programs aim to develop and recognize teachers' knowledge and expertise and to expand the knowledge and skills available to meet students' needs. For example, popular AQs include special education, English as a second language, and French as a second language. New AQs are also developed to keep current with latest needs and developments in education, such as integrating technology with pedagogy, creating inclusive classrooms, and understanding and supporting First Nations, Métis, and Inuit education. Recently, some AQ courses have become modularized to encourage greater participation and access, functioning rather like micro-credentials. As Susan Perry from Ontario English Catholic Teachers Association explained, a teacher may say, "This year I have three kids with autism, so I really want to learn more about autism." That teacher can study this very specific area to meet a particular need and expand her expertise, while also earning more money and becoming a contributor to her peers' learning.

In addition to funding teacher leadership positions for the student achievement strategy in schools and boards, the ministry also *seconds* (transfer an employee for a different, temporary assignment) experienced educators to work—usually on a time-limited basis—in the ministry to inform strategies and to support implementation in the education sector. Mary Jean Gallagher, former head of the student achievement division, explains how these strategies build a common vision for education in the province:

> So we go out and we find the people who are really good at what they do. They understand literacy and numeracy and improving instruction really well, in their school and in their Board, and then they come in and they work for three years, ideally, if we can keep them that long, in a group of different Boards. They get to see how things are done elsewhere, and learn with our internal staff, and we do a lot of development of our own staff. So they are not a group of independent operators out there; they are pretty closely connected on similar wavelengths, because we bring them in for discussions and modelling of what needs to go on. They grow so much in that three-year period. Then they go back, and we end up with new people working for us, but those old people are still working for us out there too. So we end

up with all of these people who really understand the work deeply and can lead their schools and their classrooms and their Boards in ways that make sense.

We are now at a point where we're beyond 25% of teachers who have come through student achievement roles, either student success leads out in the Boards or school effectiveness leads out in the Boards or staff that we have seconded and have gone back. It is all part of Ontario's growing focus and attention on the student achievement agenda.

Opportunities to Lead Professional Learning

As the designs of these leadership opportunities suggest, one important way for teachers to take on new roles is by leading the professional learning of their colleagues. Because much of the professional learning in high-performing systems takes place within schools, teacher leaders have a particular responsibility to organize the learning and support of their colleagues.

The support by teacher leaders starts with mentoring new teachers. As noted in Chapter 3, high-performing systems have structured induction programs in which mentors play an important role in acclimating new teachers to the school culture and providing them with instructional support. To ensure that the new teachers receive the support they need, the systems have clearly articulated the qualifications and responsibilities of mentors.

In Ontario, for example, mentorship is voluntary, although school administrators may invite individuals to take on the role to support a beginning teacher. Mentors must be an "excellent role model of a teaching professional," skilled in working with adults and students, knowledgeable about current curriculum and teaching-learning strategies, good problem-solvers and collaborators, effective listeners and communicators, able to use feedback, and lifelong learners. The province has a structured training program for mentors and provides them with release time to work with their mentees. Ontario sees the program as an informal way of developing teacher leaders.

Even more expansive is Ontario's Teacher Learning and Leadership Program (TLLP) (Link 5-3), launched in 2007 as a partnership between the Ministry of Education and the Ontario Teachers' Federation (OTF). The goals for the TLLP are as follows:

o Support experienced teachers in undertaking self-directed advanced professional development.

○ Develop teachers' leadership skills for sharing their professional learning and exemplary practices.
○ Facilitate knowledge exchange for spread and sustainability of practices.

The TLLP approach[1] is grounded in a commitment to "authentic learner led learning . . . by teachers, for teachers" (Campbell, Lieberman, & Yashkina, 2014, p. 65). Each year, experienced teachers—usually in teams—apply to conduct a TLLP project in which they take on an area of learning and then share their results with others. School board committees review applications and submit their priority choices to a provincial committee composed of teacher union and government representatives who select projects for funding. The most frequent focus areas for these projects have included differentiated instruction, technology, math, literacy, and professional learning communities. Most have included teacher collaborative learning, reviewing research, and engaging in research, in addition to other forms of professional learning and networking.

Prior to embarking on their TLLP projects, successful applicants attend a leadership skills for classroom teachers to support their preparation to take on the professional learning, project management, and leadership expectations of a TLLP. Throughout their TLLP project—and beyond—participants become part of Mentoring Moments, an online community to share resources, learning, and discussion and, at the end of their TLLP project, TLLP teams attend the Sharing the Learning Summit to showcase completed projects and to strengthen the spread and sustainability of practices.

Research on the outcomes of this initiative has found that large majorities of teachers reported improved instructional practices, including greater technological and assessment skills, as well as new knowledge and greater collaboration (Campbell, Lieberman, & Yashkina, 2015). Fully 97% of survey respondents indicated that the TLLP had supported development of their leadership skills. As one TLLP interviewee commented: "This is grassroots leadership at its finest. . . This has been some of the best and most rewarding work in my career" (Campbell, Lieberman, & Yashkina, 2015). Another said:

> The opportunity that this project gave me to utilize strategies dealing with collaboration, empowering others in the group, and motivating colleagues [who] were less confident than others at the outset of this project was incredibly valuable. Leading this project was the most useful leadership-based professional learning that I have been involved with in my teaching career.

The emphasis on knowledge exchange has supported teachers to de-privatize their practice and share their learning and practices across classrooms, schools, and districts, provincially and, in some cases, internationally. An analysis of recent projects found that the majority were sharing their learning through developing and providing professional learning sessions and also through the use of online media, including Twitter, blogs, and websites. Other forms of sharing included staff meetings, professional learning communities, conferences, modeling, mentoring, communications and publications, and events. TLLP teachers were also developing professional resources and materials including lesson plans, resource lists, assessment tools, and instructional materials.

To further spread sharing of practices, completed TLLP projects can be identified by a school board to apply for additional funding through the Provincial Knowledge Exchange (PKE) to provide resources and release time to enable sharing of practices from the TLLP with other schools in their board and school boards across Ontario. Most recently, Ontario's public broadcaster, TVO, has collaborated with advice from TLLP teachers to develop an online platform, Teach Ontario, where teachers can share their practice, explore research, collaborate on new projects, and access resources to support knowledge mobilization with, for, and by teachers across Ontario. Here is one example of how the knowledge exchange works.

The Provincial Knowledge Exchange (PKE) in Action

PKE began as part of a TLLP project in 2012 led by Kirsten Muscatt-Fennel when she was a primary junior teacher at Fieldcrest Elementary School in the Simcoe County District School Board (SCDSB). Kristen's passion for math encouraged her to bring the Balanced Math program to her classroom and the school. The program provides opportunities for modeled, guided, shared, and independent math experiences in an engaging, interactive learning community. Starting as a TLLP in one school, the Balanced Math program became a PKE involving 15 schools across SCDSB in 2013–2014. The PKE team, led by Kristen, includes her colleagues Darrell Bax, a special education resource teacher, and Stephanie Skelton, a grade 8 teacher at Fieldcrest Elementary School. The project has been strongly supported by current and past school principals as well as the board's superintendent of education.

The key learning goals of this PKE included growth in numeracy instruction and assessment using technology, strategies to enhance student achievement in the mathematical processes, and enhanced differentiation of instruction. The PKE supported a collaborative learning process in which the PKE team told teachers about the program and modeled use of resources and activities and provided practical resources for use by the participating teachers. Teacher participants observed the resources in use (through demonstration classrooms and as modeled by the PKE team). There were opportunities for teachers to co-plan and co-learn for their own use of the Balanced Math strategies. Each session built in time for the exchange of ideas and the co-planning of lessons.

The project team shared their learning using a wiki space designed to highlight a variety of instructional strategies and resources linked to the board's Essential Practices. Teachers also collaborated on the wiki space by uploading and exchanging resources, including lessons, assessment resources, tip sheets, and samples of student work. In addition, all teachers participating in the PKE received a resource binder, books, and materials for their own use in their classrooms and schools. Teachers were supported to apply Balanced Math in their own classrooms and to share their learning and resources with other staff members within and across their schools, thus further expanding the reach of the program. Teachers who participated in professional development became teacher leaders in their own right as they spread the knowledge to others. For further sharing of practices across the province, the PKE team has developed math tutorials as short video clips to be made available online.

Thus, a teacher leadership project beginning with three teachers became a districtwide program supporting hundreds and a resource for province-wide learning, as has often been the case with various TLLP initiatives.

Similarly, Singapore's career track system provides opportunities for highly capable teachers to lead professional learning within and across schools. The most prominent example of the role of teachers in leading professional learning is the AST as well as other subject-specific academies and language centers. These academies and language centers were founded, initially, to pull the master teachers together to support their learning and to enable them to chart, plan, and organize professional learning for others. There are currently 76 master and principal master teachers.

Cynthia Seto, a principal master teacher for mathematics currently assigned to AST, shared her view of the academy's role as facilitating the spread of good practice within and across schools:

I see the set of Academy of Singapore Teachers really encouraging teachers to take ownership and leadership of their professional development. It allows an opportunity for teachers to collaborate, to interact with teachers from another school. I was a senior teacher for seven years before I became a master teacher. . . In a particular school, we may have two or three senior teachers, but sometimes they are from different subjects, so we need to have a platform to know what other senior teachers are doing in their subject area. I feel that the academy is well situated to bring about this kind of collaboration, to spread good practices across schools.

Right now, my first goal as a master teacher is to raise the professional standards of the mathematics chapter of my mathematics master teachers. To do that, we conduct workshops [and] an opportunity for follow-up. . . I see myself as providing a catalyst to encourage teachers to form networked learning communities [NLCs] for us to talk further about what we are doing, for everyone to look at how can we incorporate strategies to help meet the diverse learning needs in our class for [children] to learn mathematics.

We could come together to co-design a lesson and then look at how it works in this classroom. Once the teachers observe it, we discuss. It may not be a perfect lesson, but it's an opportunity for learning. Teachers [may say], "Hey, I'm going to do something like that in my own class," and then they'll bring back their learning. It could be in the form of a video. It could be in the form of, "Oh, my students, this is what they have done." At the same time, "Oh, your school does this like that? Mine is like that. Oh, we could do something, you know?"

Shanghai's clearly articulated career ladder also provides opportunities for taking on leadership roles in professional learning. But as observers of that system have noted, the leadership can be implicit as well as explicit. The informal identification of teachers as "backbone teachers" in the *jiaoyanzu* is an example of this implicit form of leadership within the culture of teaching in China. Paine and Ma (1993) describe backbone teachers as

those who are more active in the activities of the *jiaoyanzu* and have a good reputation in teaching . . . backbone teachers contribute much to what and how the group works to improve its teaching quality. In effect they operate as assistants and resource people for the group head. When the group sets up a new program, typically they are the ones who will try it first. They also mentor or coach new teaches. If we think of the *jiaoyanzu* as a substantial level in the organization of a school, a backbone teacher should be seen as a substantial component of the group. (p. 680)

To some, the structure of the career ladder in China may seem hierarchical. To a large extent, there is a clear status difference in *jiaoyanzu* meetings, with less experienced teachers serving tea, not speaking as much as more experienced teachers, and sitting on the periphery. The head of the *jiaoyanzu* takes a central seat at the conference table, is the first person to provide feedback on a lesson, and summarizes all the feedback at the end of the meeting.

Yet, these different roles are a function of expertise rather than bureaucratic titles. As Paine and Ma (1993) explained of Chinese teacher relationships:

> Featuring Chinese teachers' working together, it is easy for one to see that they do not work in a democratic way. The principle of one person, one vote is not applied there. However, it seems not to be a static hierarchy either. A teaching research group leader or a backbone teacher does not have any legal authority. Their prestige does not allow them to dictate what another teacher must do. Such a teacher is considered an expert rather than a leader. Others will take advantage of their expertise as resources, rather than be passively directed by another teacher. The experts are at the center of an eddy rather than at the top of a ladder. (p. 689)

Recruiting and Developing School Leaders

School and system leadership roles provide another career pathway. High-performing systems actively recruit potential leaders, provide them with training and support, and guide them into their new roles. In these jurisdictions, advancing to higher levels of educational administration in schools, district or cluster offices, and state, provincial, or national ministries is typically also based on one's career accomplishments as a teacher. In Shanghai, for example, the OECD noted that

> almost all the officers in the government education authorities, both at municipal and district levels, started as school teachers. Most of them distinguished themselves as teachers or school principals with strong track records. This perhaps explains their devoted professional

attention to teaching and learning amidst all the administrative chores and political issues they normally contend with. They manage, however, to maintain this teaching focus while at the same time relying on a strategic vision that enables them to navigate a policy arena which goes well beyond education. (OECD, 2011, p. 89)

The Shanghai school principals we encountered in our study had achieved the highest rank as a teacher and talked proudly about their teaching accomplishments. They tended to link what they know about successful teaching to how they provided guidance to their school staff members and set a direction for the improvement of their school.

Similarly, in Finland, principals are typically selected from the ranks of accomplished teachers. By law, all school principals must be qualified teachers for the school they lead and must complete a specific course of academic training at the university. In most cases, this is done as part-time study while the person is teaching or working in the school. Some of the university programs are based on a peer-assisted leadership model, in which part of the training is done by shadowing and being mentored by the senior school principal.

Educational leadership operates from a locally rooted, capacity-building framework in Finland. As Andy Hargreaves and colleagues (2008) concluded in an analysis of leadership development in Finland,

> Leadership currently contributes to Finnish high performance . . . by paying attention to the conditions, processes and goals that produce high performance—a common mission; a broad but unobtrusive steering system; strong municipal leadership with lots of local investment in curriculum and educational development; teachers who already are qualified and capable at the point of entry; informal cooperation and distributed leadership; principals who stay close to the classroom, their colleagues, and the culture of teaching; and [from the principal's standpoint] being first among a society of equals in the practical and improvisational practice of school-based improvement. (Hargreaves, Halász, & Pont, 2008, p. 93)

Ontario's Leadership Strategy

Much more formal is the approach Ontario has developed for recruiting and preparing school leaders. The Ontario Leadership Strategy (OLS) (Link 5-4) is underpinned and informed by a research-based framework for leadership development (see Figure 5–3).

Figure 5–3 The Ontario Leadership Framework

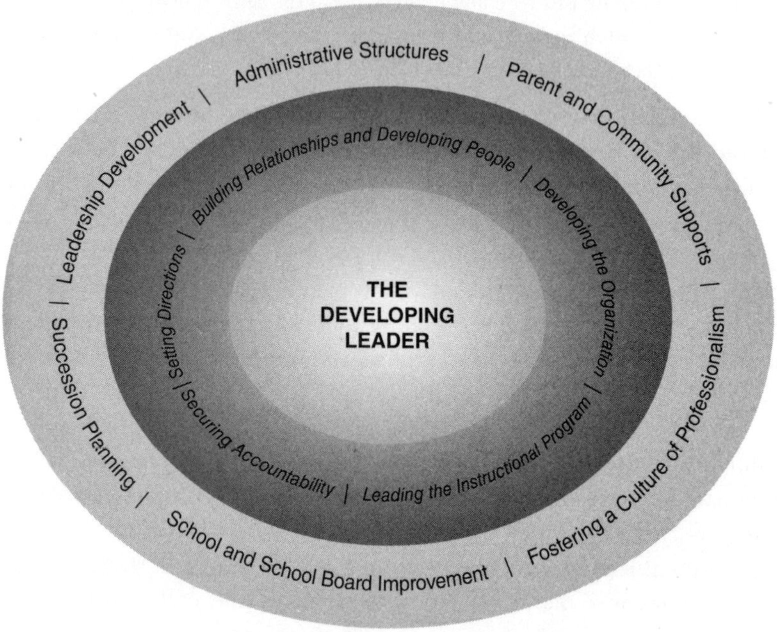

Source: Ontario Ministry of Education, Leadership Development Branch (2012).

Through the OLS, each school district in Ontario is provided with funding and support to develop and implement a board leadership development strategy (BLDS) that focuses on school and system leaders and all those within the district who aspire to take on leadership roles, whether on the academic or business side of the organization. The BLDS focuses on four key areas:

- *Recruiting and selecting leaders* through structured and innovative succession planning
- *Placing and transferring leaders* in ways that sustain school and system improvement
- *Developing leaders* through mentoring, performance appraisal, and differentiated learning opportunities that meet the needs of leaders in diverse contexts and at various stages of their careers
- *Coordinating support for leaders* to buffer them from distractions, make information easily accessible, and assist them in building coherence across different initiatives

Principals and vice principals in Ontario must attain principals' qualifications by completing the Principals' Qualification Program (PQP). Accredited by OCT and provided by faculties of education with principals' associations across the province, the program consists of two parts, each totaling 125 hours, plus a practicum. It is based on the Ontario Leadership Framework (OLF), which is a tool designed to foster an understanding of leadership and what it means to be a school and system leader, to make explicit the connections between leaders' influence and the quality of teaching and learning, and to guide the design and implementation of professional learning and development of school and system leaders. The framework contains core leadership practices to inform vice principals and principals in schools and supervisory officers in school districts. Based on this framework, the OCT (2009) set the following learning expectations for PQP candidates:

o Reflect on the standards of practice for the teaching profession and the ethical standards of practice for the teaching profession in relation to the principal's role.

o Establish a shared vision aligned with school board and provincial policies and initiatives.

o Expand leadership skills and knowledge required to shape school culture.

o Expand leadership and managerial skills related to the role of school administrator.

o Demonstrate curriculum leadership in facilitating the implementation and assessment of instructional programs to improve student achievement.

o Expand skills in managing human resources for the promotion of efficient and effective schools.

o Initiate, facilitate, and manage change.

o Expand knowledge of legislation and policy related to education in Ontario.

o Enhance the knowledge and skills needed to collaborate with parents, the community, and other educational stakeholders to meet the needs of students and advance the goals of education.

o Use current research, performance data, and feedback from students, teachers, parents, and community to make decisions related to improvement of instruction and student performance.

In addition to completing the PQP, principals must have an undergraduate degree, 5 years of classroom experience, qualifications in three divisions (administrative units) of the school system, and a master's or double-subject specialist degree. In Catholic boards, principals must also complete a specialist in religious studies.

Beyond the PQP, most board programs include a number of professional development seminars about leadership topics such as developing positive relations with parents, the link between leadership and student achievement, and work-life balance. Some programs also include a job-shadowing component where prospective administrators are placed with a practicing principal or vice principal. This enables those thinking about moving into leadership positions to get first-hand experience of the expectations and demands of such roles.

Administrators we spoke to had met all of these standards and engaged in the leadership training, finding it a valuable preparation for policy and practice. As one principal noted:

> The leadership development program was really valuable work in that we were all doing the internship at the same time. The debriefing of problems and the coming up with ideas of alternative solutions gave us a little support group to reach out to. The job shadowing was invaluable. I thought that that was one of the best things that the board did. I worked with my principal. He said, "Okay, you're just the fly on the wall. You are going to see whatever I do and follow along and we'll ask questions later," and I had the opportunity to do that once a month for 10 months, and that was really, really helpful.

As part of the Ontario leadership system, all principals and vice principals are also offered mentoring for their first 2 years in each role, funded by the ministry and delivered by school boards according to ministry guidelines. Features of the leadership mentoring program include training for mentors, a learning plan outlining how the mentor and mentee will work together, and a transparent matching and exit process to ensure a good fit between mentor and mentee.

Singapore's Leadership Track

In Singapore, leadership is seen as a key enabler for strong schools, and much attention and resources are given to identify and groom school leaders. Teachers with leadership potential are identified early and groomed for leadership positions. When teachers pursue the leadership track, they progress from teacher to subject head, head of department, vice principal, and then a principalship.

The process of being considered for a principalship is rigorous. Potential principals go through several rounds of interviews with senior management, including the permanent secretary, director-general, and divisional directors in MOE. They also undergo a leadership situation exercise, which is a 2-day intensive simulation test to gauge their leadership competencies and their readiness to take on leadership positions. After this selection process, they are required to attend a 6-month Leaders in Education Program (LEP) conducted by the NIE.

The LEP is an executive leadership program that exposes vice principals who have the potential to take on a principalship to challenging leadership experiences in the context of the school and beyond, including other industries. Participants have the opportunity to visit other countries and learn about their educational systems, structures, and the kinds of issues they are grappling with. The LEP also helps to shape the personal qualities for effective leadership and prepares participants to exercise curriculum and instructional leadership, meet the demands of school management, and establish effective stakeholder relationships with parents, the school board, and the public. Participants partner with and are mentored by experienced principals while they take courses at NIE. Beyond the LEP, new principals are given in-service training on governance, human resource management, financial management, and management of media. The placement of principals in schools is decided at the ministry, where they are matched to schools according to their leadership strengths and the profile and needs of the school.

Similar to teachers, principals are evaluated using the EPMS. They are assessed on their performance and leadership competencies. The evaluation also takes into consideration processes and results in the following areas: vision for the school, strategic planning and administration, development and management of staff members, and management of resources and school processes. They are also assessed on their overall school progress and performance, which includes student academic achievement as well as achievements in the nonacademic domains, such as arts and aesthetics, physical fitness and sports, social and emotional well-being, and student morale and leadership. These overall evaluations are used to determine their promotion and progression along the leadership track. Principals who are not performing well are counseled, coached, and, if need be, redeployed.

Principals who show strong leadership abilities and a broad vision for educational improvement are continuously evaluated for promotion to the level of cluster superintendent, and even a directorship within the Ministry of Education. Thus, Singapore aims to build a coherent system grounded in a common vision: strong, common training on shared goals and continual development of educational knowledge, skills, and talent.

Australia's Strategies for Leadership Development

There is widespread recognition in Australia of the fundamental impact school leaders have on teaching conditions, teacher learning, and through this the learning of students. The Australian Professional Standard for Principals (Link 5-5) provides a nationally consistent framework that defines what effective leaders need to understand and do to enable effective teaching and learning (see Figure 5–4). Developed through strong collaboration with professional associations, unions, and employers, the standard has strong professional validity and efficacy. The following key professional practices are identified in the standard:

- ○ Leading teaching and learning
- ○ Developing self and others
- ○ Leading improvement, innovation, and change
- ○ Leading the management of the school
- ○ Engaging and working with the community

Figure 5–4 Australian Professional Standard for Principals

Leadership context: school, local area, wider community, Australian, global.

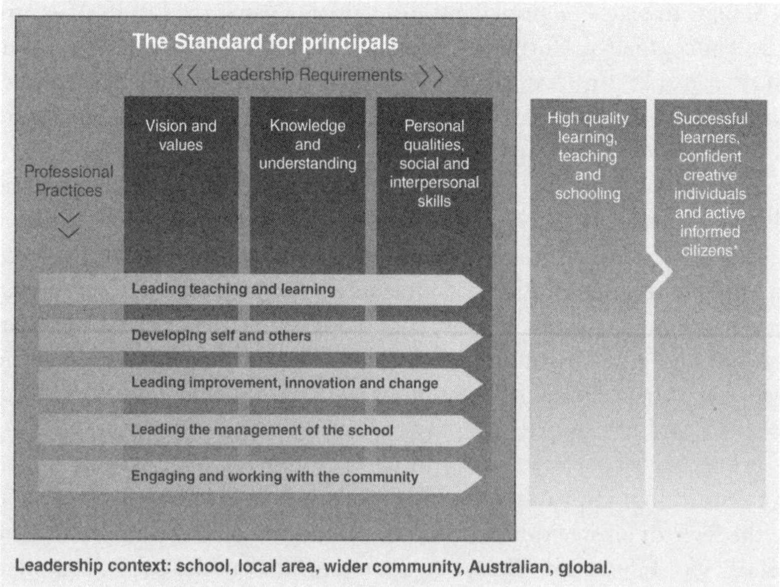

Source: AITSL (2015b).

These professional practices are underpinned by three areas of leadership requirements:

o Values and beliefs

o Knowledge and understanding

o Personal and interpersonal skills

The standard includes a set of leadership profiles that serve to guide the development of principals toward increasing proficiency. These are grouped according to three lenses—leadership requirements, professional practices, and leadership emphasis—and focused on the role of the principal in enabling and leading high-quality teaching and learning (see Figure 5–5).

The standard provides the basis for a more systematic, coherent evidence-based process for the development of school leadership capabilities. It also provides a clear framework for preparing and certifying principals, because it describes what principals need to know, understand, value, and do to effectively lead the continuous development of a school. Future developments in Australia include the development of a new national certification process. This process will require all new principals to become a "certified practicing principal." This process will include the development of a portfolio of evidence of their qualifications and demonstrated proficiency against the Australian Professional Standard for Principals.

Figure 5–5 Australian Professional Standard for Principals Leadership Lenses

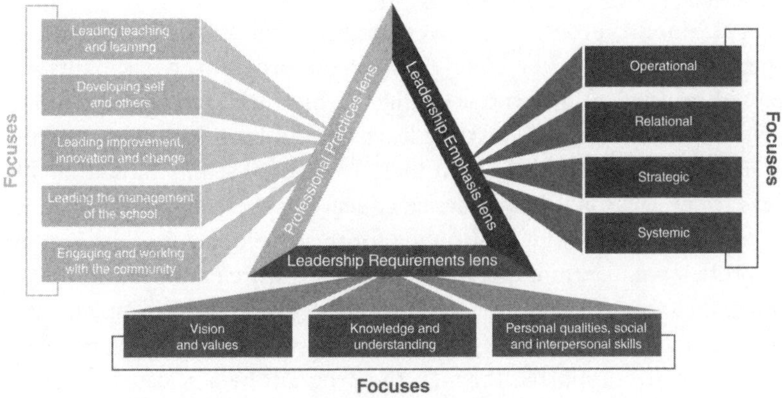

Source: AITSL (2015b).

New South Wales

In New South Wales, the Great Teaching, Inspired Learning reform heralded the development of principals' credentials, building on the continuum of professional learning programs New South Wales has offered leaders since 2005, including aspiring leadership programs, executive induction and development programs, and the Team Leadership for School Improvement program. The NSW professional learning and leadership development strategy was introduced to build the capacity of teachers and school leaders at each state of their careers. The NSW DEC Professional Learning Continuum mapped professional learning requirements from teacher preparation to school and system leadership. Each career stage was articulated in terms of the impact of the role for students, such as "making a difference in your classroom," "making a difference in your school," and "making a difference in the school next door."

An early example is the Principals Credential program that commenced in 2014 and is run by the NSW Primary Principals Association (PPA). It is based on the Australian Professional Standard for Principals and tied to the key professional accountabilities of school leaders, including transparency of education processes and outcomes and the need to personalize learning to ensure all students succeed. The program has two pathways. One pathway is for excellent teachers and school administrators who aspire to school leadership. Another pathway provides professional learning and credentialing for current principals who seek to review their leadership practices and drive improvement innovation and change. This program has been aligned to a master's of educational leadership degree, and it is envisioned that the program will inform future credentialing in New South Wales.

The 18-month program involves the formal assessment of evidence of performance. As a key component of the program, participants are required to drive an innovative change within their school and develop an e-portfolio as evidence of their learning and leadership impact. Formal learning is provided through three residential seminars that enable access to international best practice educational research and thinking. The seminars also provide scaffolding for the development of a personalized professional learning plan and a school research and learning plan. Participants work in collegial, collaborative groups in the implementation of individual action projects and their professional learning plan. Participants are supported through the program by a selected group of highly competent, practicing principals who have strong expertise in professional learning. Completion of the program, the assessment of the portfolio evidence, the presentation of an executive summary document and seminar, and refereed validation lead to recognition of leadership capacity and the award of the NSW PPA credential. These participants are also assessed to have achieved 50% of the Master of Educational Leadership program.

Participants in the 2014–2015 program gave it strong reviews (NSW Primary Principals Association, 2015) and described its value for developing their leadership skills of analysis, review, and collaboration. As Jodi Bennett, the assistant principal of Oxley Park School, stated in her validation review panel:

> I have learnt to stop and think: What is the data that [are] helping us to understand what we need to do and why? What is the evidence that informs me of the best next steps to take, and how can we work together in collaboration to ensure that in the end we are able to make a real difference for our students? I understand that our context matters greatly and that we need to establish a model for our team and work out how we can align our resources to achieve what we need to achieve.
>
> We have been breaking down those classroom walls to see teachers as leaders of learning working together to make a difference with our children. We are now able to work together and study our work, use our learning continuum, and provide each other with feedback. We needed to develop trust and focus on our learning together. The teachers can now clearly state what they are learning from their collaborative examination of their teaching. For teachers to go beyond their school gate and learn from other teachers in other schools is a great source of professional learning. I have had this opportunity to connect with other teachers in other schools through this program and the power of these professional networks for my learning has been great and I want other teachers to have this opportunity.
>
> One of the key elements of this program has been the leadership challenge. The challenge has provided a focus that I needed to see through, and through implementing the challenge, I have needed to focus on my growth as a leader. If you want to grow, if you want to be accountable, and if you want to be forced to examine your practice, this is the program for you (Bennett, 2015).

Victoria

In New South Wales and Victoria, school and system leadership are seen as key drivers of increased school performance. Featuring the greatest decentralization of schools of any state in Australia, Victoria's commitment to self-managing schools tasks principals with a tremendous number of responsibilities. These include resource allocation within the school, accountability to the community and the Department of Education and Training (DET) for continual improvement in student learning, and personnel management, including teacher performance assessment and professional learning planning. Principals must be adept organizational and financial managers and have strong instructional leadership skills. Thus the success of the self-managing schools model in Victoria depends in good measure on the ability of the state to maintain a steady flow of, and effectively train, aspiring school leaders. The DET has therefore begun developing a new talent identification system that will work with school networks to identify potential talent and draw new candidates into leadership training programs.

DET views leadership capability as representing a set of knowledge and skills that can be learned and developed over time rather than a fixed set of attributes (Matthews, Moorman, & Nusche, 2007). This was reflected in the department's 2007 Developmental Learning Framework for School Leaders (leadership framework), which identified five domains of the knowledge, skills, and dispositions of effective school leaders to create the conditions for quality teaching and learning (DEECD, 2012a; DET, 2007), including technical leadership, human leadership, educational leadership, symbolic leadership, and cultural leadership. Each was further elaborated into a set of leadership profiles with descriptors of increasing proficiency across each domain. This framework has now been superseded by the Australian Professional Standard for Principals.

Given the importance of the development of leadership capabilities to school improvement in Victoria, the state has maintained a level of investment in the direct provision of leadership training, primarily through the Bastow Institute of Educational Leadership—a specialized leadership training institute that is housed within the DET.

The Bastow facility itself is impressive. The building façade is the red brick original school building of State School no. 307 founded in 1882, one of the first school sites in Melbourne. In sharp contrast, the recently renovated interior is a spectacular piece of modern architecture with ceiling-high glass window panels connecting at oblique angles. There are courtyards and standing tables in purpose-designed, open-plan conversational spaces. The basement houses a fully electronically networked lecture theater, capable of seating about 100 people, while simultaneously webcasting to many more. The building itself is perhaps emblematic of where the government sees it has a strong direct lever in school improvement and of the way a tradition of school education can be married with a forward-looking vision for education. As Bastow director Bruce Armstrong explains (Link 5-6):

> It's symbolic of your employer investing in the development of your knowledge, skill, and disposition to lead and teach . . . to say . . . "we value you." It was to be symbolic both in its infrastructure, and with how we conceptualize change at a school level or system level. . . There's this wonderful, contemporary, modern, forward-looking fit-out, and I think it's saying that if you're to be a leader, you have to have a futures perspective.

Since its opening in 2009, Bastow has had 7,000 teachers and principals undertake training at the facility, making it the largest provider of educational leadership training in the state (interview with C. McKenzie, Bastow Institute Research and Development director, May 30, 2014).

Bastow's current course structure is based on a career-stages approach:

○ **Emerging leaders:** *Impact* for teachers in their first 3 to 5 years of teaching

○ **Middle leaders:** *Create* for teachers leading teams in schools

○ **Aspiring principals:** *Unlocking Potential* for assistant principals or leading teachers

○ **New principals:** *Evolve* for those new to principalship

○ **High-performing principals and retired principals:** Courses from principal coaching to master's degrees in instructional leadership designed for those have the potential to be system leaders

Each of these programs is intended to be contiguous with the next. It is anticipated that by identifying potential leaders earlier, they can be staircased into ongoing leadership training at Bastow at various points throughout their career. DET has developed a new system for the identification of leadership talent within the state. From 2014 through 2015, it expects to train several new cohorts: up to an additional 400 teachers as emerging leaders; 200 middle leaders, teachers who are already working in leadership roles in the school; 100 aspiring principals to complete a principal preparation program; 200 existing principals, providing them with specialized coaching; and 80 high-performing principals as network leaders (DEECD, 2013b).

The curriculum at Bastow was developed in 2009 following a research exercise that drew on school leadership research internationally. It combines the described leadership model with elements of the teaching for understanding framework of Harvard's Project Zero, emphasizing a "performances of understanding" approach in which learning can be represented and expressed multiple ways. Course curricula are also being updated to incorporate the Australian Professional Standard for Principals.

Leadership trainees are encouraged to attend in pairs or teams to reinforce learning beyond the institute, and courses are structured so as to help principals translate the skills they learn in course workshops back into the school setting. As described by director Armstrong:

> One of the big shifts in our courses from pre-Bastow to Bastow was that people would need to come and go through performance assessments. And it was within action learning, so you'd learn a little bit, [then] you'd go back to your site. You'd have a challenge project or a school-based change project or a peer-led project that you would identify, looking at your school context, and needs, and stage of development. Then you'd come back [to Bastow] and talk about your learning and there'd be a formal and information assessment and feedback.

Recently, Bastow has sought to form closer partnerships with universities in leadership development, enabling leadership trainees to receive university credit for some of their course work through the institute. This move serves to support content rigor and access to university knowledge for Bastow as well as providing a mechanism for leadership trainees to reengage with universities and perhaps go on to complete graduate-level qualifications. For example, some units in instructional leadership will be taught by faculty members from Melbourne Graduate School of Education (MGSE), and participants can receive credit for these toward MGSE's master of instructional leadership. Bastow has also entered into a credit transfer arrangement with Monash University for its master of leadership program, a 1-year program aimed at principals and middle leaders.

The Master of Instructional Leadership Program

The Bastow Institute provides a limited number of scholarships for a master of instructional leadership program offered through the University of Melbourne. Principals studying with Bastow may credit specified courses toward the program, which focuses on principals' use of evidence to understand the impact of teaching in their school on student learning, fostering teacher collaboration, and sharing teaching practices to drive school improvement. The course, taught largely over weekends and school holidays over 1 to 2 years, begins by teaching principals how to use school data to calculate effect sizes at the level of classrooms and grades and down to individual students. Principals then study how to interpret the impact they have as instructional leaders on student learning and how to work with staff members in the school to raise their effectiveness.

Professor John Hattie, one of the course instructors, explained that a key challenge for principals is how to make these data available and visible to staff members (Link 5-7) in a way that is nonthreatening and can be used to establish a common conception or standard for progress in student learning:

> The one [method] that I use the most is the bookmark method. We have a levels-based curriculum, not a years-based curriculum, which makes this a lot easier. We ask the teachers to bring out artifacts of kids' work. . . We get them to place two pieces of work, a pre and a post, usually over eight to ten weeks. We ask the teachers to first individually put it across a [curricular] line, then have a debate [on student progress]. And then they go back and do it again as a group. The role of the principal is to moderate that debate. If you get it wrong, teachers will never do this exercise again, because you're questioning their judgment. It's a massive skill. I take them through simulations on how to do this, point out the traps that you fall into, and get them to understand what happens.

The course also looks at how principals can create learning communities within the school and improve instructional practice. As Hattie further notes, the emphasis is on school leaders harnessing teacher knowledge and expertise that may already be present in the school:

> I think we have to stop the days [when] we expect everybody in the school to be expert at everything. One of our tasks is to say to them, "If you [as principal] don't have that, you've got 20 or 30 other people in your school. . . Your job is to create the right narrative, not necessarily do everything. . . I think the mistake is that we think that a teacher's an expert with [everything]—we haven't got enough money for that.

Bastow has also begun to offer courses in coaching for school leadership teams. This typically includes the principal, assistant principal, and other senior teachers. The leadership team studies together at the institute, looks at their own school's data, seeks to develop their teamwork, and designs an improvement project for their school. Director Armstrong explains that by working with the whole leadership team at once, it has the potential to change school cultures:

> It's very powerful because that's when you start to get not [just] little pockets of reform in one or two teachers' classrooms. Often the prevailing organizational structures or cultures can [militate] against innovation and reform in a school and can be exhausting for teachers, and they give up. By bringing everybody together with a sense that we're going to lead this together, you get this whole school endeavor, which I think is absolutely critical.

Beyond its offerings through the Bastow Institute, DET provides an induction toolkit for new principals, online learning modules, and partners with professional associations to provide a range of professional learning opportunities. For example, the Principals as Literacy Leaders (PALL) program, developed by the Australian PPA, was offered through the Victorian Principals' Association. The 5-day program focuses on the use of data and evidence to evaluate school literacy needs and enhancing principals' capacity to build and lead professional learning communities for improving literacy in their school. The DET provided funding to subsidize the program and funded 10 hours of ongoing coaching to support principals in implementing the program in their schools.

In these myriad ways, the development of teacher leaders, school leaders, and leadership teams strengthens school capacity in Australia and in the other jurisdictions we studied.

Lessons Learned

High-performing systems view teaching as a profession, one that is attractive to enter and remain in and one that offers rewards—intrinsic and extrinsic—to those who excel. In doing so, the systems help ensure that well-qualified individuals go into teaching, thus enhancing the respect for the profession throughout society.

As people in other professions do, teachers in these systems take on additional responsibilities based on their interests and abilities. This is valuable for teachers: It enhances their interest in teaching and keeps them stimulated. At the same time, it is valuable for the education system: It distributes leadership and enables teachers to play important roles in building the capacity of their fellow teachers. In that way, the career-ladder structures are integral parts of the human capital systems in high-performing systems.

The policies and practices described here differ from country to country, but they share some common themes:

Career paths enable teachers to take on leadership roles. Teachers know the opportunities they have to advance in the profession and what they have to do to move ahead. They have choices and can follow their interests. They can remain in their schools, take on additional learning opportunities, or work on policy. In some countries this is a very formal progression; in others, less formal. In all, however, teachers' roles and opportunities to share their skills evolve as they continue in their career.

Teacher advancement is tied to professional learning. The career paths serve as a key component of the learning systems. Knowledgeable and experienced teachers lead professional learning for newer teachers. They become part of the school leadership team and help manage instructional leadership in the school and, in some cases, beyond the school.

Leadership development is intentional. High-performing systems proactively recruit prospective leaders and provide them with support and learning opportunities to take on leadership roles. They seek strong teachers with knowledge of instruction and a demonstrated ability to lead adult learning as well as student learning. They provide the same kind of clinical experiences for prospective leaders that they provide for prospective teachers so that leaders can be prepared for their jobs from the day they start.

The practices described in this chapter and the previous two represent a complete system. They are designed to complement one another. Strong recruitment policies help ensure that well-qualified individuals enter teaching, but these will only be effective if there are opportunities for teachers to grow and advance in the profession. Strong preparation programs help ensure that teachers begin their careers well qualified, but professional learning helps teachers continue their learning and growth throughout their career. Career paths provide opportunities for teachers to lead professional learning and grow into leadership positions. Such pathways also provide opportunities to "bend" the professional continuum so that experienced teachers come back around to the start of the career with novices whom they mentor and support (Sato, Roehrig, & Donna, 2010).

Yet although these practices have enabled high-performing systems to demonstrate high levels of student learning, the systems are not resting.

They are learning organizations themselves; they are continuing to study their systems, determine what is working and what needs improvement, and make changes when necessary.

NOTE

1. This is a video profiling the TLLP: http://www.youtube.com/watch?v=3DCi HTSaZu8&feature=youtube.

6

PERSEVERANCE IN THE PURSUIT OF EQUITY

HIGH-PERFORMING SYSTEMS NOT ONLY attain high average levels of performance on international tests but their performance is equitable as well. That is, the gaps between the high and low performers in each system are relatively narrow. Thus these systems manage to raise the floor even while they raise performance overall.

This is no accident. These high-performing systems have put in place policies and practices designed to support historically low-performing students and groups of students. And, as their success makes clear, these efforts have not come at the expense of high-performing students. Equity and excellence are not a zero-sum game: They reinforce one another. This is because teacher quality policy is a critical component of a larger system driving toward equity—and because policies supporting a broader equity agenda enable capable teachers to accomplish their goals with the supports that they need.

These policies take several forms. First, the high-performing systems have taken substantial policy and funding steps to invest in children's welfare, and they work to provide resources equitably so that all schools have adequate services, teacher salaries, and working conditions, and schools with students with high needs receive additional support. This may take the form of additional funding, special programs, training, or specialized staff members. As a result, teachers in all schools have many supports they need to teach their students effectively.

Second, these systems recruit and support teachers and leaders for high-needs students and schools. The systems create strong incentives to place well-qualified educators in schools with the greatest needs—often with special preparation to teach well in students' particular cultural contexts.

Third, the systems train all educators in equity pedagogies—strategies to address disparities and meet the needs of diverse learners—and construct curriculum that will support greater success for underserved groups. They recognize that one size of teaching does not fit all, and they ensure that schools and teachers are prepared to address the learning needs of all students, including immigrants and migrants, special education students, and those from historically underserved groups.

Finally, the systems create school improvement strategies that continually improve teaching and learning; within these, they target resources and supports to students and schools with the greatest needs.

This chapter examines the equity-related policies and practices in high-performing systems. These augment the foundation laid by seeking to ensure uniformly well-prepared teachers to all schools—itself a form of equity—by giving these teachers and schools the range of tools they need to address diverse students' distinctive needs. This, in turn, makes it more likely that teachers, being supported, will stay in these schools. We describe features of these policies that are unique to each country, and we underscore themes that are common to all countries.

Resourcing Student Learning

At the heart of educational equity is the availability of resources: ensuring that all students, regardless of where they go to school, have adequate opportunities to learn what they are expected to learn. In that respect, equity ensures that all children have the outside-of-school conditions that enable them to thrive and the conditions in schools that ensure access to strong programs, well-qualified teachers, and positive school climates that enable students to feel safe and supported while also supporting teachers to stay and develop their professional careers.

Supporting Children's Welfare

In practice, this means that governments ensure that children are healthy, housed, fed, and have access to good early care and learning opportunities as well as being well supported in school. In the jurisdictions we studied, these investments in children's welfare were quite substantial.

Finland's social democratic system offers free health care for all citizens and a policy framework that supports sources of housing and income for all families. Beyond these foundational resources, there are special investments in the welfare of children: Since the 1930s, on the occasion of the birth of a new baby, the Finnish government has provided every new mother with a cardboard box filled with clothes, sheets, toys, diapers, and other essential items. The box even includes a small mattress, and the box can actually serve as a simple crib (and often does for many newborns). The intention of the box is to ensure that all children in Finland have an equal start—but it serves also as a symbol of the centrality of equity for children in Finland (Lee, 2013).

In addition to the baby box, Finland offers an equally good start to schooling for every child: A long parental leave system that provides income to stay-at-home parents guarantees that parents can remain home with the child until the infant is a year old. All children in Finland have access to high-quality and safe early childhood programs that are heavily subsidized by public authorities. Preschool, offered to all at age 6, is free. Well-qualified professionals in this system work closely with parents to deeply understand and support the process of child development; when the child transitions to primary school, these professionals ensure that educators there are made aware of each child's needs and interests so that their healthy development continues without interruption. The notion of caring for students educationally and personally is also central principle in the schools. All students receive a free meal daily as well as free health care, transportation, learning materials, and counseling in their schools so that the foundations for learning are in place (Sahlberg, 2007).

Other high-performing systems also provide a range of social and health benefits for children and families. They help ensure that children arrive at school with the support they need to be ready to learn. In Australia, there is a strong awareness that the well-being of the whole child is essential and is a fundamental requirement of social policy. Core national services that are designed to provide a safety net to underpin child well-being in Australia include health and social security support services. Since the 1970s, the Australian government has funded a universal public health insurance scheme to provide free or subsidized health treatment. The government also provides a range of social security payments and services, including income supports, youth allowances, study allowances, and rental assistance that support children and families. This system is among the strongest family safety nets in the world.

Canada also provides health and social services for children and youth. Each province in Canada has mandatory and universal health care coverage. The health care delivery and financing system is a mixed public-private system, but the public sector provides 70% of the funding. Canada also provides direct financial support to families with children, with greater payments to low-income families. Under the Canada Child

Tax Benefit, the federal government provides monthly payments to families with children. In addition, the government provides the Universal Child Care Benefit, which helps families with children under 6 pay for childcare and early education.

In Singapore, the government provides extensive subsidies for health care, which is universally available, and housing: About 80% of the population lives in clean, safe, and well-designed publicly supported housing estates that typically are also connected to a well-equipped school. Early childhood care and education are increasingly supported with subsidies from government and businesses and staffed by professionally trained teachers.

Financing Schools

In addition, the governments we studied all work on creating equitable systems of schools. Finland's education finance system is founded on this principle. Ninety-eight percent of the cost of education at all levels is covered by the government, which creates a strong, equitable foundation for access and quality. Although education is mostly funded by local municipal taxes (about two-thirds of the total), the central government provides funding to boost the resources available in municipalities with lower levels of wealth. In doing so, the Finnish National Board of Education uses an equalizing formula that takes into account specific needs of the region and attends to any differences in wealth so that districts all gain the support they need (Link 6-1). Some districts are heavily supported by government subsidies; meanwhile, others are able to support their work largely through municipal funding. This calculation and effort to equalize funding means that the wealthier districts do not end up with an unequally high proportion of funding. Government subsidies to municipalities are not earmarked—which means that locally elected politicians and school boards in municipalities decide how the overall local budgets will allocate resources to education and other public services.

Alberta's funding system is based on a similar principle, but the finance system is somewhat more complicated because the government provides funding for private schools and Catholic as well as for public schools. Funding for the education system in Alberta (Link 6-2) comes from general government revenues, which make up about two-thirds of the funding, and education property taxes, which fund the remainder of the K–12 education budget (Alberta Education, 2016). All of the money is collected centrally and allocated by the Ministry of Education in Alberta. Funds for staffing are protected; otherwise, local school boards and school district authorities have considerable flexibility in determining how to best use these resources.

In addition to base funding—determined on a per-student basis in grades K–9 and a per-credit basis in grades 10–12—differential funding is allocated to support students with severe disabilities, English as a second language instruction, French language and enculturation (Francisation), First Nations, socioeconomic status, northern (geographic reach) funding, learning resources, transportation, and plant operations and maintenance funding. Targeted funding is provided for special school improvement initiatives, as well as for things such as technology and capital funding. Although local school boards can get approval to levy a special school tax, it can comprise at most 3% of the board's budget for a given year (School Act, 2000). This ensures that if a board does choose to raise money locally, the amount does not significantly undermine the broader equality and equity principles of the funding system.

Similarly, in Ontario, the provincial government provides funding to compensate for discrepancies in local taxing capacity. Currently, the Ontario Ministry of Education provides funding to school boards (Link 6-3) through a series of annual grants for student needs (Government of Ontario, 2015). In 2013–2014, these grants consisted of a pupil foundation grant (teacher salaries, educational assistants, textbooks, learning supplies, and library and guidance services); a school foundation grant (principals, vice principals, secretaries, office supplies); 12 special purpose grants (special education, First Nations, learning opportunities, safe schools, facilities, student transportation, etc.); and debt service (interest expense), which totaled a projected $20.8 billion. These grants are distributed equitably to ensure that all districts are able to provide comparable student programming, with additional funding available to high-needs schools. Most categories are broad in scope and boards have discretion in determining the direction and focus of the allocations in each area.

Similar to Canada, Australia has long had a state-run education system, but the national government began to provide funding for schools in 1964, first for science laboratories, then for libraries, and then, in 1970, for ongoing support. In 2008, the federal government began to take a stronger role in education funding and policy with the Melbourne Declaration on Educational Goals for Young Australians, signed by the education ministers of all nine states, territories, and the federal government. The Melbourne Declaration was explicitly focused on equity and on eliminating disparities in opportunity to learn across states (MCEETYA, 2008).

One outcome of the Melbourne Declaration was the creation of the Review of Funding for Schooling, named the Gonski Report (Link 6-4) after the chair of the panel who wrote it, David Gonski, a prominent businessman and philanthropist. The report recommended comprehensive changes in the balance and alignment of funding between state governments and the Commonwealth, and between government and nongovernment schools (Gonski, Boston, Greiner, Lawrence, Scales, & Tannock, 2012). The core principle was a movement to needs-based funding on a per-student basis, rather than on historical spending patterns and to add "loadings" for students with a disability, from a low SES background, who are Aboriginal or Torres Strait Islander, have a low level of English proficiency, or who come from a remote school or one not located in a major city. These allocations are intended to provide greater resources to students who may require more support. As Gonski said in a 2014 speech to the Australian College of Educators:

> One of the easiest decisions we [the review panel] were able to take is what we as a review team believed "equity" should mean in determining a suitable funding system in Australia. We felt strongly and unanimously that a funding system must ensure that differences in education outcomes are not the result of differences in wealth, income, power, or possessions. Flowing from this, a funding system based on need was both obvious and important. (pp. 14–15)

The Australian government committed to the core recommendations of the review and pledged 6 years of a funding model in which signatory states would increase funding by $1 for every $2 increased by the federal government. As the terms of the review required that no school receive less money as an outcome, it also recommended a significant increase in funding in real terms (Gonski et al., 2012). The National Partnership for School Improvement was released in 2013 under the banner of "Better Schools." State governments signed onto the plan in June 2013, and the funding scheme was included in the Australian Education Act 2013, signed into law shortly before the national election in September 2013, which took effect on January 1, 2014.

However, following a change of federal government in the election that year, the new administration initially committed to just 1 year of funding. This was later increased to 4 years of funding (to 2018) following significant protest from state governments, which had already budgeted on the basis of increased funding from the Australian government. Decisions about the level of investment in the plan after 2018 are still being made, but the needs-based framework has been established. The states of New South Wales and Victoria have introduced a needs-based funding model for schools in an attempt to address the issues of resource inequity for students from less-advantaged backgrounds. In addition, a recent state-level funding review in Victoria has recommended further strengthening equity funding by introducing new resources to support underperforming students (based on NAPLAN scores in year 5) and new resources and initiatives for students who are at risk of disengaging with school or who have already dropped out (Bracks, 2015).

Similar to Canada and Australia, Chinese provinces are largely responsible for funding schools and the national government allocates additional resources—about 17% of the total—to bring up spending in the lowest-wealth areas. In Shanghai, which is one of the wealthiest provinces, the Municipal Education Commission also employs strategies to help equalize funding between the more-advantaged urban schools and less-advantaged rural schools within the province. It sets a minimum threshold for per-student funding, and it provides funds to schools in rural areas to invest in infrastructure, materials, and teacher salaries (Cheng, 2011). As part of its equity efforts, Shanghai was the first jurisdiction to disestablish "key schools," essentially model schools that received a higher level of funding, more qualified teachers, and selective admission practices, in order to invest more equitably in all of its schools.

The Municipal Education Commission is also making an effort to expand education for migrant students who live in Shanghai but are registered to another province (through the Chinese *hukou* system, which registers citizens to their home province, where they are entitled to receive services). It has sought to expand access to public schools for migrant students, rather than requiring them to attend only private schools designated for migrant students. In addition, the Municipal Education Commission has announced that it will help supplement the funding these private schools receive from the national government when they are registered as a school serving a province where its migrant population is from.

Singapore's school history is fairly unique among these nations: It inherited a mix of private and religious schools on independence and then built a public system around these, gradually incorporating private schools into the public system in ways designed to enhance equity. Expanded investments during the 1990s improved and equalized public school conditions and curriculum and allowed greater access to diverse educational pathways. Regardless of the school, primary education is now free to all, and the government offers funding for tuition, textbooks, and uniforms to those in any school—including independent or autonomous schools—who cannot pay for them.

Because the public housing estates where most Singaporeans live are organized to be racially or ethnically integrated, and because well-resourced schools are attached to each estate, the government schools are also substantially integrated and offer a high-quality education across communities. Respondents in Singapore noted that the government schools are considered generally of high quality—and are viewed as very desirable by most families, including those who are affluent.

Higher education is now available to virtually all Singaporeans. Higher education is heavily subsidized so that tuitions are low, and need-based aid is available to make up any difference between what families can afford and the costs of a program students have been admitted to. Virtually everyone completes some postsecondary education. About 75% of young people complete postsecondary education in a college or a polytechnic, and nearly all of the remainder go on to pursue vocational education at the well-resourced institutes of technical education, which give them a certificate or a diploma in fields that enable them to find employment in the many multinational companies and industries that are based in Singapore.

A history of Singapore notes how the combination of an egalitarian ethos with a goal of integrating diverse ethnic groups is joined with a meritocratic culture in a unique blend that has created the nation's unusually strong and increasingly equitable educational outcomes.

> More clearly than any other social institution, the school system expressed the distinctive vision of Singapore's leadership, with its stress on merit, competition, technology, and international standards, and its rejection of special privileges for any group. Singaporeans of all ethnic groups and classes came together in the schools, and the education system affected almost every family in significant and profound ways. Most of the domestic political issues of the country, such as the relations between ethnic groups, the competition for elite status, the plans for the future security of the nation and its people, and the distribution of scarce resources were reflected in the schools and in education policy. . . It was in the schools, more than in any other institution, that the abstract values of multiracialism and of Singaporean identity were given concrete form. (LePoer, 1989, p. 116)

Recruiting and Supporting Teachers in High-Needs Schools

In addition to their efforts to provide an even start for children and equitable funding for schools, high-performing systems also take affirmative steps to recruit and support teachers in high-needs schools. This is made easier when government funding is structured to allow local schools or districts to offer comparable salaries and working conditions to educators. In places where this is not the case, as in most parts of the United States, there is evidence that teachers tend to gravitate toward schools with students from more advantaged socioeconomic backgrounds, in large part because the unequal funding system often enables these schools to offer better salaries, facilities, and working conditions, including smaller class sizes, more up-to-date and plentiful materials, and more supportive leadership (Borman & Dowling, 2008; Johnson, Kraft, & Papay, 2012; Ladd, 2011; Loeb, Darling-Hammond, & Luczak, 2005).

Even where salaries and working conditions are equitable, there are other factors that operate in the labor market: It is harder to recruit employees to remote areas or other communities that have fewer amenities and more social or economic challenges. It is also often more difficult to recruit educators to contexts farther from where they grew up or went to school or where they have less cultural familiarity or linguistic expertise to communicate with children and families.

To ensure that all students, particularly those with the greatest needs, have access to high-quality teachers, high-performing systems create incentives and other programs to ensure a more equitable distribution of excellent teachers:

o Educator assignment and promotion policies
o Incentives for teaching in high-need schools
o Preparation for teaching effectively in specific high-needs locations

Assignment and Promotion Policies

In Singapore, teachers are hired by the ministry when they are accepted into teacher education, and they are paid a salary while receiving their preparation, which is funded by the ministry. When they complete preparation they are expected to serve in the school system for at least 3 years or repay the cost of their education. Teachers are assigned to schools where they are needed. School postings are determined by the Ministry of Education depending on person power needs; the ministry then recruits teachers according to vacancies in schools and in response to shortages in specific subject areas. This arrangement benefits the schools, which are assured of teachers who are well prepared and who have been carefully selected to meet their needs. It also benefits prospective teachers, because they are assured of employment on completion of their preparation program. The ministry administers an open posting each year for all teachers after they have completed at least 2 years of service in their first placement. Principals are free to identify suitable candidates for their schools but must first seek the consent of principals of the schools where teachers are currently serving.

Later, as educators are moving up the career ladder, especially in the leadership track, they are encouraged, and sometimes assigned, to take positions in schools that have greater staffing needs in order to develop and deploy their skills in a wider set of contexts and to demonstrate that they have the range of abilities needed for responsibilities they will take on. The deployment of principals takes into consideration each school's unique leadership needs and principals' experience and fit for each school. Principals are typically rotated after 4 to 8 years in a school. This gives them sufficient time to initiate, implement, and consolidate new programs for the school. Principal rotation thus supports the ministry's goal of "Every School a Good School," enabling principals to contribute their knowledge and experience in different school contexts and bring fresh perspectives and best practices to their schools. It also provides principals with the opportunity to take on different challenges as part of their professional development. The ministry seeks to tap the special talents and expertise of teachers and leaders to meet needs where they emerge across the system.

China also assigns teachers to positions where they are needed, and it has long required teachers to move to rural areas, for example. In addition, a reform plan adopted in 2010 called for improving the conditions in rural schools and created additional incentives for teachers to choose those schools. Specifically, the plan calls for teachers in rural areas to receive increased stipends, better housing arrangements, and teaching awards for distinguished contributions in rural areas. In addition, the plan proposes changing the process of rotating teachers and principals to rural areas by requiring urban primary and middle school teachers to "work at least one year in rural schools or schools with disadvantaged teaching facilities and faculty before they can apply for senior titles and positions" (Communist Party of China Central Committee and the State Council, 2010, p. 38). With this proposal, the central government is aiming to scale up pilot programs of teacher rotations and make it a requirement for the most experienced teachers to take a turn teaching in the lesser resourced areas of the country.

Incentives for Teaching in High-Needs Schools

A number of countries provide service scholarships (structured as forgivable loans) to underwrite the preparation of teachers who will teach in high-needs fields or high-needs locations. These are repaid with a term of service in the schools or the loan itself is repaid in full or in part.

Australia has several incentive programs in place to attract teachers to rural and remote schools, which are harder to staff than those in the metropolitan areas of Sydney and Melbourne. For example, the NSW Department of Education and Communities offers a number of scholarships for high school graduates, current university students, and professionals seeking a career change to train in an initial secondary teacher education program or special education program for fields and locations with high needs. These scholarships are designed to support work in NSW public schools in noncoastal rural areas of the state. Scholars receive a AU$5,000 training allowance while studying full time as a teacher for up to 5 years. On completion of their studies, they are awarded an additional AU$3,000 to assist with expenses such as relocation costs. Following graduation, teachers may be eligible for an added student loan repayment benefits from the Commonwealth Government.

In the 2014 year, up to 300 scholarships were made available for students to train as teachers in secondary mathematics, science (physics), technological and applied studies, English, and special education. Eighty of these scholarships were available exclusively for Aboriginal or Torres Strait Islander students who met the eligibility requirements. Recipients of this scholarship must remain in their full-time teaching positions for a minimum of 3 years or else refund a proportion of the financial support they had received.

Beyond these scholarships, teachers who accept positions in rural or remote sections of the state, typically in noncoastal areas, receive a range of benefits. Altogether, 10% of NSW government schools are on the incentive program. The benefits vary from school to school:

o Additional training and development days

o A rental subsidy of 70% to 90% in isolated locations

o Special provisions for priority for a later transfer after serving a required number of years in a rural or remote school

o Compassionate transfer status for your teaching partner, if you are appointed to and moving out of some rural and remote schools

o An annual retention benefit of AU$5,000 for teachers in about 40 isolated schools

- ○ A number of locality allowances such as a climatic allowance, an isolation from goods and services allowance, vacation travel expenses, reimbursement of certain expenses related to medical or dental treatment, and an allowance for dependents
- ○ One week of additional summer vacation for schools in the western areas of NSW

Similarly, in Victoria, the Department of Education and Training's Teaching Scholarships scheme provides payments to new graduate teachers for accepting a job in a designated priority school, rural school, or hard-to-staff subject area. The payments are between AU\$3,000 and AU\$7,000, depending on the combination of school category and subject area in which the teacher works. Recipients must stay in employment in that capacity for at least 2 years or are required to repay a portion of the scholarship. In addition, teachers who stay in the position into their fourth teaching year may be eligible for a retention bonus of up to AU\$4,000.

In Shanghai, the East China Normal University and Shanghai Normal University offer Ministry of Education scholarships to students who declare their interest in being a teacher during the college examination and placement process. Scholarships are awarded based on competitive college-entry exam scores and are available to students throughout the country. The intention of the scholarship program is for talented students who want to be teachers to be prepared as teachers in highly reputable universities and then return to their home province to build stronger instructional capacity in rural as well as industrialized areas.

Alberta and Ontario, meanwhile, have taken steps to strengthen the teaching of their Aboriginal population (Link 6-5), known as FNMI (First Nations, Métis, and Inuit). One program, organized by the University of Alberta and funded by the Ministry of Education, is the Aboriginal Teacher Education Program (ATEP). It recruits one to two cohorts a year in the northern parts of the province. Teacher candidates in these cohorts tend to have been working as support staff at schools in the First Nations communities and are then selected for recruitment into the cohorts. By offering a blended model of instructional delivery, the University of Alberta prepares these individuals to become teachers. Some of the course work is offered online by university faculty members, and other aspects of the course work are offered closer to the teacher candidate's communities at partner institutions. Much of the focus of the ATEP program remains on educating teachers who are already members of these communities to remain in and find success in teaching students in these communities.

A pilot of this program graduated 27 new teachers for northern FNMI communities in 2014. In addition to the ATEP program, the University of Calgary and University of Lethbridge offer First Nations courses specific to the bands in their areas.

Preparation for Teaching Historically Underserved Students Effectively

Teaching FNMI students was also a focus of a wide range of projects funded by the Alberta Initiative for School Improvement (AISI), a 12-year project that funded action research partnerships between teachers and community partners aimed at improving instruction and learning. These included improving the academic potential of FNMI students, increasing the involvement of and communication with FNMI parents and guardians, creating a more inclusive sense of belonging for FNMI students within cooperating schools and districts, and enhancing cultural awareness within cooperating schools and districts (Gunn, Pomahac, Striker, & Tailfeathers, 2011, p. 332). Many of the successful projects were expanded to other schools and districts across the province.

Ontario has a substantial Aboriginal population as well, though smaller than Alberta's, and several programs in that province are aimed specifically at preparing teachers to teach native students. The most extensive is at Lakehead University, in the Northern Ontario city of Thunder Bay, which has Canada's only Department of Aboriginal Education. The department offers two unique undergraduate degree programs that focus on Aboriginal cultures and traditions.

One, an honors bachelor of education (Aboriginal) program, is specifically designed to prepare people of Aboriginal ancestry to become teachers and leaders in Aboriginal communities. The degree consists of 2 years of courses from the faculties of social sciences/humanities and sciences/environmental education, including required courses in native languages (Cree and Ojibwa) and indigenous learning, followed by a 2-year education component, which includes courses exploring the literacy of Aboriginal children, the context of teaching in Aboriginal settings, and Aboriginal ways of child-rearing. Additional education courses include subject-specific methods courses as well as courses in classroom management, educational psychology, and teaching exceptional learners.

Students must undertake two teaching practicums to be completed either in a band school or a provincial school with a significant Aboriginal population. In addition, during the final year of the program, students must complete an honors project that demonstrates meaningful learning through one of a variety of media, including learning portfolios, apprenticeships with elders or other cultural leaders, research projects, or the design of culturally relevant teaching resources. On completion of the degree, students are eligible to receive Ontario College of Teaching certification to teach grades K–6 in Ontario schools. This program, similar to others, will be extended to a 5-year model as part of the new requirements for teacher education in Ontario.

A second program at Lakehead is the Native Teacher Education Program (NTEP). This program consists of four undergraduate programs open to people of Aboriginal ancestry as well as non-Aboriginals with a desire to teach in Aboriginal contexts. The programs include course work in Aboriginal languages and cultures as well as pedagogy and subject-area content.

In addition to these programs, NTEP also offers a specialization as a teacher of Aboriginal learners to students enrolled in any of Lakehead's consecutive or concurrent initial teacher education program. To earn this certificate, students must complete courses in native arts and crafts; literature of Canada's First Nations, Ojibwa, or Cree; introduction to indigenous learning; and an additional elective in indigenous education, alongside their other course work.

Developing an Equity Pedagogy

In addition to programs focused on the needs of specific schools and groups of learners, these countries seek to prepare all teachers to work effectively with a diverse student body, and this is a growing emphasis in every jurisdiction.

Finland's teacher education programs have long focused on preparing teachers for diverse learners. To that end, teacher preparation in Finland emphasizes learning how to teach students who learn in different ways, including those with special needs. It includes a strong emphasis on "multiculturality"—also reflected in the national curriculum—and the "prevention of learning difficulties and exclusion," as well as on the understanding of learning, assessment, and curriculum development (Buchberger & Buchberger, 2004, p. 6). Teachers at the University of Helsinki take courses such as "Facing Specificity and Multiplicity: Education for Diversities" and "Cultural Diversity in Schools," along with a course on "Education and Social Justice," for example.

From early childhood education through primary and secondary school, there is a strong commitment to meeting the needs of all students. All Finnish children are bilingual, and many are trilingual, with Finnish,

English, and a mother tongue always taught. In Helsinki, whenever there are at least three children in a school speaking the same native language, the school seeks to create a class for them and other students: Common languages taught include Somali and Arabic, as well as Sami, Swedish, and Russian. Classes are also taught in culture and religions for different regions and people represented among the student body. The goal is to be sure all children feel a sense of belonging, are encouraged to maintain their language and heritage, and are joined by other children who learn their language and heritage as well, to create a true multicultural, multilingual educational experience.

Finland's schools are also designed to provide in-classroom and extra supports to struggling students, regardless of whether they are designated as "special education" students. Finnish education policy intentionally reflects an inclusive approach to children with special needs—in contrast to a more traditional approach that focuses on the "disabilities" of children who must fit into the institutions who provide for them. Teachers must be well prepared to enable this approach in the classroom.

The development of the comprehensive school in Finland was intended to keep *every* student in the same school system, and one approach that emerged was a practice of "part-time special education" for those students in need (Graham & Jahnukainen, 2011), which has been the strategy in use since the 1980s in Finland. In clear contrast to a "wait-to-fail" approach, the way this policy is enacted means that a child with special needs is seen as *any* child who needs additional support or help—whether the child has particular and long-term challenges that might fit particular categories of special needs definitions or whether the child just happens to be struggling at the moment with a particular concept, such as multiplication or understanding similes. This conception frames children with special needs as fitting within a broad and naturally occurring *continuum of variation* rather than designating children with special needs as having *disabilities*. Thus, the development of children's abilities is supported rather than labeled and categorized.

About 30% of Finnish students in grades 1–9 receive some form of special support (Graham & Jahnukainen, 2011; see also Statistics Finland, 2014a). Because they receive sophisticated instruction and supports when they need them (rather than having to wait for long tortuous identification and labeling processes and legal decisions about services), most do not continue to need extra support in the long term. Thus, the number of students identified as requiring special education is *lower* in secondary schools, and first-time graduation rates are extremely high, reaching 93% in 2012 (Sahlberg, 2015b, p. 36; Statistics Finland, 2007).

An understanding of diverse cultures and of how to teach a wide range of students is also strong component of teacher education in Australia. According to national teaching standards, teacher education programs are expected to ensure, among other things, that graduates understand the following:

○ *Students and how they learn:* including student and child development (physical, social, and intellectual); differentiated teaching for students from different backgrounds; strategies for teaching Aboriginal and Torres Strait Islander students; and strategies for students with different learning needs, including disabilities

○ *The content of the school curriculum and how to teach it:* including matters relating to assessment and reporting; particular attention in the standards is given to several emphasis areas—literacy, numeracy, ICT, and knowledge of Aboriginal and Torres Strait Islander histories, cultures, and languages; these standards convey the expectations that teachers will personalize the new national curriculum developed by ACARA, the Australian Curriculum, Assessment and Reporting Authority (and adapted for implementation by states) in ways that build on their students' experiences and take account of their progression in acquiring literacy, numeracy, and other skills

○ *How to create safe, supportive, and inclusive learning environments* (AITSL, 2011)

The diagnostic cycle now being implemented in teacher education and in teacher appraisal systems aims to help teachers address diverse learners' needs, because teachers learn to deeply understand students' learning needs, implement productive learning strategies matched to those needs, and evaluate and refine those strategies. In addition, universities and schools are infusing more course work and clinical work on cultural knowledge and competency (see Chapter 3).

In New South Wales, one strategy for deepening teachers' and school leaders' cultural competency has been launched under the Connected Communities initiative (DEC, 2011). Participating schools have an executive principal appointed for 5 years, along with a community engagement leader who is an Aboriginal person able to provide cultural links to the community while also being a cultural mentor to the school leadership team. The local Aboriginal Education Consultative Group also assists in planning a strategy in each school designed to build strong cultural understandings. All staff members participate in Aboriginal cultural education in partnership with their local Aboriginal community and undertake professional learning to increase their knowledge of Aboriginal students and how they learn. This work is designed to support teachers in planning and implementing effective teaching, learning, and assessment for Aboriginal students. Eight key concepts that convey an assets-based, antiracist model of engagement have been established to guide this and other government work (NSW Government, 2013):

○ Partnerships over paternalism

○ Opportunity over disadvantage

○ Successes over shortfalls

○ "Listening to" over "talking at"

○ Local solutions over one size fits all

○ Evidence over assumptions

○ Participation over marginalization

○ Practice over theory

School Improvement Strategies

A significant component of the equity strategies in high-performing systems is purposeful school improvement. Although large-scale improvement efforts are aimed at schools overall, they particularly benefit the schools with the least capacity, and they build a strong infrastructure for high-quality schooling by strengthening teaching knowledge and skills, as well as planting strategies for continual analysis and reflection on practice. These efforts provide support for strong instruction.

Ontario's literacy and numeracy strategy is one example. The strategy was created in 2004 when the new provincial government reversed the approach of the previous government and focused on building capacity for instruction and learning. The government set a goal that 75% of students in grade 6 would reach the provincial standard in reading, writing, and mathematics, and they created a division within the Ministry of Education to support schools in reaching that goal. The division, known as the Literacy and Numeracy Secretariat, provides a broad range of support services to school systems and schools:

○ Working with school boards to set ambitious student achievement goals at the system and school levels

○ Working with school boards to identify ways to improve student achievement and to provide the resources—such as funding for special projects—necessary to do so

- o Providing professional learning opportunities to teachers, principals, and other educators
- o Sharing research on effective teaching
- o Building partnerships with principals' councils, teachers' federations, faculties of education, and other organizations
- o Sharing successful practices within and across school boards
- o Providing funding to boards to hire tutors who work under the direction of classroom teachers to reinforce previously taught concepts and skills

At the school level, this has involved a focus on supporting all schools to improve with additional supports for schools identified as lower achieving or struggling to improve. Consistent with the theory of action of "support and positive pressure," the Ontario ministry's approach has been to identify schools that are struggling to improve and provide targeted resources and professional development support to build the capacity of teachers and school administrators to improve teaching, learning, and educational outcomes. At first, the ministry targeted for additional resources elementary schools in which fewer than 33% of students met provincial targets, a total of 20% of the province's schools. But once the number of low-performing schools shrank, the ministry targeted for support schools in which fewer than 50% of students met provincial standards.

The strategy has shown great success. At the start of the initiative, 54% of students reached provincial standards in reading, writing, and mathematics; in 2013–2014, 72% met or exceeded those targets. The number of low-performing schools has dropped to 6%, the gap between English speakers and English learners has narrowed substantially, and there are no significant differences in performance between immigrant students and Canadian-born students.

In Australia, specific school improvement strategies were developed to affect the outcomes of schools that had traditionally underperformed. In New South Wales these schools were supported through a program that developed teacher and school leadership though a focus on instructional improvement including the use of assessment and structure to guide teaching practice. The program focused on leadership development across the school through the implementation of an integrated leadership and curriculum program. Schools engaged in the Team Leadership for School Improvement and Focus on Reading programs demonstrated significant and sustained gains in student achievement.

Targeting Improvement and Support in High-Needs Schools

While school-improvement plans are designed to raise overall performance and build a strong infrastructure of school capacity, high-performing systems also provide additional resources to those schools by targeting their improvement efforts at struggling students and schools. In this way, the schools that need the most resources receive the most support.

In some systems, the accountability and improvement system is designed to direct resources and attention to the schools with the greatest needs. In others, the resources are widely available but directed at struggling students, regardless of where they attend school.

Ontario's Student Success Strategy, an initiative to raise performance in high schools, contains elements of both. As part of the effort, the Ministry of Education identifies schools with low levels of achievement and sends to them a team that works closely with the principal and a team of teachers to build their capacity for instructional improvement. For example, the team might identify courses in which students appear to be struggling and start an inquiry process with teachers in those courses. The ministry team identifies high-yield strategies for instruction; the teachers then try those approaches, gather data on their effectiveness, and review the data among themselves and the ministry team.

In addition, the strategy also includes the appointment of a student success teacher and a student success team in each secondary school. According to one educator (Link 6-6), the team zeroes in on students who are struggling and develops plans for improving their performance:

> There's one [student success teacher] in every school. . . It is the expectation that there be a minimum of half-time release. . . The student success teacher is an advocate for students who are struggling. The term we typically use is "students with persistent achievement challenges," but the students could be at risk for any reason that the school identifies. So there may be a critical event or more persistent challenges facing the young person, but if they are on the radar for the student success teacher, the idea is that that teacher is working with those students; they're watching the student, they're tracking how the student is doing, and they are advocating for those students with other teachers, as well. In the description of a student success teacher, there's also an opportunity for them to work with staff to promote some of the ideas that will support the students. As it is with many things, how that actually plays out is really a question of the context of the school; every school and every student success teacher

situation is different. (Rob Andrews, Student Success/Learning to 18 Implementation, Innovation and Support Branch)

Dual-credit teachers are also identified as part of the Student Success Strategy. At the elementary level, student work study teachers collaborate and co-learn with host classroom teachers to understand students' learning and to inform improvements in instruction and assessment practices. The Ministry of Education provides school boards with funding for these positions and, through the Student Achievement Division, support sharing of learning and local practices across the province.

Similarly, in Singapore, a number of programs focus on students with distinctive learning needs. Specialized early intervention programs support lower-primary students who are at-risk of having literacy and numeracy difficulties. For example, the Learning Support Program, introduced since 1992, supports students with weaker language literacy on entry to grade 1. Specially trained teachers provide support daily to these students in small groups of 8 to 10. Similarly, the learning support for mathematics is an early intervention effort aimed at providing additional support to students who do not have foundational numeracy skills and knowledge to access the grade 1 mathematics curriculum. Specially trained teachers work with these students for 2 to 3 additional hours a week.

Beyond the lower primary grades, there are additional learning programs targeted at supporting low-progress learners, particularly in English and mathematics. Since 2013, the training of primary and secondary teachers was stepped up to equip them with teaching strategies to help students acquire numeracy skills. These teaching strategies could be used in class or in small-group instruction within and outside curriculum hours. They enable students to learn at their own pace and strengthen their numeracy skills.

There is also growing recognition of the importance of students' socioemotional needs, especially for students from less-advantaged backgrounds. As of January 2015, 105 of Singapore's 187 primary schools were equipped with a school-based student care center that provides additional after-school guidance and a productive after-school environment for students who need it. MOE will be expanding this scheme progressively to provide a student care center in every primary school.

Shanghai focuses its improvement efforts at the school level. One of the most recent innovative reform efforts in Shanghai has been its approach to bringing up low-performing schools through its "empowered management" program (Jensen & Farmer, 2013). What was once a focus on identifying a few key schools for strong investment is now an effort to raise the overall quality of the system. In this approach, school district leaders match a low-performing school with a high-performing school. The high-performing school is contracted to support and develop the low-performing school in specified areas—for example, teaching quality, school management, and relationships within parents. The performance of the low-performing school is carefully monitored through evaluations conducted by the district bureaus. The high-performing school is only paid if the terms of the contract have been met, meaning that the low-performing school is demonstrating some success. The contract can be ended and payments can be withheld if the relationship does not result in improved performance.

The empowered management approach to school reform relies on the expertise of Shanghai's best principals and teachers to reform its lower-performing schools. For the high-performing schools, the opportunity to enter into such contracts brings more prestige to their staff members and their schools. The Shanghai government promised career advancement opportunities and autonomy if educators could turn around low-performing schools, and this policy has shown success.

The empowered management approach happens within the city and also through exchange program with poor rural schools:

> In 2007, the Shanghai municipal government asked 10 good schools in downtown and other educational intermediary agencies to take charge of 20 schools providing compulsory education in 10 rural districts and counties. The good schools/agencies and the rural schools signed a two-year contract that required the former to send senior administrators and experienced teachers to the latter. The city government bears the cost of the partnership (Shanghai Municipal Education Commission, 2008). Such an arrangement not only benefits the poor schools; it also gives the good schools more room to promote their teachers. (OECD, 2011, p. 97)

Shanghai also has in place other policies to support low-performing schools. For example, principals from high-performing schools may be asked to manage multiple schools, or schools in geographic proximity with each other can be formed into clusters to share resources, including sharing teachers. Clusters can include public and private schools, and they may also receive input from higher education institutions.

Schools and Teachers Learning From Each Other in Shanghai

Over the last 5 years at Qibao Experimental Middle School, dramatic gains have resulted from the opportunity to work with and learn from a better performing school. Zha Jian Sheng, principal and a lead teacher, describes how their school has experienced professional development under the guidance of a higher-performing school:

> [The strategy] has several components. After being hosted by prestigious schools, it works in practice with different components. The first component is that we send outstanding young teachers to prestigious schools to learn, for a year, to teach. They send outstanding teachers in their middle ages, lead teachers, to our school for a year. Every year, we send three teachers over and host three teachers from them. We send three young teachers, young and outstanding, while they send us three middle-aged outstanding teachers.

A teacher chimes in:

> Actually we go to their school to learn how to teach and they come to our school to lead us to teach and demonstrate how they teach in prestigious schools.

In addition, the schools maintain communication among groups of teachers for lesson design and planning. And master teachers from Qibao School are matched up as mentors with teachers in the Experimental School who need assistance.

Five years ago, Shixi Middle School, ranked near the bottom of Shanghai middle schools, was taken into the Qibao Education Group, a school management group built from the strategies used in Qibao School.

Zha Jian Sheng, who was previously an award-winning teacher in Qibao School, attributes his current school's success to two areas of focus in their improvement efforts: active classroom instruction for the students and attention to the development of young teachers. As he describes teaching practices that are actively engaging, Zha Jian Sheng explicitly draws on what he calls Eastern and Western values. From the Eastern perspective, the students' commitment is to hard work and diligence—a focus on effort as opposed to a focus on inherent ability. In this Eastern mind-set, you can be successful if you put the time and effort into the work. From the Western perspective, Zha

Jian Sheng speaks of independent learning, cooperation, curiosity, teamwork, and creativity. To illustrate what this looks like in instruction, he references John Dewey and his ideas of learning from experience.

For the teachers in Qibao Experimental School, shifting instructional practices to ones that engage students in experience and activity was challenging at first. They had to learn new processes of student activity and give more thought to how to build on experience over time. They report today that they find more enjoyment in teaching because the students do not seem bored. They also see even the weakest-performing students doing better. If they were to go back to their traditional ways of teaching, they say that they and their students "would be miserable."

Finally, Zha Jian Sheng emphasizes the importance of investing in his youngest and newest teachers. He wants to lead the beginning teachers to learn to teach in more active ways from the beginning of their careers and not have to relearn how to teach later. He advocates for more opportunities for teachers to go out and learn from others, to arrange opportunities for experienced teachers to work with beginning teachers, and to take care of the beginning teachers with special care. The partnerships within the Qibao Education Group enable him to provide these opportunities for his least-experienced teachers. His mantra is to "cultivate a strong team of leaders to help students, teachers, and the school develop."

Yet another strategy involves district pairings, in which an urban district signs a 3-year agreement with a district in a rural area. The districts exchange information including planning, teacher professional learning, curricula, and teaching materials. A third strategy involves transferring teachers from urban schools to rural schools and vice versa given the difficulty of the latter in recruiting and retaining qualified teachers (Cheng, 2011). High-achieving principals from urban districts were also sent to lead several rural schools. The initiative aimed to redress the balance in the distribution of qualified and experienced teachers.

Victoria also targets support to particular schools as an outgrowth of that state's system of peer review. Under the system, once every 4 years schools are evaluated through a peer-review process as long as the school is scoring above key thresholds. The peer review analyzes performance data as well as leading indicators, such as curriculum, teaching practice, and school leadership; the quality of relationships between the school and the wider community; and how effectively resources are used.

Peer reviews are conducted by two peers selected by the school under review and facilitated by an externally accredited reviewer, who documents the peer-review activities. The peers are typically principals from other schools in the state, and the process is intended to build the professional knowledge and capacity of those peers (DEECD, 2013c). DET provides principals with accreditation training for school review via the Bastow Institute for Educational Leadership. There is an exemplary practice review process conducted alongside the peer review to capture elements of best practice for dissemination across the system.

Schools that fail to meet key thresholds undergo a more intensive priority review. DET contracts a review team that spends 4 days examining the school's data and identifying the factors inhibiting school improvement (DEECD, 2013c). Outcomes of the priority review are used as the basis for an intervention program designed by representatives from the school, along with regional and central offices of DET.

"Interventions focus on strengthening the capacity of teachers and leaders to build the school's ability to self-improve, and to sustain improvement" (DEECD, 2013c, p. 11). These may include structured peer-support programs or mentoring and coaching for the principal or staff members in areas such as leadership, teaching and learning, school governance, strategic partnerships, and literacy and numeracy. In each case, the focus of intervention is on targeting support for capacity building and school improvement. Thus, the self-evaluation and peer-review processes in Victoria serve to embed the principles of reflective inquiry, professional engagement, and the use of networks to share best practices. These principles are seen in school improvement processes in every one of the jurisdictions we studied.

Lessons Learned

High-performing systems aim not only to raise student performance overall but also work to ensure that all students attain the knowledge and skills they need to succeed in the future. And they act on the principle that "all means all;" that is, every student from every background deserves high-quality instruction and support.

In carrying out this principle, the high-performing systems use a variety of approaches. They support children's welfare, provide adequate financial support to all schools, and provide additional support to address students with particular needs. They take steps to ensure an equitable distribution of well-qualified teachers and leaders. They monitor performance and target resources to students and schools that are struggling. And they prepare teachers to teach in diverse settings and address the needs of all students, regardless of their background.

To be sure, these efforts are not perfect. These systems, similar to every system around the world, continue to experience opportunity and achievement gaps. But the steps they are taking to work toward equity are noteworthy. The policies and practices described here differ from country to country, but they share some common themes:

Equity begins with support based on need. Although the funding systems in all of these countries provide a base of adequate support for all students and all schools, the systems also recognize that students with additional needs require additional support. The finance systems provide for that by basing aid to schools on student need—schools serving students with disabilities, second-language learners, and students from low-income families receive additional funding. But in addition, the countries provide targeted financial support for low-performing schools and students so that they receive the instructional help and other services they need.

Equity requires sophisticated teacher and leader knowledge, coupled with cultural competency. Teacher education programs help teachers learn to see and understand each child and develop a wide repertoire of strategies to teach all children successfully. Success also requires an understanding of and support for cultural experiences and languages. These efforts help educators understand their students as people as well as learners.

Equity is tied to school improvement. The equity strategies employed by high-performing systems are integrally tied to their efforts to improve schools. The additional funding ensures that schools are equipped to educate all students effectively. The programs designed to ensure an equitable distribution of well-qualified teachers are aimed at improving the hard-to-staff schools overall. And the targeted assistance programs, such as Shanghai's pairing of low- and high-performing schools, aim to raise the level of quality of all schools.

Support for equity is aimed at building educator and school capacity. The support that states and national governments provide to schools to address the needs of diverse students is intended to strengthen their ability to teach and lead schools. This begins in teacher preparation programs, in which prospective teachers learn about diverse cultures and pedagogies appropriate for them. It continues in support programs, such as that in Ontario, in which provincial officials work with faculty members in low-performing schools to conduct an inquiry-led improvement strategy.

Throughout this book we have emphasized that the teacher quality systems in high-performing jurisdictions are just that—systems. These countries and provinces do not focus solely on an aspect of teacher quality, such as preparation or evaluation, but rather see all the components as complementary and mutually supportive. As a result, they are able to recruit, prepare, and retain excellent teachers year after year.

The policies and practices to support equity make clear that the teacher quality policies are themselves part of coherent and mutually reinforcing systems as well. The school-finance systems support school improvement by supporting teacher quality and building the capacity of school faculties. The accountability systems provide data and direct resources to build capacity and support teacher quality. And the educator preparation programs reinforce those systems by ensuring a steady supply of teachers and leaders who are capable of teaching and leading in high-performing, equitable systems.

Achieving these kinds of systems is an ongoing, challenging task. In Chapter 7 we examine how these jurisdictions are continually involved in learning to meet the challenges they face, in part by borrowing successful ideas from each other, in part by demonstrating the will to evaluate and overcome the ever-present set of obstacles facing reforms, and in part by continuing to set explicit goals for greater quality and equity in teaching and learning.

7

GLOBAL LEARNING FOR ONGOING IMPROVEMENT

DESPITE THE MANY DIFFERENCES AMONG these very distinctive countries, each has established strong mechanisms for attracting and selecting high-quality individuals into teaching, academically grounded preparation that offers significant clinical learning, and ongoing opportunities to sharpen practice to support ever-more sophisticated and effective teaching.

Part of the success of jurisdictions with well-developed policy systems is the ability to draw on, adapt, and integrate effective practices from other countries. This transfer is a process that has accelerated since the 1990s as education has become increasingly viewed as a lever for international economic competitiveness. Successful borrowing takes some policy skill, because "traveling policies" are only successful in a new venue if they are responsive to the particular challenges facing a jurisdiction and fit well within existing policy systems, cultural norms, and professional practices. When a policy is not adapted sufficiently to find such coherence in a new context, it may be implemented without deep understanding or conviction, proving a weak and often short-lived lever on practice.

Another feature of well-developed policy systems is that they are dynamic rather than static. Even in jurisdictions that perform well on international assessments, policy makers are continually seeking opportunities to make policy adjustments that can enhance student learning. For the jurisdictions in our study, these changes often involve increasing teacher professionalism, centered on a vision of a teaching as involving collaborative engagement with colleagues and ongoing learning to continually improve practice.

This approach stands in contrast to efforts to engage in the "remote control" of teaching (Shulman, 1983), which produces the kind of top-down policy that seeks to prescribe and constrain teaching through mandates and stringent rules to follow. Instead, the policies provide guidelines and set conditions under which good decisions can be made by professionals in response to local contexts and student needs. This approach, which has been called *professional policy* (Darling-Hammond, 2009; Thompson & Zeuli, 1999), uses professional standards to hold educators accountable for developing shared expertise and applying it appropriately, rather than imposing standardized prescriptions for practice that would fail to meet clients' different needs. Because knowledge is always growing and its appropriate application is contingent on many factors, this strategy aims to build a set of bottom-up structures, norms, and cultures that are more likely to lead to effective changes in local practice by activating processes such as standard setting, accreditation, preparation, and professional learning.

In this chapter, we briefly outline the different ways these jurisdictions have conceptualized these kinds of policies, including how they learned and borrowed from others. We illustrate examples of teacher and teaching policies that have been shared across our study jurisdictions, and we look at where each is moving in the next phase of policy development. We end with a summary of our conclusions, drawing all of these themes together.

Policy Borrowing: Learning From Success

Increasingly, countries engage in benchmarking their system against others to seek policy solutions used by high-achieving jurisdictions. This process has become more visible with the advent of international comparative assessments, such as PISA, TIMSS (Trends in International Mathematics and Science Study), and PIRLS (Progress in International Reading Literacy Study). In addition, policy makers are informed by comparative studies of education systems led by such organizations as the World Bank and OECD and newer research programs from the National Center on Education and the Economy's Center on International Education Benchmarking.

Growing public interest in, and awareness of, international comparative assessments can increase pressure on (or create opportunities for) governments to make changes in educational policies. For example, following a dip in Australia's relative achievement on PISA 2009, then–prime minister Julia Gillard announced in 2012 that "by 2025, Australia should be ranked as a top five country in Reading, Science, and Mathematics" (Gillard, 2012). Soon after, Australia passed new education legislation that included major reforms to equalize and increase education funding—the so-called Gonski reforms—which were justified by this perceived need and announced goal and which might have been politically impossible without them.

Intentions to pursue international benchmarking can also be found in policy documents at the state level. For example, Victoria's strategic plan indicates that the state should borrow policy from other countries:

> Realizing world-leader status is an ambitious but realistic goal. Top performing jurisdictions like Finland, Hong Kong and Canada have systems and cultures that are as different from each other as ours are from theirs. Our challenge is to learn from the experience of other high-performing jurisdictions, select the most effective strategies for our context, and implement them well. (DEECD, 2013a, p. 9)

The very notion of investing in teaching quality has been a key aspect of this global borrowing. Noting that the state had not "achieved the same improvement in learning outcomes experienced by other highly autonomous systems," the Victoria DEECD, for example, argued,

> We know from the experiences of high-performing jurisdictions, like Finland and Singapore, that education reform will succeed where it is anchored in the professionalism of teachers and leaders and focuses on building professional practice. (DEECD, 2012b, p. 6)

Ideas about how to strengthen the teaching profession have traveled in part through international education forums, such as the International Summit on the Teaching Profession. Cohosted by the OECD, Education International (the international federation of teachers' unions), and a host country, the event has, since 2011, annually convened "governments and teacher organizations from a number of high-performing and rapidly improving education systems" in a forum for "open and constructive exchange on effective teacher policies and practices" (Kultusminister Koferenz, 2016). The annual summit features conference sessions comparing policies and their implications in participant countries, as well as reports from the OECD on specific topics using data from international benchmarking surveys such as the TALIS.

These and other international conversations have contributed to broadened ideas about how a teaching profession might be structured and a range of ideas about what the key elements might be. These can include ideas associated with traditional professions—professional autonomy over technical decision making, manifested as collective control over the work, control over entry standards, a shared knowledge base, and a foundational code of ethics, as well as those associated with public accountability and managerial oversight—standards of practice as part of appraisal—and those associated with the knowledge society, such as teachers as reflective practitioners (Snoek, 2014).

The following are policies and practices that have traveled among the jurisdictions we studied:

o The use of professional standards to guide teaching practice

o The development of teacher registration and certification systems to ascertain teachers' competence to enter the profession and for advancement in the profession

o Designs for teacher preparation focused on clinical practice

o Professional development strategies such as lesson study and action research

Professional Teaching Standards

The development of professional teaching standards has been a linchpin for reforms to create a more coherent approach to developing knowledge, skills, and dispositions for the profession. A defined knowledge base undergirded by ethical expectations for its use on behalf of clients is a hallmark of traditional professions, such as medicine and law. Professional standards are commonly administered by a representative body, often composed of members of the profession, with a measure of autonomy from government prescription or intervention (Snoek, 2014). As professional standards in teaching are used to underpin functions such as accreditation of initial teacher education programs, registration, professional learning, and career pathways, they can help create the glue for a more coherent system to guide and support teaching practice (Darling-Hammond, Wise, & Klein, 1999).

Professional teaching standards were first launched in the United States, led initially by the National Board for Professional Teaching Standards, which set standards for the advanced certification of teachers in 1987; the Interstate New Teacher Assessment and Support Consortium, which set standards for beginning teachers in the early 1990s; and the National Council for Accreditation of Teacher Education, which incorporated these teaching standards into its long-standing approach to approving educator preparation programs. The National Board standards focused for the first time on competencies—what teachers should know, be like, and be able to do—and this approach has spread throughout many countries in the world, including the jurisdictions we studied.

Among the jurisdictions we studied, each except Finland had adopted a set of standards through similar governmental or professional bodies.

In Finland, a different process accomplished similar ends: The 2004 Government Decree on University Degrees, revising a version from 1995, based in turn on one from the 1970s, establishes the criteria for initial teacher education degree programs, which constitute expectations for what teachers should learn about content, pedagogical knowledge, and aspects of teaching practice. Teaching standards thus operate through the schools of education, which are trusted as the cornerstones for professional practice in that country. Elsewhere, professional bodies have descriptions of teacher knowledge, professional practice, and engagement with colleagues in professional collaboration and learning.

Teaching standards traveled over the US border to provinces in Canada during the 1990s. In Alberta, the Teaching Quality Standard Ministerial order put forth by the Ministry of Education establishes the standard that teachers are expected to meet for certification and to maintain throughout their careers. The ministry also accredits and monitors initial teacher education programs against the standard. The standards, first adopted in 1997, reflect a professional view of teachers, who are expected to understand the legislative and ethical frameworks in which they work, know and be able to implement a variety of pedagogical methods, have deep content understanding and be able to translate it into curricula, and be lifelong learners able to establish effective relationships with parents, their communities, and school colleagues (Alberta Education, 1997).

Ontario's Professional Standards of Practice, adopted in 1999, are established by the Ontario College of Teachers, composed of peer-elected and government-appointed members of the profession. The standards underpin initial teacher education programs and teacher certification and are intended to anchor the teaching profession. They include a "commitment to students and student learning," "professional knowledge," "professional practice," and "leadership in learning communities." Appended to the Professional Standards of Practice are ethical standards for teachers, who are expected to demonstrate "care," "respect," "trust," and "integrity" (Ontario College of Teachers, 2000). The standards set high expectations and are regarded as aspirational, elaborating a teaching ideal, rather than a mandatory minimum checklist.

Australian states such as New South Wales and Victoria developed teaching standards in the early 2000s, and the standards of these states later informed the national Australian Professional Standards for Teachers developed by AITSL in 2011. The new national standards are administered by professional bodies in each state (by the Victorian Institute of Teaching, for example, and the Board of Studies, Teaching and

Educational Standards in New South Wales) where they underpin the accreditation of initial teacher education programs, teacher registration, and, in some cases, career advancement. States can elect to certify teachers at the higher levels of the standards. The seven standards with 37 descriptors at each of four career stages provide a common language through which to inform teacher self-reflection and professional learning throughout the teaching career.

In Singapore, two complementary sets of teaching standards were developed, the first in 2005 to guide teacher evaluation and the second, 4 years later, to guide teacher education. The seven competencies are grouped into three dimensions: teachers' professional practice, leadership and management, and effectiveness. The standards broaden as teachers progress through the career ladder to include such things as contributions to their school and cluster, professional collaboration and networking, and contributions to a culture of professionalism.

In Shanghai, teaching standards for primary and secondary teachers were developed by the national Ministry of Education in 2011. The standards were developed to give stronger guidance to initial teacher education programs about the professional expectations for teachers. The 61 standards are divided into four broad categories:

○ Student-centered teaching: supporting independent development, stimulating curiosity, fostering learning interests, and creating freedom to explore

○ Teacher ethics: expectations of the teacher as a role model and professional

○ Knowledge and skills: pedagogical knowledge and strategies, understanding students' thinking and cultural characteristics, classroom management, and supporting students' creativity and independent thinking

○ Teachers' lifelong learning: working with colleagues to constantly reflect and improve education and teaching, identify practice needs and problems, and address them through exploration and research

Interestingly, the Shanghai teaching standards are being used to convey a new image of teaching for deeper understanding, along with critical and creative thinking and stronger strategies for meeting the needs of diverse students. This is leveraging changes in preservice teacher education, including extending and redesigning the clinical experiences of candidates, and in in-service learning, especially including the kind of teaching that is rewarded in the career ladder process and in teaching competitions. As the government makes explicit the kind of teaching that is desired and viewed as excellent, it creates incentives for teachers to learn these kinds of new pedagogies on a wider scale and for principals to support the pedagogies themselves and the teachers' quest to develop them.

Teacher Licensure or Registration

Standards have been coupled with teacher licensing (also variously called *registration, accreditation,* or *certification*) in several jurisdictions. Licensure also has its roots in the United States, but it has spread to many jurisdictions internationally. Professional certification is also present among other professions, such as doctors and nurses, which has facilitated its adoption for teachers internationally. Among the countries we studied, Australia, Canada, and China have forms of licensure or certification, and discussion about a registration system has taken place recently in Finland.

Teacher licensure can serve as method of supporting public confidence in the teaching workforce; meanwhile, the nature of teacher licensure processes can also serve to support teaching quality. For example, in Ontario, a key function of teacher licensure is to provide assurance that teachers have met a threshold level of preparation from an approved education provider. This is particularly important in jurisdictions where there may be a large number of teachers whose training took place outside the area. The Ontario College of Teachers accredits teacher education providers, ensuring that they meet government regulations for teacher education programs and that they are consistent with the College's standards of practice. Teachers who have completed an approved program then apply to the college for certification to practice as a teacher. The applicants must show that they have the methodological and subject background to teach students at one of the designated school levels. As teachers undertake learning to complete additional qualifications, they can add them to their annual certification.

The notion of licensure or registration as a two-stage process is also one that has traveled from the United States. Candidates receive an initial license when they have completed preparation and must apply for a longer-term professional license within 2 or 3 years or when they have demonstrated a capacity for ongoing improvement or a level of competence articulated in the professional teaching standards. For example, in Alberta, teachers receive interim credentials for up to 3 years on the successful completion of a teacher education program that meets quality standards. To move to permanent professional certification requires the recommendation of a school authority. The recommendation must show that the teacher has had at least 2 years of successful teaching and has had at least two evaluations based on the knowledge, skills, and attributes outlined in Alberta's Teaching Quality Standard.

Similarly, Australian teachers begin at graduate teacher status and have 2 to 3 years within which to advance to proficient teacher status through a process known as *registration* in Victoria and *teacher accreditation* in New South Wales, in which they are evaluated against the national teaching standards. The way the process is shaped incentivizes teachers to familiarize themselves with national standards to guide and reflect on their teaching practice as well as their learning and development. To achieve full registration or accreditation, provisionally registered teachers collect evidence of their professional practice and how it meets the standards. This evidence is then submitted to a school-based panel or principal who then writes a recommendation report to the state teaching authority—a process that helps connect early-career teacher learning with school-level supports and mentorship.

In Victoria, for example, teachers must document their ability to implement the cycle of reflective inquiry discussed in Chapter 3. Their evidence report must demonstrate their ability to formulate an inquiry question focused on student learning, identify their students' context and particular learning needs, develop a unit plan with desired learning outcomes, create an action plan for their own learning that includes professional conversations with colleagues and professional development activities, write a reflection evaluating the effectiveness of their practice in meeting learning needs, and plot next steps for student learning.

This process was designed to make the standards meaningful in the support system for teaching. As Fran Cosgrove from the Victoria Institute of Teaching explained,

> Our view was if we've got this requirement for beginning teachers to meet the standards, then we're going to use it as a vehicle for really strong support. What we've done is driven the way teachers are inducted into the profession. We said, "If teachers have to meet the standards, then what we're going to do is prescribe the process." It is an evidence-based process; it's school-based, so it has to be what you're doing in your current practice now. It was about defining practice but [also] it was about support for practice. We decided we would build into our process the idea that experienced teachers have to work with beginning teachers. The evidence has to show that there

have been professional conversations and interactions [that] focus on student learning [between] a beginning teacher and an experienced teacher. The experienced teacher has to spend time in the beginning teacher's classroom. . . We've said [the Timperley cycle of reflective inquiry] works really nicely with our evidence-based process. You work from student learning into your own professional learning. You develop your action plan. You implement it with your group of students. You reflect on the learning that occurs from that. You continue the cycle. . . We ask our teachers to undertake this cycle as a way of gathering their evidence.

The process does not end with professional registration at the beginning of the career. Once full registration (to proficient teacher status) has been achieved, it must be maintained. Australian teachers must undertake and provide evidence of an average of 20 hours a year of standards-referenced professional development activities and write a personal reflection that explains how their professional learning addresses the standards, contributes to professional knowledge and teaching practice, and supports student learning. The standards are also used to guide an evidence-based process of advancement through a career ladder to lead teacher status. As the standards reflect professional knowledge, practice, and engagement with colleagues, the relicensure and advancement processes are intended to support and reinforce ongoing teacher development that is focused on student learning and collaborative professional engagement.

The goal is the development of professional teaching practice that values ongoing learning, fosters teaching quality and innovation, and supports 21st-century student learning, as articulated by former AITSL chair, Tony Mackay (Link 7-1):

> We've got to be confident at the point of graduation that we're as prepared as we can be, but it's only the beginning. Think about the nature of the early years, induction, orientation, coaching, mentoring, observation, feedback. Any profession that really wishes to say that it's going to make a difference through the quality of its practice embraces all of that, and understands there's going to be a commitment over your professional life . . .
>
> I want to inspire the profession to not only think about how they can become great practitioners of current knowledge but [also] how they can actually be constructors of new knowledge. That new knowledge is going to make a big difference to the way in which young people will learn, what they learn, and their capacity to thrive and survive. (Interview with A. Mackay, former AITSL chair, January 2014)

In some jurisdictions, teacher licensure is the responsibility of the teaching profession. This is the case in Ontario, where the College's governing council is composed primarily of present or former teachers who are elected by peers and several members appointed by the provincial government. In Victoria, the Victorian Institute of Teaching is independently managed, but it reports to the state government; while in New South Wales, the Institute of Teachers was incorporated with the government's Board of Studies in 2014 and is composed of members who are appointed by each government, the teachers' federation, and nominees from the school sectors. Teacher certification remains a function of the Ministry of Education in Alberta and Shanghai.

Since the 1990s, China has required that all teachers hold a national certification regardless of whether they teach in a public or private school. The majority of teachers are supported toward this certification through normal school and university-based preparation programs, and currently all teachers must pass a three-part national examination for their teaching license (described in Chapter 3). Following this process, teachers hold permanent lifetime certification.

In Singapore, some of the aims of licensure are accomplished through alternative means. After an investiture ceremony that includes new teachers' pledge to engage in ongoing learning, exemplary practice, and ethical standards, which marks formal entry to the profession (see Chapter 3), beginning teachers are placed on probation for 1 year. During this time they are periodically observed by grade- and subject-level leaders and by heads of department, receive mentoring, and receive additional feedback and coaching if underperforming. At the end of the probationary year, they are assessed by school leaders, and, if they meet the standards, they are confirmed as permanent teachers.

The spread of teacher licensure is associated with efforts to professionalize teaching. Its adoption into a local policy context may be strengthened where it connects to teaching standards, teacher learning and growth, and the work that teachers do in the classroom, as one NSW teacher noted:

> I think that the standards really put us at a level where we are respected just like other professions that have standards are respected. It also helps to have that common drive or vision or understanding. . . We're working towards a common level of profession practice.

Clinically Based Initial Teacher Preparation

The strengthening of clinical preparation for new teachers provides a further example of policy borrowing and transfer. This process was stimulated in part by the increased recognition of the role played by well-developed initial teacher education programs in Finland's achievement on international assessments. As discussed in greater detail in Chapter 3, Finnish teachers receive not only academic training to the master's level but also experience significant time in monitored teaching practice throughout their time in model training schools appended to the nation's research universities.

Also, as the name suggests, clinically based teacher preparation draws on ideas regarding professional preparation from the medical field. Specifically, it suggests that teachers should not only become expert in their content areas and in theoretical knowledge about practice but also, much like physicians, teachers should experience significant time observing and practicing under the supervision of experienced mentors throughout their training prior to taking sole charge of a classroom.

The adoption of such programs gained impetus with the launch of initiatives such as the Carnegie Foundation's Teachers for a New Era, which emphasized that teaching should be an "academically taught clinical profession" featuring residencies for clinical practice (Carnegie Corporation, 2006) as well as the blue ribbon report on clinical preparation issued by the National Council for Accreditation of Teacher Education (NCATE, 2010). The integration of theory and practice was already a concern for University of Melbourne Graduate School of Education's dean Field Rickards, who had himself initially trained in audiology, following the medical model, and was looking for ways to improve teacher education. Rickards noted,

> One of the documents I read was *Teachers for a New Era*. It said, "Teaching should be considered as an academically taught clinical practice profession." As soon as I read the words "clinical practice" and "clinical practice profession," I thought, "Perfect. That's where we've got to take teaching. If ever we got the opportunity to reinvent the professional training of teachers, it's got to be focused around that." For me, clinical practice is a framework of thinking.

The University of Melbourne's MTeach program, which grew out of this commitment, is strongly based on a clinical practice approach similar to that used in medicine.

Master of Teaching Program

The Master of Teaching at the Melbourne Graduate School of Education is intended to train teachers to become clinical interventionist practitioners. Teacher candidates are instructed in a research inquiry model that emphasizes identification of one or more students' learning needs, research and selection of an intervention strategy, implementation of the strategy, and reflection and assessment of its effectiveness in promoting student learning.

The program was developed drawing on elements of audiology and second-language learning. It thus takes a clinical analytic approach and a developmental paradigm to student learning, observing all students as being on a continuum of increasing competencies. This draws teacher candidates' focus to the process of student learning as well as outcomes. The role of the teacher is to identify what students are ready to learn next, using evidence about what they understand and can do, and then to establish interventions and learning programs to facilitate that development. Differentiated teaching within the same classroom is an important element of the pedagogical approach. As professor Patrick Griffith noted how training for this approach helps teachers observe students carefully with a diagnostic eye:

> The idea of evidence is pretty clear. Almost all of our graduates would talk about skills, not scores, and all of them would talk about evidence not inference as a way of monitoring growth. And they would all talk about readiness to learn, rather than achievement levels.

Clinical training occurs as candidates are taking relevant courses 3 days a week at the university while spending 2 days a week in school, interweaving theory and practice throughout the four semesters of the program. This practice is supported by clinical specialists and teaching fellows who are in constant communication with teacher candidates, reviewing and giving feedback on lesson plans, observing lessons, and providing coaching.

Evaluation of teacher candidates is conducted using a clinical praxis exam that assesses candidates based on their ability to integrate theory and practice and to conduct research, design interventions, and evaluate their efficacy in facilitating student learning.

From their initial start in Finland, approaches to an "academically taught clinical practice profession" have spread to universities in Australia and Canada that are developing 2-year master's programs with extensive student teaching in partner schools, and these are beginning to take root in Singapore and Shanghai as well.

Under this model, the practice of teaching is transformed from the teacher-centered stand-and-deliver approach to transmission of content to a student-centered approach that focuses as much on what the student is ready to learn as it does on what the teacher is ready to teach. Teachers' abilities to inquire into student learning and plan for productive next steps is central to this approach, as is figuring out how to solve specific problems of practice. Teacher research and analysis, evaluation of effectiveness, and further reflection and refinement of practice are also beginning to inform inquiry-oriented teacher development practices that have traveled across continents, such as lesson study and action research.

Lesson Study and Action Research

We were struck by the extent to which a variety of teacher inquiry practices, grounded in the teaching of specific curriculum content and the teaching of specific students, were spreading throughout the jurisdictions we studied. As we described in the previous section, teacher inquiry practices are nurtured for novice teachers in leading universities in these jurisdictions and carried into the schoolhouse in a variety of forms, including lesson study and other forms of action research.

Lesson study is a specific form of action research focused on the design, implementation, and refinement of lessons on core topics. With origins in Japan and China, it has strong roots in Asia—including Shanghai and Singapore—and has recently traveled to Australia, Canada, Sweden, the United Kingdom, and the United States, among other locations (Dudley, 2011). Traditional lesson study and other forms of teacher action research (described in Chapter 4) engage teachers in looking at practice with a critical eye, often in collaboration with others, to test and evaluate which strategies are most successful for students. Action research takes several forms, but similar to lesson study, it involves teachers jointly conducting observation and examination of a practice, analyzing and interpreting findings, and proposing and enacting strategies for improvement.

Whereas lesson study focuses on testing and fine-tuning individual lessons, other forms of action research take up broader curriculum issues and issues associated with meeting the specific needs of individuals or groups of students. Both serve as forms of job-embedded and context-specific professional development. They are able to leverage improvements in teaching by providing opportunities for teachers to draw on the collective capacity of colleagues in addressing specific learning needs.

From the collaborative school-based action research groups in Singapore and Shanghai to the inquiry cycle taken up by teachers in

Australia to the teacher-led projects funded by governments in Ontario and Alberta to the organic teaching evaluation process common in Finland, the spread of this approach transforms the role of teachers in the knowledge production process (Zeichner, 1995). As one defini-tive description of teacher action research notes, engagement in action research has deep implications for the teaching profession:

> Action research is a process of concurrently inquiring about problems and taking action to solve them. . . Although it is focused on actions leading to change, action research is also a mental disposition—a way of being in the classroom and the school—a lifelong habit of inquiry. . . Action research empowers teachers to own professional knowledge because teachers—through the process of action inquiry—conceptu-alize and create knowledge, interact around knowledge, transform knowledge, and apply knowledge. Action research enables teachers to reflect on their practice to improve it, become more autonomous in professional judgment, develop a more energetic and dynamic envi-ronment for teaching and learning, articulate and build their craft knowledge, and recognize and appreciate their own expertise. As knowledge and action are joined in changing practice, there is grow-ing recognition of the power of teachers to change and reform educa-tion from the inside rather than having change and reform imposed top down from the outside. (Pine, 2008, pp. 30–31)

New Horizons

None of the jurisdictions we studied is resting on its laurels or remain-ing static. Each is continually pushing ahead with policy reforms to improve the quality of teaching. Despite their different contexts, there are some common threads that emerge across countries. In particular, most are continuing their efforts to focus curriculum, pedagogy, and assess-ments on 21st-century learning needs; to improve welfare for children and ensure greater equity of educational opportunity; and to strengthen the continuum of support they have built to prepare, retain, and develop high-quality teachers.

Transforming Systems to Meet 21st-Century Learning Expectations

A striking feature of the policy systems we studied was the ongoing transformation of the curriculum and related supports to better prepare students for work and society in the 21st century. These shifts involve redirecting the focus of schooling beyond the acquisition of predefined content toward the application of knowledge to new situations. As noted in Chapter 2, each jurisdiction has recently revised, or is in the process of revising, its curriculum guidance to place greater emphasis on the development of critical thinking and performance skills in addition to content coverage. Such competencies typically involve fostering interpersonal and communications skills, critical and creative thinking, and capacity for lifelong learning. All of the systems recognize that these curriculum changes also require transformations in teaching, which they plan for with the profession as the revisions are under way.

Perhaps the most dramatic curriculum development project is taking place in Finland. The country has begun moving toward greater use of "phenomenon-based learning," particularly upper secondary school, as its national curriculum is being revised (Sahlberg, 2015a). In this approach, student learning is centered on a specific topic or research question, and students draw on knowledge from a range of subjects to address this area of study. Not unlike the conception of project-based or problem-based learning popularized at various times in the United States, this approach appears designed to foster student inquiry into questions and ideas, pulling on knowledge across disciplines. In Finland, this shift has involved schools restructuring some teaching time to deemphasize discrete, traditional subjects in favor of including several units each year built on multidisciplinary topics that address real-world issues. An example is a unit on the European Union, integrating elements of history, geography, languages, and mathematics into multiple-session teaching units.

Phenomenon-based learning is expected to play a greater role in a new national curriculum framework to be introduced in late 2016, and it represents a significant shift in approach for many Finnish teachers. Yet it is useful to note that teachers have significant input into revisions of the national curriculum framework via curriculum groups. The open nature of the process means that teachers are able to be well informed about curricular changes long before they are actually implemented. According to one account, 70% of Helsinki's teachers have already received training in implementing phenomenon-based learning (Garner, 2015). As previously noted, the curriculum framework is a lean set of standards, and each school can determine the kind of programming and the length of lessons devoted to each unit. Thus teachers will continue to have significant input into lesson planning and adapting the curriculum framework to meet the needs of the school.

Changing the what of education in these jurisdictions is also shifting the how, notably in terms of pedagogical approach. This can involve greater student participation and questioning to develop students' curiosity and critical thinking skills and enhance their engagement with learning, connecting school lessons to real-life problems to foster students' problem-solving abilities, and using project-based learning to integrate knowledge from several domains. The movement to phenomenon-based learning in Finland, for example, involves students having greater voice in lesson design, working with teachers to develop research projects. Similarly, in Australia, some school networks have a professional learning strategy aimed at developing student curiosity through inquiry-focused teaching and specific strategies such as the framing of higher-order questions (DEECD, 2011).

In Shanghai, ongoing curriculum reform is shifting curriculum and pedagogy from a more traditional exam-focused approach to a student-centered one, oriented toward more engaged learning, higher-order thinking, and the greater application of knowledge to real-world problems (Tan, 2013). Through networks such as those run out of the Institute of Schooling Reform and Development at East China Normal University, a "new" basic education is starting to take hold in Shanghai schools (Ye, 2009). Teachers are encouraged and taught how to allow students to think for themselves and create new ideas.

Schools are encouraged to develop curricula for new elective subjects and to extend learning beyond the classroom to places such as science centers and museums (Zhang, Ding, & Xu, 2016). As noted in Chapter 2, teachers in Shanghai are increasingly encouraged to devote more of their class time to student activities over didactic instruction, including student-led research and greater interaction with other students (OECD, 2011; Tan, 2013). This kind of pedagogy is further incentivized through the work of the action research groups and the standards used for teaching competitions.

Concomitantly, jurisdictions are also adapting by reshaping policies for the assessment of student learning. In Shanghai, recent policy gives greater flexibility to schools to develop their own student assessments. Some schools have been experimenting with presentations of student projects and assessing students on their problem-solving skills and application of knowledge. Others have developed student growth records that can involve a combination of self- and peer appraisal, a portfolio of students' best work, contributions to community and physical well-being, and include input from teachers and parents (Tan, 2013). Similarly, upper secondary schools in Finland are introducing e-portfolios as a means of tracking and assessing a range of student work.

In Singapore, the increased use of open-ended assessments designed to assess critical thinking skills includes activities such as essays, research projects, and science experiments. In addition, admission to all levels of the system is being opened up to a wider range of indicators of student ability beyond test scores, particularly those that emphasize critical thinking and problem-solving. Project-based components can compose up to 20% of a student's examination grade. Students may also select specific projects to be submitted along with examination scores for consideration in university admissions.

Transforming teaching and learning is not a simple endeavor. It requires efforts to change multiple parts of the policy system. It also requires a change in student and teacher identity. Students have to be encouraged and inspired to take control of their learning. Teachers must become more than conveyors of content, and are "designers of learning opportunities" (Koh, Tan, & Ng, 2012). Such a transformation requires a change in the way teachers are trained and the construction of a range of supports for teachers to support learning throughout their career.

Educational Equity and Meeting Student Needs

As these nations are transforming curriculum and assessment to meet 21st-century learning needs, they are also determined to bring this quality of education to all of their students. As described in Chapter 6, considerable new policy in each jurisdiction is targeted at addressing educational inequities and supporting children's welfare so that they are ready and able to learn. These efforts go beyond national and provincial investments in teaching, and they are understood as essential for enabling teaching investments to pay off so that all students—not just a lucky few—have the necessary skills to be successful in a rapidly changing world (Tucker, 2011). As we noted in Chapter 1, international data support the assertion that high educational achievement and equity are not only possible but also they can be mutually reinforcing.

However, the nature of equity challenges differs by jurisdiction and thus also do the emphases of policy going forward. In Australia, in addition to the Gonski funding reforms that have been adopted only partially at the federal level, new state-level policy is aimed at achieving greater equity of school funding. In New South Wales, progressive iterations of school resource allocation models are extending additional per capita student funding for schools with students with disabilities, students from low socioeconomic backgrounds, indigenous children, refugees or new immigrants, and additional professional learning funds for teachers. In Victoria, new policy has recently introduced a 70% increase in needs-based funding, mainly to schools in rural and regional areas (DET, 2015), and increased training for mathematics and science specialists to work with students in the most disadvantaged schools. A new funding measure will also extend that needs-based funding formula to include students deemed to be "at risk of falling behind."

Policy strategies for addressing educational equity in Singapore have combined increased funding and supports and smaller classes for programs for lower-achieving students, together with differentiated curricula that include "ladders and bridges" for students to move back to more academically demanding courses. Additional early diagnosis and intervention are available to students in early primary school who may be struggling with English literacy or mathematics. Learning support programs that feature daily small-group instruction with specially trained teachers are intended to improve equity of educational opportunity for underperforming students (Teh, 2014).

Chinese schools create specialized roles for some teachers. In China, it is typical for each class group to be assigned a teacher called a *banzhuren* (Link 7-2)—translated as "class director"—who serves as an advisor for the class group. This teacher consults with the families of the students, keeps track of the academic progress of the students in the class, and provides counseling to students on social and emotional issues they are facing. Some *banzhurens* are expected to visit the homes and families during the academic year on Saturdays or Sundays or on holidays. The *banzhuren* provides instruction for the class on issues of social importance or will help the class organize themselves into club activities. The *banzhuren* will also sit in on other subjects so she can monitor the progress of her students with other teachers and support them. The *banzhuren* gets to know the students and their families by staying with them for multiple grades.

Coupled with this is increased attention to student well-being. Jurisdictions with well-developed policy systems increasingly recognize that students are more likely to succeed when their cultural, emotional, and social needs are also supported. This is particularly so for students from minority or underserved backgrounds. There are extensive efforts under way in this regard in Australia and Canada. For example, the Australian Curriculum sets the learning of Aboriginal cultures as a cross-curricular priority to be woven throughout learning in all subjects, noting that when "Aboriginal and Torres Strait Islander students are able to see themselves, their identities and their cultures reflected in the curriculum of each of the learning areas, [they] can fully participate in the curriculum and can build their self-esteem" (ACARA, 2015). The nationally agreed Melbourne Declaration encourages schools to establish stronger connections with communities, noting that "the development of partnerships between schools and Indigenous communities, based on cross-cultural respect, is the main way of achieving highly effective schooling for Indigenous students" (MCEETYA, 2008, p. 10). Likewise, the national professional standards for teachers require that teachers "provide opportunities for students to develop understanding of and respect for Aboriginal and Torres Strait Islander histories, cultures and languages" (AITSL, 2011, p. 11).

Similarly, a goal of Ontario's Achieving Excellence policy vision is to "increase knowledge and understanding of First Nation, Métis, and Inuit cultures and histories to enhance the learning experience of both Aboriginal and non-Aboriginal students" (Government of Ontario, 2014, p. 13). At the national level, Canadian policy makers have established a commitment to strengthening and integrating indigenous histories, cultures, and perspectives through curricula, initial teacher education, and professional learning (ISTP, 2016).

Shaping the education system to support student well-being may be more challenging in the historically competitive and exam-oriented systems of Shanghai and Singapore, particularly where the students' families have deep-rooted cultural expectations of academic achievement and will invest as many family resources as possible in activities such as additional tutoring and specialized programs to accelerate their child. Nonetheless change is being led in these jurisdictions, too. In China, the 2020 plan policy vision seeks to reduce the heavy burden of homework on students in order to reduce stress and foster creativity and greater student engagement in learning. Shanghai was among the first districts in China to impose a limit on the amount of homework that can be prescribed, and it has also set a required minimum number of hours of physical activities during the school week (Cheng, 2011).

In Singapore, a range of policies are oriented toward providing a holistic approach to student learning, understood as developing well-rounded students and capturing the cognitive, aesthetic, spiritual, moral, and social dimensions. This approach is reflected in the Framework for 21st Century Competencies, which articulates the skills and competencies students need to live and work in the 21st century and should guide student learning and development. Similarly, "learner-centered values" including a "belief that every child can learn" and a "commitment to nurturing the potential in each child" form a core strand underpinning teacher education policy and the teacher growth model that guide teacher professional development in the country (Singapore MOE, 2012; Singapore NIE, 2012, p. 6). Students also participate in cross-curricular activities in which they work with teachers on community-oriented projects.

Building a Continuum of Support for Teaching

Each jurisdiction is continuing to work in policy areas that strengthen support for teachers throughout the course of their career. Each jurisdiction is working on different parts of the system to fill in the supports needed to develop a teaching workforce that is characterized by high standards, values teacher knowledge, promotes professional collaboration that supports ongoing learning, and provides career pathways that support teacher leadership.

New policy in Australia is working to strengthen public confidence in the quality of teacher graduates. There is thus a focus on teacher preparation programs and ensuring that teacher graduates are classroom ready. This involves strengthening the selection criteria for teaching candidates into initial teacher education, with new guidelines that include academic capability and personal qualities such as "motivation to teach," "interpersonal and communication skills," and "willingness to learn" to be instituted from 2017.

New accreditation guidelines for professional practice in training require structured agreements that facilitate closer communication between universities and placement schools, with guidelines for greater diversity of professional experiences in training, opportunities to observe and participate effectively earlier in their placement, and processes for early identification of preservice teachers at risk of not meeting standards. The country is investigating additional pedagogical and teacher performance assessments, designed to ensure teacher graduates' abilities to plan high-quality lessons, provide effective instruction, and assess and provide feedback to students on their work as they enter the classroom. Together with new guidelines introduced in 2016, these recommendations aim to ensure teachers enter the classroom equipped with the professional experience to reach their potential earlier in their career.

Finland is increasing its emphasis on induction and mentoring, an area that has previously received much less attention because of the strength of initial teacher training in the country. The decentralized structure of education in Finland means induction for teachers is primarily the responsibility of the school and municipality. In recent years, the Ministry of Education and Culture has funded a mentoring program coordinated through a collaborative network of teacher education institutions known as *Osaava Verme* (the Finnish Network for Teacher Induction), involving more than 120 of Finland's 300 municipalities (Pennanen, Bristol, Wilkinson, & Heikkinen, 2016).

Mentoring in Finland has taken on quite different characteristics to that in some other jurisdictions, shifting from the familiar one-on-one or mentor-protégé model to one of peer-group mentoring, which focuses on generating collegiality and dialogue rather than assessment (Kemmis, Heikkinen, Fransson, Aspfors, & Edwards-Groves, 2014; Pennanen et al., 2016). Participants meet in small groups often facilitated by an experienced teacher to discuss their work among colleagues who serve as co-mentors and co-mentees. Mentoring is thus understood as collaborative self-development that helps shape teachers' professional identity and strengthens the teaching community (Geeraerts, Tynjälä, Heikkinen, Markkanen, Pennanen, & Gijbels, 2015; Kemmis et al., 2014).

Other jurisdictions are providing increased support in the area of teacher-led professional development. In Shanghai, the Municipal Education Commission commonly sponsors action research, often as part of pilot programs to investigate scalability. Zhang et al. (2016) report that the amount of action research in Shanghai—over 100 school-based projects in 2013—has more than doubled since 2010, and teacher and principal action research, often published in journals, is forming a growing proportion of all school research. The authors note that

> Action research has become a crucial part of Shanghai's schools. A survey of principals found that almost all schools have drafted regulations about the conduct of educational research, supported teachers' participation or applications for research projects, set up research teams on teaching various subjects, included teachers' research performance in their performance evaluations, and/or allocated funds for the research. (Zhang et al., 2016, pp. 17–18)

Additional changes include the revision of the career ladder in 2013 to include a title for senior teachers, equivalent to that of a university professor, reflecting the value that is placed on teachers' knowledge.

This is also the case in Ontario, where the province is expanding its Teacher Learning and Leadership Program. The program provides government grants for individual classroom teachers or groups to engage in research and professional learning projects of their own design. The teacher-led program funds about 80 projects a year, ranging from lesson study to innovative classroom strategies or methods, and has covered more than 4,000 teachers since its inception. As part of the program, teachers participate in online learning communities and are required to share their learning experiences with other teachers within and beyond their school. The program builds on teacher knowledge and experience to foster increased teacher leadership and share good practices that builds teacher capacity.

Conclusion

It is clear that these countries, states, and provinces have undertaken an ongoing quest to support high-quality teaching for every child. In Chapter 1, we identified 10 key themes that capture some of the commonalities across these jurisdictions. To reprise these themes, the jurisdictions share these characteristics:

1. *A high social regard for teaching,* expressed in government statements and actions about teaching. Competitive salaries, investments in recruitment and training, participation in decision making, and opportunities for leadership all stem from a view that teachers and teaching are of critical importance to the welfare of the society—and if there are problems to surmount, teachers must be part of the solution, not positioned as the source of the problem.

2. *Selectivity into the profession,* enabled by teaching's high status and strong support. Candidates are carefully selected for their commitment and demonstrated strong capacity for working with children as well as other adults, along with their academic ability. Preparation is rigorous and is typically followed by high standards for licensure, hiring, and induction. With this on-ramp into the profession, candidates have demonstrated their competence early on, and schools can focus on developing them throughout the career rather than weeding them out later.

3. *Financial support for preparation and professional learning:* With preparation largely or entirely subsidized, all candidates can be fully prepared before they enter teaching. Governments also support teachers' time and costs for ongoing professional development. As a result, rather than acquiring only as much training as they can afford, teachers have ready access to learning and are expected to develop substantial expertise throughout their careers. Annual professional learning plans for teachers and schools guide purposeful development toward shared goals.

4. *Professional standards that outline teaching* expectations for knowledge, skills, and dispositions undergird preparation,

professional licensure or registration, professional learning, appraisal, and career development. The vision of teaching and learning embedded in these standards values the whole child's physical, social, emotional, and moral development—and views teachers as committed to using their knowledge and skills to advance growth and learning for each and every child using a wide repertoire of strategies to achieve success.

5. *Preparation and induction grounded in well-defined curriculum content and well-supported clinical training:* Teaching and teacher preparation are grounded in thoughtful national or state curriculum guidance, in each case recently revised to reflect 21st-century skills and competencies for students. Strong content preparation is coupled with increasingly strong preparation for teaching diverse learners, with an ever more intense focus on extended clinical training for teacher candidates, frequently through school-university partnerships much like teaching hospitals in medicine. This clinical support continues with mentoring and induction by expert veterans who are trained to coach, co-plan, and problem-solve with novices.

6. *Teaching as a research-informed and research-engaged profession:* Teachers use and conduct research about how to strengthen student learning from preservice preparation throughout their careers. In various jurisdictions, their capacity to engage in practice-based action research is part of admissions and graduation from teacher education, the work of professional learning communities, and a criterion for career advancement. As a result, teaching practice is deliberately reflective, with teachers conducting inquiries with colleagues to meet specific teaching challenges, collecting and using evidence to inform teaching practice.

7. *Teaching as a collaborative, not isolated, occupation,* where accomplishments are collective, not an individual act of courage. Teachers plan and problem-solve collaboratively and generally have scheduled time to do so. Teachers observe other teachers in action and are observed and mentored so that teacher knowledge and expertise are shared. Expertise is shared within and across schools to extend quality practices system-wide. Successful practices and results of teacher research are published for conferences and in professional journals for teachers.

8. *Teacher development as a continuum:* Each of the countries treats teacher professional learning as a continuum toward ever more effective work in support of student learning and, over time,

toward the learning of colleagues as well. Collaboration with colleagues is a key aspect of the evaluation process and helps identify teachers for leadership roles. Teacher evaluation processes are connected to teacher growth and development rather than punitive accountability. Teaching is regarded as a learning profession, with opportunities for even senior teachers to continually learn new skills and develop new expertise, which they also then share.

9. *Opportunities for leadership* are well developed in each jurisdiction—tied to formal career ladders in Australia, Singapore, and Shanghai and to organic opportunities to engage in research, mentoring, curriculum leadership, and school improvement activities as part of the teaching role in these countries as well as Canada and Finland. In each case, there is a range of formal and informal opportunities for teachers to develop pedagogical innovations, share them with others, and participate in school and system decision making.

10. *Systems organized to support quality teaching and equity* provide an infrastructure for the work of the individuals in the profession. A national or state curriculum, designed by members of the profession and used as a road map rather than a straitjacket, provides a centerpiece for teachers' work and collaborative planning. Stable, reliably funded systems of preparation, mentoring, and professional learning, along with scheduled in-school and professional development time, enable coherent and skillful teaching. Equitable funding and a conscious focus on improving education in traditionally underserved communities aim to ensure that all students will have access to high-quality teaching and learning opportunities.

As these themes suggest, widespread access to quality teaching does not occur by happenstance or through random acts of innovation that are exciting in the moment but come and go without ever spreading, getting deeply embedded, or scaling up. Among the things that became clear in this study were several principles that are critical for policy makers to understand.

Systemic Approach

First, *high-performing systems develop teachers and teaching systemically.* They do not try to raise teaching quality by focusing on a single policy lever. Instead, high-performing systems have developed systems of teacher development that take into account each aspect of teaching practice and that span teachers' careers. Although some systems might place greater emphasis on a particular aspect of the system, the systems are comprehensive in each jurisdiction; each element of the system complements the others and provides a supporting structure that has created a strong, purposeful, coherent system (as shown in Figure 7–1). What teachers learn is related to what they are expected to teach; schools are funded and organized to enable them to do so; and professional standards, learning opportunities, and career incentives reinforce this vision for practice.

We also saw that as countries or states make changes in one area, they also make complementary changes in another. For example, as curriculum changes, there is a concerted effort to bring preparation,

Figure 7–1 Policies in a Teaching and Learning System

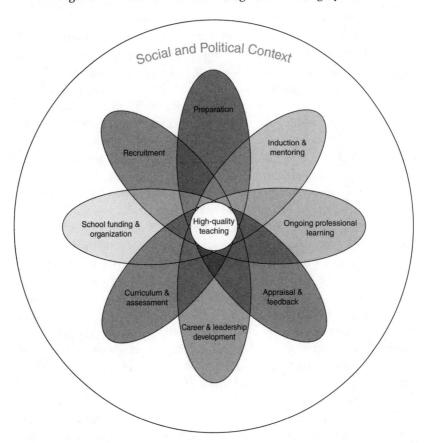

professional learning, and school-based practices and incentives into alignment. When new teaching practices are desired—whether these are pedagogical innovations or strategies such as lesson study or action research—supports for learning these practices are put in place. These may include creating seminars or institutes for teachers to learn the practice, training senior or lead teachers who can help organize learning for others in the schools, training coaches who can work with others to develop practices in the classroom, or finding time for teachers to collaborate on designing and testing new curriculum units and lessons.

When new forms of teacher learning are desired, such as action research, they are infused in preservice and in-service preparation, and administrators learn about them and how to support them, just as teachers do. The fact that teachers and principals have a shared knowledge and experience base, because principals are drawn from among the ranks of the most expert teachers—and the fact that this shared base of knowledge carries through to those who advance to work in the ministry or Department of Education—also creates coherence and a unified system.

A systematic learning and implementation process is enhanced by the fact that the ministries of education are typically occupied by practitioners with substantial knowledge of teaching, learning, and the systems they oversee and who are charged with examining research and successful practice at home and abroad. Ensuring that the ministry or state department includes the right mix of knowledgeable individuals has been part of the career ladder system in Singapore, the rigorous selection processes in Shanghai, and the strategies for tapping expert practitioners and policy advisors in Australia, Canada, and Finland.

When nations had previously emphasized some areas of work, they are now focused on strengthening the other parts of the system. For example, although Finland placed a strong emphasis on initial teacher preparation, it is now working to develop more formal mentoring systems and investing new funding streams in ongoing professional development. And although Shanghai built a very sophisticated system of mentoring and induction as well as teacher collaboration on action research, it is now working to strengthen recruitment and preservice teacher education. New clinical models of preservice education are taking hold in many places to strengthen teachers' abilities to enter teaching with more fully developed skills and judgment. All of these changes are aimed at strengthening the system as a whole and ensuring that all the parts are working together optimally.

A corollary is that these systems work toward this holistic vision in a steady manner over a long period of time. Rather than changing direction every few years, most of these jurisdictions have engaged in a regular process of researching, developing, and scaling up new approaches to curriculum, teaching, and teacher development to respond to their needs; then evaluating and refining those approaches; and then building on them to meet additional needs that have been identified. In most cases, they are buffered from many of the political winds that can easily overturn serious work and progress in places such as the United States, Great Britain, and other countries that expose education decisions to changing political forces.

Coordinated Approach

Second, teacher policies in high-performing systems work in synch with other education policies. For example, systems such as those in Victoria, New South Wales, and Singapore use student performance assessments that measure students' ability to apply their knowledge to solve complex problems and communicate effectively. Teachers are actively engaged in developing and scoring these assessments. This in turn provides powerful professional learning for teachers, who develop a strong understanding of the standards students are expected to reach and the curriculum and instructional strategies that would enable students to develop those competencies. They also develop similar standards of quality that they apply in their own classrooms.

Accountability policies in high-performing systems are also used to support teaching quality. In Shanghai, for example, when schools identified as low performing are matched with high-performing schools to support their learning, professional development is organized, and teachers are traded between the schools so that expertise is shared in multiple ways. Schools in Finland with high proportions of students with special needs receive additional funds for the express purpose of supporting teachers and instruction. Ontario, likewise, targets resources to low-performing schools focused specifically on developing the instructional capacity of school leaders and teachers in those schools, and accomplished teachers are made available to those schools to lead the instructional improvement process. As these nations take up virtually any area of education policy aimed at improvement, educators' capacity is at the center of attention.

Balancing Innovation and Control

Third, these high-performing systems encourage innovation while maintaining quality control and equity. Just as they expect teachers and schools to improve continually, the high-performing systems themselves are constantly seeking to improve their policies and practice. To this end, the systems evaluate the results of their policies and refine or change them in light of what is learned. They also find ways to disseminate successful practices and implementation strategies, even as they encourage local schools and teacher preparation institutions to develop their own innovative practices. These innovations are monitored carefully and evaluated to ensure that they are achieving their desired ends. At the same time, the systems are strongly committed to maintaining practices that ensure quality and equity so that these remain stable, reliable aspects of the system and innovations do not put children at risk.

In Australia and Canada, for example, the state maintains quality control over teacher education through professional standards and state or provincial accreditation standards. Yet it also has allowed considerable flexibility for institutions to develop innovative practices, as seen in the development of new clinically based models that governments are also in some cases supporting with grant funds. Alberta and Ontario sponsored bold initiatives to encourage teachers to form partnerships with communities and other professionals to develop innovative ideas. The Alberta Initiative for School Improvement provided CA$75 million per year, for 12 years, for teacher-led projects designed to improve instruction and learning. The Ontario Teacher Learning and Leadership Program has provided significant funding since 2007 to support teacher innovations coupled with action research and widespread dissemination to improve learning. Teachers' initiatives undergirding action research projects in Shanghai and Singapore are part of a culture of innovation that is supported, applauded, and widely disseminated through teacher journals, conferences, and recognitions.

Invest in Teaching

In sum, high-performing systems invest in the profession of teaching. When systems invest in teacher's knowledge and skill, teachers are acknowledged as expert educators who are trusted to make judgments about practice and how to improve it. Further, there are structures to enable teachers to use their expertise to support other teachers and participate in policy making. This in turn makes teaching a more attractive profession to thoughtful and creative individuals, supporting recruitment and retention in the field.

Perhaps the best example of this virtuous circle can be seen in Finland, where confidence in teachers' judgment is inspired by the nation's deep investment in initial teacher preparation: a 2-year master's degree for all teachers that places a strong emphasis on content knowledge and clinical preparation coupled with extensive preparation to use and conduct research. Teacher candidates enter through an examination that evaluates their ability to read and understand research and graduate having completed a master's thesis based on empirical research on teaching so that teachers have a solid grounding in methods to evaluate the effects of their own instruction. In addition, they have deep preparation in curriculum and assessment. Because of the great trust in teacher judgment, the country does not use external tests of student achievement but relies on the classroom performance assessments teachers create and grade to evaluate student progress. Teachers are also deeply involved in developing and reviewing the national curriculum, and they work together to develop the school-based lessons and units that flow from it so that they deeply understand the goals and outcomes of the work they are doing.

In Singapore and Shanghai, the profession's evolution and contribution to the leadership of practice are enhanced by well-developed career ladders that enable teachers to pursue advancement in their careers without leaving teaching and that enable excellent teachers also to pursue paths to formal teacher and school leadership positions. Teachers with demonstrated expertise take on additional roles in schools, such as curriculum development, professional learning, or instructional mentoring, or they can move into school leadership positions, from department chair to principal all the way through positions in the Ministry of Education. All of these are rooted in the knowledge base of the profession and translate the respect accorded to teachers into concrete engagement in professional decisions.

In Ontario, the ministry brings in experienced educators—usually on a time-limited basis—to inform strategies and to support implementation in the schools. Teachers' federations are involved in the development of policy through the Education Partnership Table, which brings together groups and associations representing students, parents, trustees, directors of education, supervisory officers, teachers, early childhood educators, support workers, principals, and relevant provincial organizations to meet with the Minister of Education and senior government officials. Those at the table consult their members in the field so that decisions are informed by expert knowledge and practical experience to improve the likelihood of their success.

There are several lessons that can be drawn from the orientation of these jurisdictions toward change. Each is working to improve the quality of education focusing on orienting their systems toward the anticipated needs of the 21st century, seeking to foster learning for all students regardless of background. Among policy levers available, enhancing teacher and teaching quality is seen as a key mechanism for educational improvement. Teaching in these jurisdictions is increasingly regarded as a profession, understood in terms of collaborative engagement with colleagues and ongoing professional learning that improves practice.

The nations and provinces we studied demonstrate that it is possible to think and act systemically to create a strong, knowledgeable teaching force in all communities for the benefit of all children. Although they would be the first to argue that they have further to go to fully accomplish their goals, these jurisdictions are firmly planted on a path to success in ensuring that every child is taught by caring, competent, and qualified teachers who work collaboratively in schools organized for their own and their students' success.

Appendix A

RESEARCH METHODOLOGY

THE INTERNATIONAL TEACHER POLICY STUDY (ITPS) employed a multimethod, multiple case study design in order to investigate the policies and practices that support teaching quality within education systems. Seven jurisdictions across five countries were selected for the study based on their highly developed teaching policy systems as well as indicators of student performance on international assessments such as the Program for International Student Assessment (PISA). In larger countries, national and selected state or provincial policies were examined to develop an understanding of the policy system. In these cases, the state or province was treated as a case nested within the larger country case.

Each jurisdictional team was composed of one or more locally based researcher(s) and one or more US-based colleague(s). This approach provided an insider perspective and an external lens on the data in each case.

We followed the same research design in each jurisdiction with adaptation to local circumstances. We developed common protocols for data collection, including interviews of policy makers, principals, teachers, and teacher educators, as well as observations of professional learning opportunities in schools and universities.

The research was conducted in several phases:

○ First, we conducted extensive document analysis, including education policy documents and descriptions of curriculum, instruction, and professional development practices and programs in primary, secondary, and higher education institutions. Reviews of the academic literature within and about each jurisdiction were also completed.

○ These were supplemented with analyses of international, national, and, where applicable, state data sources. Quantitative data were used to support document analysis prior to the interview phases and later to triangulate findings from interviews. Quantitative data sources consulted included country and state or provincial government statistics; the latest PISA and TALIS reports; OECD country profile documents; and surveys conducted by ministries, universities, teacher federations, and other professional teaching bodies.

o Two interview phases were conducted in 2014, beginning with interviews with policy makers and education experts in each jurisdiction. These interviews were followed by interviews with agency administrators, principals, teachers, teacher educators, and other education practitioners. In each case interviews were audio- or video-recorded and transcribed for analysis. In total, we interviewed 190 respondents: 52 teachers, 23 principals, 23 teacher candidates, 27 university academics and staff members, 46 policy makers and ministry of education staff members, 11 union representatives, and 8 administrators or professional development providers.

o The interviews were supplemented with detailed observations of activities in schools, universities, and classrooms, along with other key meetings and professional learning events.

o Observations included classroom instruction, grade-level planning meetings, teacher professional development sessions, instructional rounds, and classes in initial teacher education. Additional data sources included teacher schedules, appraisal or evaluation forms, school strategic plans, annual implementation plans, school budgets, instruction and assessment schedules, minutes of teacher meetings, school brochures, teacher education curriculum documents, textbooks, student learning assignments, and examples of school curricula.

Within each country case, the data about policies, perceptions, and practices were assembled and analyzed by topic area—recruitment, preparation, induction, professional learning, career development, compensation, and status of the profession. Researchers triangulated the different sources of data and sought evidence as well as counterevidence for emerging findings. As the individual cases were developed, the cross-case themes were identified through a recursive process in which researchers nominated themes and tested their applicability, accuracy, and limitations across jurisdictions, seeking additional evidence as needed to evaluate them and elaborate on the data.

Appendix B

QILUN ELEMENTARY SCHOOL LESSON PLAN

School: Qilun Elementary School in Minhang District	Class: 5th grade, class 2	Instructor: Jiaying Zhang
Topic: Learning about features of parallelogram	No. of students: 22	Date: November 19, 2013

1. Teaching objectives

1) To transfer methods of studying rectangle and square, and lead students to self-discover features of parallelogram from the dimensions of "side" and "angle".

2) To experience the instability of parallelogram in creative activities, and discover relationships between parallelogram, rectangle, and square.

2. Rationales for the objectives

1) Textbook analysis

Parallelogram appears in lesson 5, volume 10, of the elementary math textbook. In the textbook, parallelogram is introduced through two transparent color bands in parallel intersecting, then acknowledging two opposite sides to be of equal length and opposite angles to be of equal degrees, followed by an exploration of its diagonal, base, and height. I think this process takes separate approaches to understanding its sides and angles, and it lacks a comparison and connection with rectangle and square that have been introduced. As a matter of fact, learning of shape features falls into two stages: the first one is an understanding of features based on an understanding of elements, learning about superordinate concept, superordinate method and structure, and learning about features of rectangle and square through numbers of sides and angels, and the degrees of the angles. The second stage is based on an understanding of connections, when learning is about the numbers and degrees as well as about the locations of sides and degrees. This lesson falls into the second stage.

In learning about features of two-dimensional shapes that have similar structure, it works to test hypotheses and draw conclusions, continuously exploring its features, and being creative in using the features. The learning of parallelogram is based on learning about features of rectangle, square, and triangle. From the latter students have acquired knowledge, methods, and process and could transfer these to the learning of parallelogram. Then, they can be supported to make further comparison with features of rectangle, square, and triangle, to discuss their connections, and to enhance their understanding of these shapes. It is important to help students learn in a process of understanding features from different perspectives, thus to solidify their knowledge structure of shapes.

243

2) Student learning analysis

Before this lesson, students have observed parallelogram. Although they are not yet able to articulate its features, they can tell which shape is a parallelogram. In the first stage of learning, they have explored features of rectangle, square, and triangle, and learned to explore features of shapes from the two dimensions of "side" and "angle", and acquired the basic process of exploring features of shapes: making hypotheses — test hypotheses — summary and conclusion — making connections. The prior knowledge that students have lays a foundation for an active discovery of the topic in this lesson.

There are challenges in the discovery indeed. First, they might not know how to describe the angles in parallelogram because the concept of opposite angles has not been introduced yet; second, due to possible measure errors, the best way to prove opposite sides to be of equal length is to see if they coincide. Yet parallelogram is not of axial symmetry, it is hard to prove the opposite sides coincide; third, rectangle is a parallelogram with four right angles. It involves a complex process to learn the concept that rectangle is a special parallelogram; fourth, a rectangle is a parallelogram with four right angles. If four sides were equal in a rectangle, it becomes a square. The path from a parallelogram to a square involves changes in side and then in angle. How to make students think further about the connections in addition to an understanding? These challenges need a breakthrough from previous research methods.

Teaching procedures			
Stages	Teacher activities	Students' activities	Purpose
1. Regular accumulation	Display: square, rectangle Summary: We can explore features of two-dimensional shapes from the dimensions of "side" and "angle".	Talk about features and connections to your desk neighbors.	Review prior learning and get ready for the learning that comes up next.
2. Exploring features of parallelogram	Step 1. Making hypotheses Question: The instructor gives each student a parallelogram. You all know that parallelogram is a shape with four sides and four angles. Please mark the four angles with <1, <2, <3, <4. Take a close look at the four sides and angles, and see what features they have.	Think, write, and talk with your desk neighbor. Share and make hypothesis. Test hypothesis.	Based on students' prior experiences of studying rectangular, square, and triangular, lead them to actively apply the same knowledge structure in the process of "making hypothesis — test hypothesis — draw conclusion", to experience and learn about the features of parallelogram.

	Ask students to share their thoughts:
	  1) side: opposite sides in parallel and of equal length
	  2) angle: <1=<3, <2=<4
	
	Step 2. Exploring features
	
	Question: Do all parallelogram share the features? You will see many types of parallelogram in the bag. Please test if your hypothesis is correct.
	
	Group sharing:
	1) features of side:
	Hint: Could you use a tool to see if the opposite sides coincide?
	2) features of angle:
	Introduction: the concept of opposite angles
	
	Step 3. Drawing conclusions
	
	Question: Through hypothesis testing, what conclusions can you draw about features of side and angle in a parallelogram?
	
	Definition: Parallelogram is a shape with four sides, of which opposite sides that are in parallel.
		Explore: Given the possibility of measure errors, it works to see if opposite sides coincide. It is hard to prove that opposite sides in parallelogram coincide. You can do so by rotating it.
		
		Clarification: In a parallelogram, opposite sides are in parallel and of equal length. Opposite angles are of equal degrees.
			The process will focus on the challenges students might have. For example, let students experience if opposite sides can coincide.

| 3. Exploring instability of parallelogram | Task: With short sticks, how will you create a parallelogram? Why? Make a parallelogram using the short sticks.

Question: With the same sticks, the parallelograms you've created are different. Compare the sides and angles of your parallelograms; are there anything similar and different?

Task: Now try making a stable parallelogram using four short sticks. See how many types of parallelograms can you make? Is there any special case?

Guide: When observing changes in angles, you may focus on one angle and see how the others change accordingly.

Comparison: I have a triangle here. Let's twist it. What can you find?

Summary and further exploration: Parallelogram is not stable. Can you recall where in our life parallelogram is used because of its instability? | Clarification: Because parallelogram has two opposite sides of equal length, you may select two short sticks of equal length.

Compare thoughts: Sides being the same, angles have changed.

Thoughts on the experiment. Focus on one particular angle. Mark the degrees of each angle, like 30, 45, 60, 90, 120, 135.

Share findings: Rectangular is a special type of parallelogram with all features of parallelogram. The unique feature of rectangular is that it has four right angles.

Thoughts: It is not easy to twist the triangle. It is much easier to twist the parallelogram. Share the application in life. | In the discovery, students will go through scientific and logic process. In twisting parallelogram, they will see changes in the angles, and learn that rectangular is a special type of parallelogram. In comparing parallelogram with triangle, they will further understand the instability of parallelogram. |

| 4. Exploring connections between parallelogram and other shapes | Question: This is a parallelogram. How can we make it a rectangle? How can we make a rectangle a square?

Share findings.

Follow-up question: Change the angles, and then the sides. Is there any other way to make a parallelogram a square?

Summary: Shapes can be transformed according to their features.

Task: There seems to be close connections between parallelogram, rectangle, and square. Can you draw a picture to display the connections?

Summary: Square is a special type of rectangle. Rectangle is a special type of parallelogram. | Think and share.

Thoughts: Change the angles to 90 degrees, and the side to equal length.

Share findings: You may change side length first to a diamond shape, and then angles to make a square.

Share with your desk neighbor.

Try drawing a picture.

Exploring the connections:

From the outer layer to the center:

Parallelogram

Rectangle

Square | The exploration of connections will further enhance their understanding of the features and help make connections.

The picture vividly displays the connections among the three shapes, which also lays a foundation for future learning. |
| 5. Summary of the lesson | Summary: How have we explored the features of parallelogram? We can study other shapes using the same method. | Pair and share. | This is to further build the knowledge structure, and inspire students to actively apply learning in related study. |

Appendix C

QIBAO TEACHING CONTEST EVALUATION FORM

Grade		Subject		Project			
Teacher		Years of teaching		Title /rank		Other responsibilities /jobs	
Evaluation categories	Evaluation content	Evaluation items	Evaluation results (Please tick √ the one that fits)				
			Excellent	Relatively good	Average	Relatively poor	
Teacher behaviors	Teaching content	1. Teaching content is effective and reasonable; teaching objectives is appropriate for the context.					
		2. Lesson plan design is an organic component of the curriculum, emphasizes integration with other knowledge, and is connected to the school context.					
	Teaching methods	3. The instruction reflects the learning-before-teaching theory; there is a scientific and effective instructional support for learning.					

	4. The teacher respects, motivates, and appreciates students; the teacher gives timely feedback and uses quantifiable evaluation for students' group performance.				
	5. The teacher guides, prompts, inspires, and challenges students responsively and appropriately; there is timely and appropriate feedback and adjustment.				
	6. The teacher attends to all students and differentiates instruction according to individuals; the teacher cares for struggling students and uses various ways to involving them in learning.				
Student behaviors — Learning	7. Classroom dynamic is good; students are engaged and energetic.				
	8. It includes diversified ways of learning; it involves independent, explorative, and cooperative learning.				
	9. The majority of the students are engaged; no students is off task; more than 80% is in a good learning condition.				

		10. Group work is used in a meaningful way and has a strong connection with learning content.				
		11. The time spent on exploration, cooperation, presentation, and communication takes up to more than 80%; it's clearly student-centered.				
	Learning effects	12. Most students can reach the learning goals, have a good grasp of key learning contents, and make progress in challenging areas.				
		13. Students at all levels have successful learning experiences; struggling students participate in learning and are not off task.				
Overall evaluation	Positives and analysis:					
	Major areas for improvements and analysis:					

REFERENCES

ABS. (2015, January 29). *Overseas born Aussies hit a 120 year peak*. Canberra, Australia: Australian Bureau of Statistics. Retrieved from http://www .abs.gov.au/AUSSTATS/abs@.nsf/Previousproducts/3412.0Media%20 Release12013-14

Academy of Singapore Teachers. (n.d.). MOE Teacher Induction Framework. Retrieved from http://www.academyofsingaporeteachers.moe.gov.sg/ professional-growth/professional-development-programmes/moe-teacher-induction-framework

ACARA. (2015, December 15). The Australian curriculum v 8.1. Australian Curriculum Assessment and Reporting Authority. Retrieved from http:// www.australiancurriculum.edu.au/

Adamson, F., & Darling-Hammond, L. (2015). Policy pathways for twenty-first century skills. In P. Griffin & E. Care (Eds.), *Assessment and teaching of 21st century skills: Methods and approaches* (pp. 293–310). New York, NY: Springer.

AEU. (2014). Teacher Education Ministerial Advisory Group Consultation 2014: Submission. Retrieved from http://aeufederal.org.au/application/ files/6114/3273/1821/TEMAGConsultation.pdf

AITSL. (2011). *National Professional Standards for Teachers*. Melbourne, Australia: Australian Institute for Teaching and School Leadership. Retrieved from http://www.aitsl.edu.au/australian-professional-standards-for-teachers

AITSL. (2015a). *Action Now: Selection of entrants into initial teacher education*. Melbourne, Australia: Australian Institute for Teaching and School Leadership. Retrieved from http://www.aitsl.edu.au/initial-teacher-education/ite-reform/selection

AITSL. (2015b). *Australian Professional Standard for Principals and Leadership Profiles*. Melbourne, Australia: Australian Institute for Teaching and School Leadership. Retrieved from http://www.aitsl.edu.au/docs/default-source/school-leadership/australian-professional-standard-for-principals-and-the-leadership-profiles.pdf

Alberta Education. (1997). *Teaching quality standard applicable to the provision of basic education in Alberta* (Ministerial Order# 016/97). Edmonton, Canada: Author.

Alberta Education. (2014). Questions about . . . teacher salaries. Retrieved September 18, 2014, from http://education.alberta.ca/admin/workforce/faq/teachers/teachersalaries.aspx

Alberta Education. (2016). *Education funding in Alberta: Kindergarten to grade 12, 2016/2017 school year.* Edmonton, Canada: Alberta Ministry of Education. Retrieved from https://education.alberta.ca/media/3255924/education-funding-in-alberta-handbook-2016-2017.pdf

Alberta Learning Information Services. (2013). 2013 Alberta wage and salary survey, jobs, skills, labour, and training. Average wages by industry and economic region. Retrieved from http://alis.alberta.ca/pdf/wageinfo/2013_AWSS_Wages_By_Industry_and_Region.pdf

ATA. (2010). *A framework for professional development in Alberta.* Alberta, Canada: The Alberta Teachers' Association.

ATA. (2014). *Reflections on teaching: Teacher efficacy and the professional capital of Alberta teachers.* Edmonton, Canada: The Alberta Teachers' Association. Retrieved from https://www.teachers.ab.ca/SiteCollection-Documents/ATA/Publications/Research/PD-86-27%20Reflections%20on%20Teaching.pdf

Auguste, B. G., Kihn, P., & Miller, M. (2010). *Closing the talent gap: Attracting and retaining top-third graduates to careers in teaching: An international and market research-based perspective.* McKinsey.

Banks, C. A., & Banks, J. A. (1995). Equity pedagogy: An essential component of multicultural education. *Theory into Practice, 34*(3), 152–158.

Barber, M., & Mourshed, M. (2007). *How the world's best-performing school systems come out on top.* London, UK: McKinsey & Company.

Bennett, J. (2015, August). *Presentation to the NSW PPA Credential Validation panel.* Presented at the NSW Primary Principals' Association, Australian Technology Park, Sydney, Australia.

Borman, G. D., & Dowling, N. M. (2008). Teacher attrition and retention: A meta-analytic and narrative review of the research. *Review of Educational Research, 78*(3), 367–409.

Bracks, S. (2015). *Greater returns on investment in education: Government schools funding review.* Melbourne, Australia: Victoria State Government. Retrieved from http://www.education.vic.gov.au/Documents/about/department/government-schools-funding-review-march.pdf

Buchberger, F., & Buchberger, I. (2004). Problem solving capacity of a teacher education system as a condition of success? An analysis of the "Finnish case." In F. Buchberger & I. Buchberger (Eds.), *Education policy analysis in a comparative perspective* (pp. 222–237). Linz, Austria: Trauner.

Campbell, C., Lieberman, A., & Yashkina, A., with Carrier, N., Malik, S., & Sohn, J. (2014). *The Teacher Learning and Leadership Program: Research report 2013–14.* Toronto, Canada: Ontario Teachers' Federation. Retrieved from http://www.otffeo.on.ca/en/wp-content/uploads/sites/2/2014/08/TLLP-Final-Report-April-2014.pdf

Campbell, C., Lieberman, A., & Yashkina, A., with Hauseman, C., & Rodway Macri, J. (2015). *The teacher learning and leadership program: Research report for 2014–15.* Toronto, Canada: Ontario Teachers' Federation.

Carnegie Corporation. (2006). *Teachers for a new era: Transforming teacher education.* New York, NY: Carnegie Corporation.

Casserly, M. (2012, May 11). 10 jobs that didn't exist 10 years ago. *Forbes.* Retrieved December 26, 2015, from http://www.forbes.com/sites/meghancasserly/2012/05/11/10-jobs-that-didnt-exist-10-years-ago/

Cheng, K. (2011). Shanghai: How a big city in a developing country leaped to the head of the class. In M.Tucker (Ed.), *Surpassing Shanghai: An agenda for American education built on the world's leading systems* (pp. 21–50). Cambridge, MA: Harvard Education Press.

Cheng, K., & Yip, H. (2006). *Facing the knowledge society: Reforming secondary education in Hong Kong and Shanghai* (Education Working Paper No. 5). Washington, DC: World Bank.

City, E. A., Elmore, R. F., Fiarman, S. E., & Teitel, L. (2009). *Instructional rounds in education: A network approach to improving teaching and learning.* Cambridge, MA: Harvard Education Press.

Clotfelter, C. T., Ladd, H. F., & Vigdor, J. L. (2006). Teacher-student matching and the assessment of teacher effectiveness. *Journal of Human Resources, 41*(4), 778–820.

COAG. (2012, June). National partnership agreement on rewards for great teachers. Council of Australian Governments. Retrieved from http://www.federalfinancialrelations.gov.au/content/npa/education/rewards_for_great_teachers/national_partnership.pdf

Communist Party of China Central Committee and the State Council. (2010, July). *Outline of China's national plan for medium and long-term education reform and development.* Beijing, People's Republic of China. Retrieved from http://planipolis.iiep.unesco.org/upload/China/China_National_Long_Term_Educational_Reform_Development_2010-2020_eng.pdf

Council of Ministers of Education, Canada. (2008, April 15). Learn Canada 2020. Retrieved from http://cmec.ca/Publications/Lists/Publications/Attachments/187/CMEC-2020-DECLARATION.en.pdf

Crocker, R. (2009). Rethinking the AISI research model: Secondary data analysis and future applications. In A. Hargreaves, R. Crocker, B. Davis, L. McEwen, P. Sahlberg, D. Shirley, D. Sumara, & M. Hughes, *The learning mosaic: A multiple perspectives review of the Alberta Initiative for School Improvement (AISI)* (pp. 9–33). Edmonton, Canada: Alberta Education. Retrieved from http://education.alberta.ca/aisi

Crowley, R. (1998). *A class act: Inquiry into the status of the teaching profession.* Canberra, Australia: Parliament of Australia, Education and Training Reference Group.

Darling-Hammond, L. (1998). Strengthening the teaching profession: Teacher learning that supports student learning. *Educational Leadership, 55*(5).

Darling-Hammond, L. (2000). How teacher education matters. *Journal of Teacher Education, 51*(3), 166–173.

Darling-Hammond, L. (2006). *Powerful teacher education: Lessons from exemplary programs.* San Francisco, CA: Jossey-Bass.

Darling-Hammond, L. (2009). Teaching and the change wars: The professionalism hypothesis. In A. Hargreaves & M. Fullan (Eds.), *Change wars* (pp. 45–68). Bloomington, IN: Solution Tree Press.

Darling-Hammond, L. (2010). Recruiting and retaining teachers: Turning around the race to the bottom in high-need schools. *Journal of Curriculum and Instruction, 4*(1), 16–32. http://doi.org/10.3776/joci.2010 .v4n1p16-32

Darling-Hammond, L. (2013). *Developing and sustaining a high-quality teaching force* (Global Cities Education Network). Stanford, CA: Stanford Center for Opportunity Policy in Education. Retrieved from https:// edpolicy.stanford.edu/sites/default/files/publications/developing-and-sustaining-high-quality-teacher-force.pdf

Darling-Hammond, L., & Bransford, J. (Eds.). (2005). *Preparing teachers for a changing world: What teachers should learn and be able to do.* San Francisco, CA: Jossey-Bass.

Darling-Hammond, L., & Richardson, N. (2009). Research review/teacher learning: What matters. *Educational Leadership, 66*(5), 46–53.

Darling-Hammond, L., & Wentworth, L. (2014). Reaching out: International benchmarks for performance assessment. In L. Darling-Hammond & F. Adamson (Eds.), *Beyond the bubble test: How performance assessments support 21st-century learning* (pp. 93–130). San Francisco, CA: Jossey-Bass.

Darling-Hammond, L., Wise, A. E., & Klein, S. P. (1999). *A license to teach. Raising standards for teaching.* San Francisco, CA: Jossey-Bass.

DEC. (2011). *Connected communities strategy.* Sydney, Australia: NSW Department of Education and Communities.

DEC. (2013). *Great teaching, inspired learning: A blueprint for action.* Sydney, Australia: NSW Department of Education and Communities. Retrieved

from http://www.schools.nsw.edu.au/media/downloads/news/greatteaching/
gtil_blueprint.pdf

DEECD. (2011). *Curiosity and powerful learning*. Melbourne, Australia:
Department of Education and Early Childhood Development. Retrieved
from http://www.aiz.vic.edu.au/Embed/Media/00000025/Curiosity-booklet-
single-pages-for-web-21-Oct-11.pdf

DEECD. (2012a, December 1). *Principal selection policy*. Melbourne, Australia: Department of Education and Early Childhood Development.

DEECD. (2012b). *Towards Victoria as a learning community*. Melbourne, Australia: Communications Division for Flagship Strategies Division, Department of Education and Early Childhood Development.

DEECD. (2013a). *DEECD 2013–17 strategic plan*. Melbourne, Australia:
Department of Education and Early Childhood Development. Retrieved
from http://www.education.vic.gov.au/Documents/about/department/
stratplan201317.pdf

DEECD. (2013b). *From new directions to action: World-class teaching and
school leadership*. Melbourne, Australia: Department of Education and
Early Childhood Development. Retrieved from http://www.eduweb.vic
.gov.au/edulibrary/public/commrel/about/teachingprofession.pdf

DEECD. (2013c). *Professional practice and performance for improved learning:
School accountability*. Melbourne, Australia: Department of Education
and Early Childhood Development. Retrieved from http://www.education
.vic.gov.au/school/principals/management/Pages/schoolperformance.aspx

DEECD. (2014a). *Professional practice and performance for improved learning: Performance and development*. Melbourne, Australia: Department
of Education and Early Childhood Development. Retrieved from http://
www.education.vic.gov.au/Documents/school/principals/management/
ppilperfdevt.pdf

DEECD. (2014b, October 22). School centres for teaching excellence. Retrieved
April 4, 2014, from http://www.education.vic.gov.au/about/programs/
partnerships/pages/partnernationalsteach.aspx

DET. (2007). *The Developmental Learning Framework for School Leaders*.
Melbourne, Australia: Department of Education and Training. Retrieved
from http://www.education.vic.gov.au/Documents/school/principals/
profdev/developmentallearn.pdf

DET. (2015). *Education state: Schools*. Melbourne, Australia: Department of
Education and Training. Retrieved from http://www.education.vic.gov.au/
Documents/about/educationstate/launch.pdf

Dolton, P., & Marcenaro-Gutierrez, O. (2013). *2013 global teacher status
index*. London, UK: Varkey GEMS Foundation. Retrieved from https://

www.varkeyfoundation.org/sites/default/files/documents/2013GlobalTeac
herStatusIndex.pdf

Dudley, P. (2011). Lesson study: A handbook. Retrieved from http://lessonstudy
.co.uk/wp-content/uploads/2012/03/Lesson_Study_Handbook_-_011011-1
.pdf

DuFour, R., & Marzano, R. J. (2011). *Leaders of learning: How district,
school, and classroom leaders improve student achievement.* Bloomington, IN: Solution Tree Press.

Elmore, R. F., & Burney, D. (1997). Investing in teacher learning: Staff development and instructional improvement in Community School District #2,
New York City. Retrieved from http://eric.ed.gov/?id=ED416203

Finnish National Board of Education. (2007). Futures education. Retrieved
from http://www.oph.fi/download/47651_netengtulevaisuuskasvatus
2007.pdf

Finnish National Board of Education. (2014). *Opettajat Suomessa [Teach-
ers in Finland]* (Koulutuksen seurantaraportit No. 8). Helsinki, Finland:
National Board of Education.

Frey, C. B., & Osborne, M. A. (2013). The future of employment: *How
susceptible are jobs to computerisation (Working paper).* Oxford, UK:
University of Oxford. Retrieved from http:// www.oxfordmartin.ox.ac.uk/
downloads/academic/future-of-employment.pdf

Gang, S. (2010). *National survey and policy analysis for teacher professional
development in primary and secondary schools.* Shanghai, China: East
China Normal University Press.

Garner, R. (2015, March 20). Finland schools: Subjects scrapped and replaced
with "topics" as country reforms its education system. *The Independent.*
Retrieved from http://www.independent.co.uk/news/world/europe/finland-
schools-subjects-are-out-and-topics-are-in-as-country-reforms-its-educa-
tion-system-10123911.html

Geeraerts, K., Tynjälä, P., Heikkinen, H. L., Markkanen, I., Pennanen, M., &
Gijbels, D. (2015). Peer-group mentoring as a tool for teacher development. *European Journal of Teacher Education, 38*(3), 358–377.

Gillard, J. (2012, September). A national plan for school improvement. Presented at the National Press Club, Canberra, Australia.

Goddard, Y. L., Goddard, R. D., & Tschannen-Moran, M. (2007). A theoretical and empirical investigation of teacher collaboration for school
improvement and student achievement in public elementary schools.
Teachers College Record, 109(4), 877–896.

Goh, C. T. (1997, June 2). Shaping our future: Thinking schools, learning
nation. Speech by Prime Minister Goh Chok Tong at the opening of the

7th International Conference on Thinking, Singapore. [Press release]. Retrieved from http://www. moe. gov. sg/speeches/1997/020697

Gonski, D. M. (2014, May). Thoughts of a reviewer of school funding, two years on. Presented at the Australian College of Educators' Inaugural Jean Blackburn Oration, Melbourne.

Gonski, D. M., Boston, K., Greiner, K., Lawrence, C., Scales, B., & Tannock, P. (2012). *Review of funding for schooling.* Canberra, Australia: Department of Education, Employment and Workplace Relations.

Government of Ontario. (2014). *Achieving excellence: A renewed vision for education in Ontario.* Toronto, Canada: Ministry of Education. Retrieved from http://www.edu.gov.on.ca/eng/about/renewedVision.pdf

Government of Ontario. (2015). *2015–16 education funding: A guide to the grants for students' needs.* Toronto, Canada: Queen's Printer for Ontario. Retrieved from http://www.edu.gov.on.ca/eng/funding/1516/2015GSNguideEN.pdf

Graduate Careers Australia. (2013). *Graduate salaries 2012: A report on the earnings of new Australian graduates in their first full-time employment.* Melbourne, Australia: Graduate Careers Australia. Retrieved from http://www.graduatecareers.com.au/wp-content/uploads/2013/07/Graduate%20Salaries%202012%20[secured].pdf

Graham, L. J., & Jahnukainen, M. (2011). Wherefore art thou, inclusion? Analysing the development of inclusive education in New South Wales, Alberta and Finland. *Journal of Education Policy, 26*(2), 263–288.

Gunn, T. M., Pomahac, G., Striker, E., & Tailfeathers, J. (2011). First Nations, Métis, and Inuit education: The Alberta initiative for school improvement approach to improve indigenous education in Alberta. *Journal of Educational Change, 12*(3), 323–345.

Halinen, I. (2014, September 19). Curriculum reform 2016: Building the future together. Presented at the Enirdelm Conference, Vantaa, Finland.

Hargreaves, A., Crocker, R., Davis, B., McEwen, L., Sahlberg, P., Shirley, D., Sumara, D., & Hughes, M. (2009). *The learning mosaic: A multiple perspective review of the Alberta Initiative for School Improvement (AISI).* Edmonton, Canada: Alberta Education. Retrieved from http://education.alberta.ca/aisi

Hargreaves, A., & Fullan, M. (2012). *Professional capital: Transforming teaching in every school.* New York, NY: Teachers College Press.

Hargreaves, A., Halász, G., & Pont, B. (2008). The Finnish approach to system leadership. In B. Pont, D. Nusche, & D. Hopkins (Eds.), *Improving school leadership* (Vol. 2: Case studies on system leadership, pp. 69–109). Paris, France: OECD.

Hart, D. (2012). *The 18th OISE survey of educational issues: Public attitudes towards education in Ontario 2012.* Toronto, Ontario: Ontario Institute for Studies in Education. Retrieved from http://www.oise.utoronto .ca/oise/UserFiles/File/OISE%20Survey/18th_OISE_Survey/OISE%20 SURVEY%2018.pdf

Hatch, T. (2013). Beneath the surface of accountability: Answerability, responsibility and capacity-building in recent educational reforms in Norway. *Journal of Educational Change, 14*(1), 1–15.

Heng, S. K. (2012, September 12). Keynote address. Presented at the Ministry of Education work plan seminar, Singapore. Retrieved from http://www .moe.gov.sg/media/speeches/2012/09/12/keynote-address-by-mr-heng-swee-keat-at-wps-2012.php.

Henry, G. T., Bastian, K. C., & Fortner, C. K. (2011). Stayers and leavers early-career teacher effectiveness and attrition. *Educational Researcher, 40*(6), 271–280.

Herbert, M., Broad, K., Gaskell, J., Hart, D., Berrill, D., Demers, S., & Heap, J. (2010). *Teacher preparation and success in Ontario.* Prepared for the Ontario Ministry of Education. Toronto, Canada: University of Toronto; Trent University; Université Laurentienne; Brock University.

Ingersoll, R. (2007). *A comparative study of teacher preparation and qualifications in six nations* (CPRE Research Reports). Philadelphia, PA: Consortium for Policy Research in Education.

Ingersoll, R. M., & Strong, M. (2011). The impact of induction and mentoring programs for beginning teachers: A critical review of the research. *Review of Educational Research, 81*(2), 201–233. http://doi. org/10.3102/0034654311403323

International Alliance of Leading Education Institutes. (2008). *Transforming teacher education: Redefined professionals for 21st century schools.* Singapore: National Institute of Education. Retrieved from http://website .education.wisc.edu/inei/wp-content/uploads/Documents/Transforming_ Teacher_Education_Report.pdf

ISTP. (2016). Country commitments from the International Summit on the Teaching Profession 2016. Retrieved from http://www.istp2016.org/ fileadmin/Redaktion/Dokumente/documentation/2016_ISTP_Country_ Commitments.pdf

Jackson, C. K., & Bruegmann, E. (2009). Teaching students and teaching each other: The importance of peer learning for teachers. National Bureau of Economic Research. Retrieved from http://www.nber.org/papers/w15202

Jensen, B., & Farmer, J. (2013). *School turnaround in Shanghai: The empowered-management program approach to improving school performance.* Washington, DC: Center for American Progress.

Jensen, B., Sonnemann, J., Roberts-Hull, K., & Hunter, A. (2016). *Beyond PD: Teacher professional learning in high-performing systems*. Washington, DC: National Center for Education and the Economy.

Johnson, D. R. (2013). *Teachers and their salaries—Some evidence from the Labour Force Survey*. Laurier Centre for Economic Research & Policy Analysis. Retrieved from http://navigator.wlu.ca/content/documents/Link/career%20new%20website/LCERPA_LFNews_Jan_2013.pdf

Johnson, S. M., Kraft, M. A., & Papay, J. P. (2012). How context matters in high-need schools: The effects of teachers' working conditions on their professional satisfaction and their students' achievement. *Teachers College Record*, *114*(10), 1–39.

Kaftandjieva, F., & Takala, S. (2002, June). Relating the Finnish matriculation examination English test results to the CEF scales. Presented at the Seminar on Linking Language Examinations to CEFR, Helsinki, Finland.

Kane, R., Jones, A., Rottman, J., & Conner, M. (2010). *NTIP evaluation: Final report executive summary (Cycle III)*. Ottawa, Canada: University of Ottawa. Retrieved from http:// www.edu.gov.on.ca/eng/policyfunding/memos/may2010/NTIP_Evaluation_Report_2010.pdf

Kansanen, P. (2007). Research-based teacher education. In R. Jakku-Sihvonen & H. Niemi (Eds.), *Education as a societal contributor: Reflections by Finnish educationalists* (pp. 131–146). Frankfurt am Main, Germany: Peter Lang.

Kemmis, S., Heikkinen, H.L.T., Fransson, G., Aspfors, J., & Edwards-Groves, C. (2014). Mentoring of new teachers as a contested practice: Supervision, support and collaborative self-development. *Teaching and Teacher Education*, *43*, 154–164. http://doi.org/10.1016/j.tate.2014.07.001

Kini, T., & Podolsky, A. (2016). *Does teaching experience increase teacher effectiveness? A review of the research*. Palo Alto, CA: Learning Policy Institute. Retrieved from https:// learningpolicyinstitute.org/our-work/publications-resources/ does-teaching-experience-increase-teacher-effectiveness-review-research

Koh, K. H., Tan, C., & Ng, P. T. (2012). Creating thinking schools through authentic assessment: The case in Singapore. *Educational Assessment, Evaluation and Accountability*, *24*(2), 135–149.

Kraft, M. A., & Papay, J. P. (2014). Can professional environments in schools promote teacher development? Explaining heterogeneity in returns to teaching experience. *Educational Evaluation and Policy Analysis*, *36*(4), 476–500.

Krogstad, J. M., & Keegan, M. (2014, May 14). 15 states with the highest share of immigrants in their population. Retrieved from http://www.pewresearch.org/fact-tank/2014/05/14/15-states-with-the-highest-share-of-immigrants-in-their-population/

Krokfors, L. (2007). Two-fold role of reflective pedagogical practice in research-based teacher education. In R. Jakku-Sihvonen & H. Niemi (Eds.), *Education as a societal contributor* (pp. 147–160). Frankfurt am Main, Germany: Peter Lang.

Kultusminister Koferenz. (2016). ISTP2016—International Summit on the Teaching Profession 2016. Retrieved March 10, 2016, from http://www .istp2016.org/

Ladd, H. F. (2011). Teachers' perceptions of their working conditions: How predictive of planned and actual teacher movement? *Educational Evaluation and Policy Analysis, 33*(2), 235–261.

Lavonen, J. (2008). *Reasons behind Finnish students' success in the PISA scientific literacy assessment.* Helsinki, Finland: University of Helsinki. Retrieved from http://www.oph.fi/info/finlandinpisastudies/conference 2008/science_results_and_reasons.pdf

Lee, H. (2013, June 4). Why Finnish babies sleep in cardboard boxes. *BBC.* Retrieved October 29, 2014, from http://www.bbc.com/news/magazine-22751415

Lee, K.-E. C., & Tan, M. Y. (2010, March 7–12). Rating teachers and rewarding teacher performance: The context of Singapore. Presented at the Asia-Pacific Economic Cooperation (APEC) Conference on Replicating Exemplary Practices in Mathematics Education, Koh Samui, Thailand.

Lee, S. K., Lee, W. O., & Low, E. L. (Eds.). (2013). *Educational policy innovations: Leveling up and sustaining educational achievement.* Singapore: Springer.

LePoer, B. L. (1989). *Singapore: A country study.* Washington, DC: Library of Congress, Federal Research Division.

Levin, B. (2014). Sustainable, large-scale education renewal: The case of Ontario. In S. K. Lee, W. O. Lee, & E. L. Low (Eds.), *Educational policy innovations: Leveling up and sustaining educational achievement* (pp. 201–216). Singapore: Springer.

Liang, S., Glaz, S., DeFranco, T., Vinsonhaler, C., Grenier, R., & Cardetti, F. (2012). An examination of the preparation and practice of grades 7–12 mathematics teachers from the Shandong Province in China. *Journal of Mathematics Teacher Education, 15*(5). http://doi.org/10.1007/s10857-012-9228-x

Liiten, M. (2004, February 11). Ykkössuosikki: Oppetajan ammatti [Top favorite: Teaching Profession.]. *Helsingin Sanomat.* Helsinki, Finland.

Loeb, S., Darling-Hammond, L., & Luczak, J. (2005). How teaching conditions predict teacher turnover in California schools. *Peabody Journal of Education, 80*(3), 44–70.

Lyman, P., & Varian, H. R. (2003). *How much information?* Berkeley, CA: School of Information Management and Systems, University of California, Berkeley. Retrieved from http://www2.sims.berkeley.edu/research/projects/how-much-info-2003/

Martin, A., & Pennanen, M. (2015). *Mobility and transition of pedagogical expertise in Finland* (No. 51). Jyväskylä, Finland: Finnish Institute for Educational Research, University of Jyväskylä.

Matthews, P., Moorman, H., & Nusche, D. (2007). School leadership development strategies: Building leadership capacity in Victoria, Australia. OECD. Retrieved from http://www.oecd.org/edu/school/39883476.pdf

MCEETYA. (2008). *Melbourne declaration on educational goals for young Australians*. Melbourne, Australia: Ministerial Council for Education, Employment, Training and Youth Affairs.

McIntyre, A. (2012). The greatest impact for early career teachers. Presented at the Australian Council for Educational Leaders National Conference, Adelaide.

McIntyre, A. (2013). Teacher quality evidence for action. Presented at the Australian College of Educators conference, Australian College of Educators.

McLean Davies, L., Anderson, M., Deans, J., Dinham, S., Griffin, P., Kameniar, B., . . . Tyler, D. (2012). Masterly preparation: Embedding clinical practice in a graduate pre-service teacher education programme. *Journal of Education for Teaching*, 39(1), 93–106. http://doi.org/10.1080/0260747 6.2012.733193

Mehta, J., & Schwartz, R. (2011). Canada: Looks a lot like us but gets much better results. In M.Tucker (Ed.), *Surpassing Shanghai: An agenda for American education built on the world's leading systems* (pp. 141–166). Cambridge, MA: Harvard Education Press.

Merlino, J. (2015, October 9). Raising the status of the teaching profession in the education state. Retrieved February 19, 2016, from http://www.premier.vic.gov.au/raising-the-status-of-the-teaching-profession-in-the-education-state/

Ministry of Education and Culture. (2012). *Education and research 2011–2016: A development plan* (Reports of the Ministry of Education and Culture, Finland, 2012–3). Helsinki, Finland: Ministry of Education and Culture. Retrieved from http://www.minedu.fi/OPM/Julkaisut/2012/Kehittamissuunnitelma.html?lang=fi&extra_locale=en

Ministry of Education of the People's Republic of China. (2011). Middle school teacher professional standards. Retrieved from http://www.moe.edu.cn/publicfiles/business/htmlfiles/moe/s6127/201112/127830.html

264

REFERENCES

Ministry of Education, Singapore. (2015). 21st century competencies. Retrieved from https://www.moe.gov.sg/education/education-system/21st-century-competencies

Ministry of Education, Singapore. (n.d.). Career information. Retrieved from https://www.moe.gov.sg/careers/teach/career-information

NCATE. (2010). *Transforming teacher education through clinical practice: A national strategy to prepare effective teachers.* (Report of the Blue Ribbon Panel on Clinical Preparation and Partnerships for Improved Student Learning). Washington, DC: National Council for Accreditation of Teacher Education. Retrieved from http://www.ncate.org/Public/researchreports/NCAtEinitiatives/BlueribbonPanel/tabid/715/Default.aspx

Niu, Z., & Liu, M. (2012, April 25). Teacher merit pay in China: A case study in Beijing. Presented at the Annual meeting of the 56th Annual Conference of the Comparative and International Education Society, San Juan, Puerto Rico.

NSW Government. (2013). *OCHRE—Opportunity, choice, healing, responsibility, empowerment* (NSW Government plan for Aboriginal affairs: Education, employment & accountability). Sydney, Australia: NSW Government. Retrieved from http://www.aboriginalaffairs.nsw.gov.au/wp-content/uploads/2013/04/AA_OCHRE_final.pdf

NSW Primary Principals Association. (2015). *NSW PPA principals credential phase one report 2015.* Sydney, Australia: NSW Primary Principals Association. Retrieved from http://www.nswppa.org.au/

OECD. (2007). *Science competencies for tomorrow's world* [Report]. Paris, France: OECD Publishing. Retrieved from http://www.oecd.org/pisa/pisaproducts/pisa2006/39725224.pdf

OECD. (2011). *Lessons from PISA for the United States.* Strong performers and successful reformers in education. Paris, France: OECD Publishing. Retrieved from http://dx.doi.org/10.1787/9789264096660-en

OECD. (2013a). *PISA 2012 results: Excellence through equity* (Vol. II). Paris, France: OECD Publishing. Retrieved from http://www.oecd-ilibrary.org/education/pisa-2012-results-excellence-through-equity-volume-ii_9789264201132-en

OECD. (2013b). *PISA 2012 results: What makes schools successful* (Vol. IV). Paris, France: OECD Publishing. Retrieved from http://www.oecd-ilibrary.org/education/pisa-2012-results-what-makes-a-school-successful-volume-iv_9789264201156-en

OECD. (2014a). *Education at a glance 2014.* Paris, France: OECD Publishing. Retrieved from http://www.oecd-ilibrary.org/education/education-at-a-glance-2014_eag-2014-en

OECD. (2014b). *Education at a glance country note: Canada*. Paris, France: OECD Publishing. Retrieved from http://www.oecd.org/edu/Canada-EAG2014-Country-Note.pdf

OECD. (2014c). *PISA 2012 results: What students know and can do—student performance in mathematics, reading and science* (Vol. I, Rev. ed., February 2014). Paris, France: OECD Publishing. Retrieved from http://dx.doi.org/10.1787/9789264201118-en

OECD. (2014d). *Talis 2013 results: An international perspective on teaching and learning*. Paris, France: OECD Publishing. Retrieved from http://dx.doi.org/10.1787/9789264196261-en

OECD. (2015). *Education at a glance 2015: OECD indicators*. Paris, France: OECD Publishing. Retrieved from http://dx.doi.org/10.1787/eag-2015-en

Ontario College of Teachers. (2000). *Standards of practice*. Ontario, Canada: Ontario College of Teachers. Retrieved from http://www.oct.ca/public/professional-standards/standards-of-practice

Ontario College of Teachers. (2009). *Principals' qualification program*. Ontario, Canada: Ontario College of Teachers. Retrieved from https://www.oct.ca/-/media/PDF/Principals%20Qualification%20Program%20 2009/principals_qualification_program_e.pdf

Ontario College of Teachers. (2011). *Transition to teaching 2011: Early-career teachers in Ontario schools*. Toronto, Canada: Ontario College of Teachers. Retrieved from http://www.oct.ca/-/media/PDF/Transition%20to%20 Teaching%202011/EN/transitions11_e.ashx

Ontario College of Teachers. (2012). *Transition to teaching 2012: Teachers face tough entry-job hurdles in an increasingly crowded Ontario employment market*. Toronto, Canada: Ontario College of Teachers. Retrieved from http://www.oct.ca/-/media/PDF/Transition%20to%20Teaching%20 2012/T2T%20Main%20Report_EN_web_accessible0313.ashx

Ontario Ministry of Education. (2010). *Growing success: Assessment, evaluation, and reporting in Ontario schools*. Toronto, Canada: Author. Retrieved from https://www.edu.gov.on.ca/eng/policyfunding/growSuccess.pdf

Ontario Ministry of Education. (2012). Ontario leadership framework. Retrieved from https://www.education-leadership-ontario.ca/content/framework

Ontario Ministry of Education. (2013, June 5). Giving new teachers the tools for success. Retrieved June 27, 2016, from https://news.ontario.ca/edu/en/2013/06/giving-new-teachers-the-tools-for-success.html

Paine, L., & Ma, L. (1993). Teachers working together: A dialogue on organizational and cultural perspectives of Chinese teachers. *International Journal of Educational Research*, 19(8), 675–697.

Parkin, A. (2015). International report card on public education: Key facts on Canadian achievement and equity. The Environics Institute. Retrieved from http://www.environicsinstitute.org/uploads/institute-projects/environics%20institute%20-%20parkin%20-%20international%20report%20on%20education%20-%20final%20report.pdf

Parsons, J., & Beauchamp, L. (2012). Action research: The Alberta Initiative for School Improvement (AISI) and its implications for teacher education. *Action Researcher in Education, 3*(1), 120–131.

Parsons, J., McRae, P., & Taylor, L. (2006). *Celebrating school improvement: Six lessons from Alberta's AISI projects.* Edmonton, Canada: School Improvement Press

Pennanen, M., Bristol, L., Wilkinson, J., & Heikkinen, H.L.T. (2016). What is "good" mentoring? Understanding mentoring practices of teacher induction through case studies of Finland and Australia. *Pedagogy, Culture & Society, 24*(1), 27–53. http://doi.org/10.1080/14681366.2015.1083045

Piesanen, E., Kiviniemi, U., & Valkonen, S. (2007). *Opettajankoulutuksen kehittämisohjelman seuranta ja arviointi. Opettajien täydennyskoulutus 2005 ja seuranta 1998-2005 oppiaineittain ja oppialoittain eri oppilaitos-muodoissa [Follow-up and evaluation of the teacher education development program: Continuing teacher education in 2005 and its follow up 1998-2005 by fields and subjects in different types of educational institutions.].* Jyväskyläm, Finland: University of Jyväskylä, Institute for Educational Research.

Pine, G. J. (2008). *Teacher action research: Building knowledge democracies.* Thousand Oaks, CA: Sage Publications.

Rickards, F. (2012, May 29). New course design: Building clinical skills with grounded experience in schools. Presented at the National Forum on Initial Teacher Education, Melbourne. Retrieved from http://www.education.vic.gov.au/Documents/about/programs/partnerships/natforuminitialmorning.pdf

Roberts, D. (2013, April 4). Chinese education: The truth behind the boasts. *Bloomberg Businessweek.* Retrieved from http://www.bloomberg.com/news/articles/2013-04-04/chinese-education-the-truth-behind-the-boasts

Sahlberg, P. (2007). Education policies for raising student learning: The Finnish approach. *Journal of Education Policy, 22*(2), 147–171.

Sahlberg, P. (2009). AISI: A global perspective. In A. Hargreaves, R. Crocker, B. Davis, L. McEwen, P. Sahlberg, D. Shirley, D. Sumara, & M. Hughes, *The learning mosaic: A multiple perspectives review of the Alberta Initiative for School Improvement (AISI)* (pp. 77–89). Edmonton, Canada: Alberta Education. Retrieved from http://education.alberta.ca/aisi

Sahlberg, P. (2010). Educational change in Finland. In A. Hargreaves, A. Lieberman, M. Fullan, & D. Hopkins (Eds.), *Second international handbook of educational change* (pp. 323–348). Dordrecht, the Netherlands: Springer.

Sahlberg, P. (2015a, March 25). Finland's school reforms won't scrap subjects altogether. *The Conversation.* Retrieved from http://theconversation.com/finlands-school-reforms-wont-scrap-subjects-altogether-39328

Sahlberg, P. (2015b). *Finnish lessons 2.0: What can the world learn from education in Finland?* New York, NY: Teachers College Press.

Salleh, H., & Tan, C.H.P. (2013). Novice teachers learning from others: Mentoring in Shanghai schools. *Australian Journal of Teacher Education, 38*(3), article 10, 152–165.

Sato, M., Roehrig, G., & Donna, J. (2010). Bending the professional teaching continuum: How teacher renewal supports teacher retention. In J. Rhoton (Ed.), *Science education leadership: Best practices for the new century* (pp. 177–198). Arlington, VA: NSTA Press.

School Act, Pub. L. No. Revised statutes of Alberta 2000: Chapter S-3. (2000). Retrieved from http://www.qp.alberta.ca/documents/acts/s03.pdf

Sclafani, S., & Lim, E. (2008). *Rethinking human capital: Singapore as a model for teacher development.* Washington, DC: Aspen Institute.

Scott, C., Kleinhenz, E., Weldon, K., Reid, K., & Dinhan, S. (2010). *Master of teaching MGSE: Evaluation report.* Camberwell, Australia: Australian Council for Educational Research.

Shanghai Municipal Education Commission. (2008). *Shanghai education yearbook 2008.* Shanghai, China: Shanghai Educational Publishing House.

Shanghai Municipal Statistics Bureau. (2011). *Shanghai basic facts.* Shanghai, China: Information Office of Shanghai Municipality.

Shulman, L. S. (1983). Autonomy and obligation: The remote control of teaching. In L. S. Shulman & G. Sykes (Eds.), *Handbook of teaching and policy.* New York, NY: Longman.

Shulman, L. S. (1986). Those who understand: Knowledge growth in teaching. *Educational Researcher, 15*(2), 4–14.

Singapore Department of Statistics. (2015, September). Population in brief 2015. Retrieved from http://population.sg/population-in-brief/files/population-in-brief-2015.pdf

Singapore MOE. (2012). *The teacher growth model: Fact sheet.* Singapore: Author. Retrieved from https://www.moe.gov.sg/media/press/files/2012/05/fact-sheet-teacher-growth-model.pdf

Singapore NIE. (2009). *TE21: A teacher education model for the 21st century.* Singapore: Author.

Singapore NIE. (2012). *A teacher education model for the 21st century (TE21): NIE's journey from concept to realisation—An implementation report.* Singapore: National Institute of Education. Retrieved from https://www.nie.edu.sg/files/booklet_web.pdf

Snoek, M. (2014). Theories on and concepts of professionalism of teachers and their consequences for the curriculum in teacher education. Retrieved from http://www.hva.nl/binaries/content/assets/subsites/kc-oo/publicaties/theories-on-and-concepts-of-professionalism-hungarian-publication.pdf

Spillane, J. P., Sherer, J. Z., & Codren, A. (2005). Distributed leadership. In W. K. Hoy & C. G. Miskel (Eds.), *Educational leadership and reform* (pp. 149–167). Greenwich, CT: IAP.

Statistics Canada. (2013). *Immigration and ethnocultural diversity in Canada: National Household Survey, 2011.* Ottawa, Canada: Statistics Canada—Statistique Canada. Retrieved from http://epe.lac-bac.gc.ca/100/201/301/weekly_checklist/2013/internet/w13-19-U-E.html/collections/collection_2013/statcan/CS99-010-2011-1-eng.pdf

Statistics Finland. (2014a). Statistics Finland—Education. Retrieved January 20, 2015, from http://tilastokeskus.fi/til/kou_en.html

Statistics Finland. (2014b). *Ulkomaalaistaustainen väestö 2013 [Population with foreign background]* (Suomen virallinen tilasto [Official Statistics of Finland]). Helsinki, Finland: Statistics Finland. Retrieved from http://www.stat.fi/tup/julkaisut/tiedostot/julkaisuluettelo/yvrm_ulsi_201300_2014_12286_net.pdf

Stewart, V. (2011). Singapore: A journey to the top, step by step. In M.Tucker (Ed.), *Surpassing Shanghai: An agenda for American education built on the world's leading systems* (pp. 113–139). Cambridge, MA: Harvard Education Press.

Tan, C. (2013). *Learning from Shanghai.* Singapore: Springer. Retrieved from http://link.springer.com/10.1007/978-981-4021-87-6

Tan, K. S., & Wong, Y. F. (2012). Developing quality teachers for the Singapore School System: The impact of the National Institute of Education and the tripartite relationship with the Ministry of Education and Schools. In I. Žogla & L. Rutka (Eds.), *Teachers' life-cycle from initial teacher education to experienced professional.* Brussels, Belgium: Association for Teacher Education in Europe.

Teh, L. W. (2014). Singapore's performance in PISA: Levelling up the long tail. In S. K. Lee, W. O. Lee, & E. L. Low (Eds.), *Educational policy innovations* (pp. 71–83). Singapore: Springer.

TEMAG. (2015, February). *Action now: Classroom ready teachers: Report of the Teacher Education Ministerial Advisory Group.* Canberra, Australia: Department of Education and Training.

Teo, C. H. (2001, July). Speech by Radm (NS) Teo Chee Hean, Minister for Education and Second Minister for Defence. Presented at the NIE teachers' investiture ceremony, Singapore indoor stadium, Singapore. Retrieved from http://www.moe.gov.sg/media/speeches/2001/sp04072001.htm

Thompson, C. L., & Zeuli, J. S. (1999). The frame and the tapestry: Standards-based reform and professional development. In L. Darling-Hammond & G. Sykes (Eds.), *Teaching as the learning profession: Handbook of policy and practice* (pp. 341–375). San Francisco, CA: Jossey-Bass.

Thomson, S., De Bortoli, L. J., & Buckley, S. (2014). *PISA 2012: How Australia measures up*. Melbourne, Australia: Australian Council for Educational Research (ACER).

Toom, A., Kynäslahti, H., Krokfors, L., Jyrhämä, R., Byman, R., Stenberg, K., . . . Kansanen, P. (2010). Experiences of research-based approach to teacher education: Suggestions for future policies. *European Journal of Education, 45*(2), 331–344.

Tucker, M. (Ed.). (2011). *Surpassing Shanghai: An agenda for American education built on the world's leading systems*. Cambridge, MA: Harvard Education Press.

Tucker, M. (2014). *Chinese lessons: Shanghai's rise to the top of the PISA league tables*. Washington, DC: National Center on Education and the Economy.

University of Alberta. (2004). *Alberta Initiative for School Improvement: What have we learned; An assessment of district qualitative reports and promising practices from Cycle 1, 2000–2003*. School Improvement Press. Edmonton, Alberta. Retrieved January 4, 2005, from www.education.govab.ca/K_12/special/AISI/pdfs/UniversityofA_Cycle1_Report_June_2004.pdf

Uusiautti, S., & Määttä, K. (2013). Significant trends in the development of Finnish teacher training education programs (1860–2010). *Education Policy Analysis Archives, 21*(59). Retrieved from http://epaa.asu.edu/ojs/article/view/1276

VIT. (2013, January 1). Evidence of professional practice for full registration. Retrieved September 29, 2014, from http://www.vit.vic.edu.au/prt/pages/evidence-of-professional-practice-for-full-registration-36.aspx

VIT. (2014, June). *Evaluating the supporting provisionally registered teachers program: 2013 summary report*. Melbourne, Australia: Victorian Institute of Teaching.

Wilson, S., Floden, R., & Ferrini-Mundy, J. (2001). *Teacher preparation research: Current knowledge, gaps, and recommendations*. Seattle, WA: Center for the Study of Teaching and Policy.

Wu, N. (2014). The implementation of the national professional standard for K–12 teachers, 2012 (NPST) at regional and local level in China: A case study of regional teacher professional development standards implementation in Qingyang District, Chengdu, China. *Higher Education of Social Science*, 7(3), 89–98.

Ye, L. (2009). "New Basic Education" and me: Retrospective notes from the past ten years of research. *Frontiers of Education in China*, 4(4), 558–609. http://doi.org/10.1007/s11516-009-0031-0

Zeichner, K. M. (1995). Beyond the divide of teacher research and academic research. *Teachers and Teaching: Theory and Practice*, 1(2), 153–172.

Zhang, M., Ding, X., & Xu, J. (2016). *Developing Shanghai's teachers*. Washington, DC: National Center for Education and the Economy. Retrieved from http://www.ncee.org/wp-content/uploads/2016/01/DevelopingShanghaiTeachersWEB.pdf

Zhang, M., Xu, J., & Sun, C. (2014). Effective teachers for successful schools and high performing students: The case of Shanghai. In S. K. Lee, W. O. Lee, & E. L. Low (Eds.), *Educational Policy Innovations* (pp. 143–161). Singapore: Springer.

INDEX

Aboriginal populations. *See* Diversity; First Nations; High-needs schools

Aboriginal Teacher Education Program (Canada), 196–197

Academy of Singapore Teachers (AST), 47, 58; for career development, 153–154; for leadership development, 166–167; for lesson study, 121–123; for professional development, 108, 127–128

Accreditation. *See* Registration; Standards

Action research, 15, 44, 126, 223–224

Alberta, 2; Alberta Initiative for School Improvement, 124–126, 197; Alberta Teachers Association, 53; appraisal in, 134; clinical training in, 83–84; First Nations in, 84; funding in, 125, 188–189, 238; Ministry of Education, 62; problem solving in, 125; professional learning communities in, 125–127; Professional Standards Branch, 64; salaries in, 50–51; social regard in, 53; teacher registration in, 217–218; teacher training in, 83–84; Teaching Quality Standards in, 64

Alberta Initiative for School Improvement, 124–126, 197

Alberta Teachers Association, 53

Amato, Lindy, 54

Annual learning plan (Ontario), 133–134

Anthony, Paul, 94–95

Appraisal: in Alberta, 134; in Australia, 132–133, 135–138; balanced scorecard approach for, 136–137; in Canada, 133–134; Enhanced Performance Management System (Singapore) for, 139–140, 173; in Finland, 132–135; for high-quality teaching, 132–140; incentives and, 142–146; in New South Wales, 140–141; Performance and Development Plan (New South Wales) for, 135–136; as policy, 3; professional learning and, 140–142, 147; research

on, 141; in Shanghai, 138–139; in Singapore, 132–133, 139–142, 151–152; S.M.A.R.T. goals for, 138; TALIS on, 132–133, 134; Teacher performance appraisal (Ontario), 133; in United States, 132; in Victoria, 136–138

Armstrong, Bruce, 179–180, 182

Assessment: in Australia, 24–25, 80; in Canada, 29–31; in Finland, 34–35, 117; gaokao for, 40–41; Interstate New Teacher Assessment (United States) for, 62; Matriculation Exam Board (Finland) for, 117; in New South Wales, 118; Pan-Canadian Assessment Program, 28; as policy, 4; in Shanghai, 39–41; of students, 8; of teachers, 95–96, 106; VAKAVA (Finland) for, 55–56; in Victoria, 118

AST. *See* Academy of Singapore Teachers

Aulich, Seona, 129–130, 136, 143

Australia: appraisal in, 132–133, 135–138; assessment in, 24–25, 80; Australian Curriculum, Assessment and Reporting Authority, 23–25; Australian Department of Education, Employment, and Workplace Relations, 76; Australian Education Union, 74; Australian Institute of Teaching and School Leadership, 23–24, 62–65, 159; Australian Professional Standard for Principals, 174–175, 180; Australian Teacher Performance and Development, 159; career development in, 158–161; clinical training in, 14–15, 78–79, 221–222; collaboration in, 79–80, 99–100, 113; curriculum in, 24–25; diversity in, 22, 200; educational systems in, 22–26; equity in, 187, 228–229; funding in, 22–25, 79, 99–100, 189–191; Gonski Report in, 190–191, 212–213, 227; governance in, 22–25; high-quality teaching in, 161; immigration in, 9; induction in, 96–100; leadership